# African Women's Movements

Women burst onto the political scene in Africa after the 1990s, claiming more than one-third of the parliamentary seats in countries such as Burundi, Mozambique, South Africa, Tanzania, and Uganda. Women in Rwanda hold the highest percentage of legislative seats in the world. Women's movements lobbied for constitutional reforms and new legislation to expand women's rights.

This book examines the convergence of factors behind these dramatic developments, including the emergence of autonomous women's movements, changes in international and regional norms regarding women's rights and representation, the availability of new resources to advance women's status, and the end of civil conflict. The book focuses on the cases of Cameroon, Mozambique, and Uganda, situating these countries in the broader African context. The authors provide a fascinating analysis of the way in which women are transforming the political landscape in Africa by bringing to bear their unique perspectives as scholars who have also been parliamentarians, transnational activists, and leaders in these movements.

Aili Mari Tripp is Professor of Political Science and Women's Studies at the University of Wisconsin–Madison. Her publications include *Changing the Rules: The Politics of Liberalization and the Urban Informal Economy in Tanzania* (1997), *Women and Politics in Uganda* (2000), several coedited volumes, and numerous scholarly articles. *Women and Politics in Uganda* won the 2001 Victoria Schuck Award of the American Political Science Association for best book on women and politics in 2000 and a 2001 Choice Outstanding Academic Title Award.

Isabel Casimiro is the coordinator of the Department of Women and Gender Studies at the Eduardo Mondlane University, Maputo, Mozambique. She also coordinates the Woman's Program at the university's Center of African Studies and was formerly a member of parliament in Mozambique. She is author of *Paz na Terra, Guerra em Casa: Feminismo e Organizações de Mulheres em Moçambique* (2004) and other works related to the women's movement in Mozambique.

Joy Kwesiga is Vice Chancellor of Kabale University and former Dean of the Faculty of Social Sciences at Makerere University. She is the author of *Women's Access to Higher Education in Africa: Uganda's Experience* (2002), and she coedited *The Women's Movement in Uganda* (2002) with Aili Tripp. Kwesiga was also a founding member of one of the leading women's rights organizations in Uganda, Action for Development (ACFODE).

Alice Mungwa is Senior Political Affairs Officer of the African Union Observer Mission to the United Nations. Prior to that, she served as Senior Political Officer of the African Union Commission in Addis Ababa, Ethiopia. Previously, Mungwa worked as a program officer for gender and development with the Africa Leadership Forum in Nigeria and with a Cameroonian women's nongovernmental organization.

# African Women's Movements

*Transforming Political Landscapes*

AILI MARI  TRIPP

ISABEL CASIMIRO

JOY KWESIGA

ALICE MUNGWA

CAMBRIDGE
UNIVERSITY PRESS

CAMBRIDGE UNIVERSITY PRESS
Cambridge, New York, Melbourne, Madrid, Cape Town, Singapore, São Paulo, Delhi

Cambridge University Press
32 Avenue of the Americas, New York, NY 10013-2473, USA

www.cambridge.org
Information on this title: www.cambridge.org/9780521704908

First published 2009

Printed in the United States of America

A catalog record for this publication is available from the British Library.

ISBN   978-0-521-87930-9 hardback
ISBN   978-0-521-70490-8 paperback

# Contents

# List of Tables

# Acronyms

| | |
|---|---|
| 31DWM | 31st December Women's Movement |
| AAWORD | Association of African Women for Research and Development |
| ACFODE | Action for Development |
| AMWIK | Association of Media Women in Kenya |
| APAC | Association of Professional African Women in Communications |
| AU | African Union |
| AWCPD | African Women's Committee on Peace and Development |
| AWID | Association for Women's Rights in Development |
| BAWATA | Baraza la Wanawake (Tanzanian Women's Council) |
| BLP | Better Life for Rural Women Programme (Nigeria) |
| BOMWA | Botswana Media Women's Association |
| CA | Constituent Assembly (Uganda) |
| CEDAW | Convention on the Elimination of All Forms of Discrimination against Women |
| CFR | Collectif des Femmes pour le Renouveau (Cameroon) |
| CIDA | Canadian International Development Agency |
| CNFC | Conseil National des Femmes Camerounaise (Cameroon) |
| CNU | Cameroon National Union |
| CPDM | Cameroon People's Democratic Movement |
| DANIDA | Danish International Development Agency |
| DAWN | Development Alternatives with Women for a New Era |
| EASSI | Eastern African Sub-Regional Support Initiative |
| ECCAS | Economic Community of Central African States |
| ECOSOC | United Nations Economic and Social Council |
| ECOWAS | Economic Community of West African States |

| | |
|---|---|
| EMWA | Ethiopian Media Women's Association |
| ESOCAM | Evolution Sociale Camerounaise |
| FAMWZ | Federation of African Media Women Zimbabwe |
| FEDIM | International Federation of Women Mozambique |
| FEMNET | African Women's Communication and Development Network |
| FGC | female genital cutting |
| FIDA | International Federation of Women Lawyers |
| FRELIMO | Frente de Libertação de Moçambique |
| GAD | Gender and Development |
| HIV/AIDS | Human Immunodeficiency Virus/Acquired Immune Deficiency Syndrome |
| HIVOS | Humanist Institute for Cooperation with Developing Countries |
| ICCO | Interchurch Organization for Development Cooperation |
| JICA | Japan International Cooperation Agency |
| KANU | Kenya African National Union |
| LMWA | Lagos Market Women's Association |
| MMD | Movement for Multiparty Democracy (Zambia) |
| MULEIDE | Mulher, Lei e Desenvolvimento, Moçambique [Woman, Law and Development in Mozambique] |
| MYW | Maendeleo Ya Wanawake |
| NAMWA | Namibian Media Women's Association |
| NCSLW | National Congress of Sierra Leone Women |
| NCWS | National Council of Women's Societies Nigeria |
| NDC | National Democratic Congress |
| NGO | nongovernmental organization |
| NORAD | Norwegian Agency for Development Cooperation |
| NOVIB | Dutch affiliate of Oxfam since 1994 |
| NUEW | National Union of Eritrea Women |
| OAU | Organisation of African Unity |
| ODA | overseas development assistance |
| OMM | Organização da Mulher Moçambicana |
| PNCDC | Provisional National Defence Council |
| REFJCI | Réseau des Femmes Journalistes de Côte d'Ivoire |
| RENAMO | Resistência Nacional Moçambicana |
| SADC | Southern African Development Community |
| SDF | Social Democratic Front (Cameroon) |
| SIDA | Swedish International Development Agency |
| SLAWIM | Sierra Leone Association of Women in the Media |

| | |
|---|---|
| SWAPO | South West African People's Organisation (Namibia) |
| TAMWA | Tanzania Media Women's Association |
| TANGO | Tanzania Association of Non-Governmental Organizations |
| TANU | Tanganyika African National Union |
| TGNP | Tanzania Gender Networking Programme |
| UCW | Ugandan Council of Women |
| ULA | Uganda Land Alliance |
| UMWA | Uganda Media Women's Association |
| UNDEFEC | Union Democratique des Femmes Camerounaise |
| UNDP | United Nations Development Programme |
| UNFPA | United Nations Population Fund |
| UNIFEM | United Nations Development Fund for Women |
| UNIP | United National Independence Party (Zambia) |
| UPC | Union des Populations du Cameroun |
| UPND | United Party for National Development (Zambia) |
| USAID | United States Agency for International Development |
| UWONET | Uganda Women's Network |
| UWT | Umoja wa Wanawake wa Tanzania |
| WCNU | Women's Cameroon National Union |
| WCPDM | Women's Cameroon People's Democratic Movement |
| WHO | World Health Organization |
| WID | Women in Development |
| WILDAF | Women in Law and Development in Africa |
| WIN | Women in Nigeria |
| WLSA | Women and Law in Southern Africa Research and Educational Trust |
| WLWM | Sierra Leone Women's Movement |
| WNC | Women's National Coalition (South Africa) |
| WPF | Woman's Parliamentary Forum |
| ZANU–PF | Zimbabwe African National Union–Patriotic Front |

# Preface

This book offers an explanation for some of the most significant developments in Africa since the 1990s, namely the emerging visibility of women as political actors and the adoption of a new generation of policies advancing women's rights. We raise many questions that have rarely been examined in a comparative African perspective: Why have some countries been more likely to adopt these policies than others? Why have so many of these changes taken place in countries coming out of civil conflict? Why have so many partially democratic and nondemocratic countries introduced woman-friendly reforms? What difference does democracy make to the adoption of women's rights reforms? These are just some of the questions this book tackles.

This book is one of the first to document the dramatic changes in women's mobilization and women's impact on politics across the continent in the 1990s. There are a few superb country studies (e.g., Britton 2005; Fallon forthcoming; Hassim 2006; Steady 2006; Tamale 1999) and some regional studies (Geisler 2004). An important edited volume by Gretchen Bauer and Hannah Britton (2006) examines women in African parliaments. There is a very small but growing literature on the subject in journals that focuses on aspects of the changes described in this book in one country or context (e.g., electoral quotas for women, women and land concerns, and female genital cutting). Our book brings many of the pieces together and tells a much bigger story about overall changes in women's movements and their political impact after the 1990s. Our inclusion of Francophone and Lusophone cases is particularly important since little has been written in English regarding these countries.

Africa is a continent of vast cultural, linguistic, economic, political, and ecological diversity of which we were acutely cognizant in writing the manuscript. In our effort to identify general patterns and trends in sub-Saharan Africa, we recognize that sometimes this comes at the unavoidable cost of overlooking important particularities of various regions, countries, and locales. There are trade-offs involved in telling a larger story. For this reason, we focus on the cases of Cameroon, Mozambique, and Uganda and examine the differences among these countries while situating them in a broader sub-Saharan context. These countries provide us an opportunity to compare women's movements and gender policies in countries representing the British, French, and Portuguese colonial legacies.

As a scholarly study, this work is unique in that it draws on the expertise of four scholars, several of whom were early leaders of the new women's movements in their home countries. They have also been active within international women's movements. They have observed these transformations both from within and from an academic perspective. The authors have been engaged in policy making as parliamentarians (Casimiro), in advising and engaging government agencies (Kwesiga) and donors (Tripp), and, at the pan-African level, working for the African Union (Mungwa).

Aili Mari Tripp has extensive engagement with the issues touched on in this book. She coordinated the planning and writing of the manuscript, which had an auspicious beginning at the beautiful location of the Rockefeller Foundation's Bellagio Study and Conference Center on the shores of Lake Como in Italy. Tripp is Director of the Women's Studies Research Center and Professor of Political Science and Women's Studies at the University of Wisconsin–Madison. She lived in Tanzania for fifteen years, and after 1987 she carried out extensive research in Uganda and Tanzania on women and politics and women's movements in both countries. She is author of *Women and Politics in Uganda* (2000) and editor of *Sub-Saharan Africa: The Greenwood Encyclopedia of Women's Issues Worldwide* (2003). She also coedited *Global Feminism: Transnational Women's Activism, Organizing, and Human Rights* (2006) with Myra Marx Ferree and *The Women's Movement in Uganda: History, Challenges and Prospects* (2002) with Joy Kwesiga. Tripp has published extensively on women and politics in Africa and women's movements in Africa. She coedits (with Kathleen Dolan) the journal *Politics & Gender* of the Women and Politics Research Section of the American Political Science Association. She also coedits, with Stanlie James, a book series on women in Africa and the diaspora for the University of Wisconsin Press.

Isabel Casimiro was a member of parliament in Mozambique (1994–9), and, as an historian and sociologist, she has been a Research Associate at the Center of African Studies, Eduardo Mondlane University, Maputo, Mozambique. She was instrumental in the creation of Cruzeiro do

Sul–Instituto de Investigação para o Desenvolvimento (Southern Cross–Institute for Research and Development). Dr. Casimiro was also co-founder and first coordinator of Women and Law in Southern Africa (WLSA) and Fórum Mulher (Women's Forum), the leading women's network in Mozambique. She has been a leader of Women in Law and Development in Africa (WILDAF) and Mulher, Lei e Desenvolvimento, Moçambique (Woman, Law and Development in Mozambique, or MULEIDE). She is author of *Paz na Terra, Guerra em Casa: Feminismo e Organizações de Mulheres em Moçambique* (Peace on Earth, War at Home: Feminism and Women's Organizations in Mozambique) (2004) and many other works related to the women's movement in Mozambique.

Joy Kwesiga is Vice Chancellor of Kabale University and former Dean of the Faculty of Social Sciences at Makerere University in Uganda. She served as chair of the Department of Women and Gender Studies and headed up a Gender Mainstreaming Division at Makerere. Kwesiga was a founding member of one of the leading women's rights organizations in Uganda, Action for Development (ACFODE). She published a book, *Women's Access to Higher Education in Africa: Uganda's Experience* (2002), and coedited another book with Aili Tripp, *The Women's Movement in Uganda* (2002). Kwesiga has published extensively on gender mainstreaming, women's movements, and other gender-related concerns in Uganda.

Alice Mungwa is Senior Political Affairs Officer of the African Union Observer Mission to the United Nations. Prior to taking this position, she served as Senior Political Officer of the African Union Commission in Addis Ababa, Ethiopia. She brings to the book her knowledge of women's movements in Cameroon and Francophone Africa as well as perspectives of transnational mobilization from the African Union vantage point. Previously, Mungwa worked as a program officer for gender and development with the Africa Leadership Forum in Nigeria and with a Cameroonian women's nongovernmental organization (NGO). The views expressed in this manuscript belong to the authors and should not be attributed to any institution with which the authors are affiliated, including the African Union.

The book draws on original fieldwork in Cameroon, Mozambique, and Uganda, including participant observation, in-depth interviews, and focus groups carried out by the authors in their home countries. We also draw heavily on a systematic analysis of African media reports and commentary from LexisNexis. We utilize pamphlets, newsletters, Web sites, and other unpublished documents. The book also draws on the small but growing secondary literature available on the subject.

We structure the book by building on the framework provided by Louise Chappell in *Gendering Government: Feminist Engagement with the State in Australia and Canada* (2002). She divides policies into legal/constitutional, electoral, and bureaucratic groupings. We find this approach useful in allowing us to examine the extent to which the various arenas have been utilized by women's movements in Africa. We include one additional arena – namely, peace building (Chapter 8) – because of its importance in explaining how women activists contributed to the resolution of major upheavals to advance their agendas. Peace building and involvement in peace negotiations are critical moments of influence for women activists, as they have laid the basis for further changes in women's political representation and woman-friendly policies in the postconflict context.

OUTLINE OF THE BOOK

A central claim of the book, outlined in Chapter 1, is that autonomous women's movements are one of the most important determinants of the new gender-based policies adopted after 1990 in much of Africa. Other determinants include changing international norms and influences of global and regional women's movements, the allocation of new government and donor resources to implement reforms related to women's rights, and the diffusion of female-friendly policies as a result of the influences of multilateral bodies such as the United Nations and the Commonwealth organization, regional bodies such as the African Union, and subregional institutions such as the Southern African Development Community (SADC). The end of a significant number of conflicts after the mid-1980s also created important political opportunities for women's movements. The conjuncture of all these developments created the right synergy for the emergence of many of the dynamics described in this book.

The book starts with an examination of the roots of contemporary women's activism (Chapter 2), first looking at precolonial ideologies of political motherhood and the historic continuities in the use of tactics such as shaming and grieving. We look at the impact of colonial policies on civil society and female education and the legacies to which these policies contributed. Another influence on contemporary movements came from the role of women in nationalist movements and the wide variety of economic and women's rights issues for which women fought in those struggles for independence. Finally, the chapter highlights the role of women under post-independence one-party rule, looking at both the constraints and possibilities for mobilization. It concludes by describing the early beginnings of the new women's movement, starting with the 1980s.

Chapter 3 provides an overview of the factors that gave rise to the new women's mobilization after the 1990s. We focus on (1) international influences and the diffusion of ideas and strategies across Africa with respect to women's rights; (2) the influence of international donors; and (3) democratization and political liberalization. These factors were important because they shaped the ways in which the movements sought policy changes, the kinds of issues that they took up, and their levels of success.

We contrast characteristics of the new women's movements with the earlier pre-1990 organizations in Chapter 4. This chapter looks at the importance of associational autonomy and heterogeneity; the interest in building ties across ethnicity, religion, and political affiliation; the advocacy nature of many of the organizations in contrast to the developmentalism of earlier associations; the emergence of new coalitions and networks; and the active involvement of men in supporting various women's rights causes. The chapter then identifies some of the challenges that these new organizations face from the state, from donor relations, and from problems of internal institutional weakness.

Chapter 5 examines the impact of women's movements on constitutions that have been rewritten since the 1990s as well as on legislative reform. It first engages the broader literature on policy reform to examine existing theories of why some reforms are adopted more easily than others and contrasts these with African cases, suggesting that laws pertaining to the clan and the family are harder to pass than laws relating to women's political representation, employment, labor, and citizenship. The former laws tended to be regulated by customary law, often under the jurisdiction of traditional authorities. The chapter goes on to examine legislative changes in the areas of domestic violence, family law, and land rights.

The electoral arena is another important area where women are making strides, especially in legislative elections. They are also making gains in the executive branch as ministers, vice presidents, and even, in the case of Liberia, as head of state. Women are increasingly forming and heading political parties. Chapter 6 starts out with a description of some of the constraints that women face in running for office. It then explains the dramatic increases that we are seeing in the number of women in African legislatures by looking not only at the role of women's movements but also at the impact of quotas, the end of conflict, and pressures from regional bodies such as the African Union, SADC, and the Economic Community of West African States (ECOWAS).

Chapter 7 examines the ways in which women's movements have engaged the state bureaucracy, starting with the national machineries and the eventual formation of ministries of gender/women. The chapter takes a critical look at some of the approaches that have guided the work of national machineries, from various women in development (WID) and gender and development (GAD) approaches to gender-mainstreaming approaches. The role of the women's movements is explored in relation to the cases of gender mainstreaming in Cameroon, Mozambique, and Uganda. Gender budgeting policies are analyzed as an example of gender mainstreaming.

In Chapter 8, the book investigates women's activism in the context of peace building. The chapter shows how the peace and women's movements in Mozambique and Uganda were linked and how they represented key moments in women's activism in conflict and postconflict contexts.

Finally, Chapter 9 ties the threads of the book together and returns to a discussion of the case studies in light of the general findings. It situates African women's movements in a global context to discuss the ways in which these trends in Africa are part of global trends but also how women's movements in Africa have influenced developments in the rest of the world.

## ACKNOWLEDGMENTS

We owe a major debt of gratitude to the many who have helped us along the way to bring this project to fruition, including the Rockefeller Foundation, the University of Wisconsin–Madison's International Institute's Transnational Feminism Research Circle, and the Woodrow Wilson International Center for Scholars in Washington, D.C. We also are grateful for the assistance that we received from Cambridge University Press and especially Lewis Bateman and the anonymous reviewers. Georgina Waylen provided invaluable feedback and encouragement with the final draft. The manuscript is a product of many dialogues and interactions with countless scholars and activists throughout Africa, all of whom have influenced the final product. And finally, we are most grateful for the help provided by research assistants Sara Burnes, Emma Condon, and Anne Fishback.

I

# Introduction

In the past decade, women have become visible in African politics in unexpected ways, setting new precedents. In 2003, Rwanda elected a new
parliament with the highest percentage of women in the world (close to
49 percent). Africa has some of the highest rates of female legislative representation in the world, with women claiming over 30 percent of the
parliamentary seats in Mozambique, South Africa, Tanzania, Uganda, and
Burundi. In November 2005, Liberia's Ellen Johnson-Sirleaf became the first
elected woman president in Africa. Specioza Wandera Kazibwe served as vice
president in Uganda for a decade (1994–2003). There have been six female
prime ministers in Africa since the mid-1990s, with Luísa Dia Diogo serving
as prime minister in Mozambique since 2004. At the regional level, Gertrude
Mongella of Tanzania became the first president of the Pan-African Parliament of the African Union, and half the parliamentarians are women.

Women's new engagement with politics is evident in other ways as well.
Women's movements have successfully lobbied for constitutional reforms
to include gender equity and antidiscrimination clauses. They have sought
the passage of new legislation to expand women's rights. Women are for the
first time making bids to participate in an official capacity in national-level
peace talks in countries where conflicts have come to an end. These are just a
few of the dramatic changes in women's status that are under way in Africa
today.

This book examines how and why women became more visible in politics
and began to affect policy in ways not evident in the past. It also looks at why
some countries have had more success than others in passing legislation to
advance women's rights. Although there is considerable variation, basically
the more successful countries saw a convergence of several trends: the emergence of active and autonomous women's movements; openness to changing

international norms regarding women's rights and representation as there emerged institutional mechanisms to spread those norms within Africa; the availability *and* deployment of resources to advance women; and, finally, the opening of new opportunities as a result of a major upheaval in society, such as the end of conflict. All four factors were critical in bringing about the aforementioned changes in the countries that saw the most change.

## ACCOUNTING FOR NEW FEMALE-FRIENDLY POLICIES

The introduction of new gender-related reforms has been tied first and foremost to the rise of new women's movements in Africa that started in the late 1980s, gaining full steam in the 1990s. For this reason, much of the book is preoccupied with these movements and their impact on reforms related to women's rights. The expansion of these movements often resulted in the introduction of a set of new policies that promoted women's rights. They represent a shift more directly into politics and advocacy and away from the earlier strictly "developmental" and welfare approach of women's organizations. Not only did the new women's movements focus on advocacy, they also provided women with the skills with which to advocate change. They carried out training in lobbying, research, grant writing, public speaking, civic education, and leadership skills. They also promoted consciousness raising (referred to as "gender sensitization" in Anglophone African countries). Moreover, they engaged the public through the media by publishing research findings, airing radio and TV discussions, producing newspaper features, and engaging in other such means of influencing public opinion.

Women's movements included organizations that represented a wide range of activities directed at advancing women's status, including both international and domestic nongovernmental organizations (NGOs) engaged in advocacy, social service provisioning, leadership training, business promotion, media reform, financial empowerment arrangements, as well as professional and labor associations and organizations that address the concerns of special groups such as disabled women. They also included a wide variety of local-level informal and formal associations. Femocrats, or feminists within the state and international bureaucracy, can also be credited with bringing about some of the changes discussed in this book, as can women and men parliamentarians, lawyers, media workers, academics, and many other sectors of society.

A growing body of scholarship has linked policy outcomes to women's agency. Many of the studies examine individual countries or policy areas and therefore the dynamics described are fairly country-specific. In a nuanced study of women's movement agency and its limitations, Shireen Hassim (2006) looks at the various ways in which the state and the broader political movements created political opportunities for women's collective action from the late 1970s and 1980s, when the women's movement engaged in grassroots organizing, to the transition from apartheid to democracy in the 1990s, when women's formal political participation became possible. Hassim wrestles with the way the political discourse of nationalism constrained the women's movement in South Africa and the challenges of creating an autonomous movement that at the same time could draw strength from alliances with other progressive forces.

Some have emphasized the pretransition mobilization and its impact on posttransition gains by women's movements. Hannah Britton (2002, 2005), for example, links women's earlier mobilization in the anti-apartheid movement in South Africa to their ability to ensure later constitutional changes, influence party politics, and increase female representation. During the transition, women successfully built a broad coalition that developed a platform for action and raised awareness of women's issues nationally, built cross-party alliances to press for constitutional provisions regarding women, and adopted strategies to get women elected and into positions of power. These steps laid the basis for future gains. However, women's movements were by no means the only factor contributing to these changes in policy agendas, although they were critical. As Georgina Waylen (2007a, 2007b) has observed, they were necessary but not sufficient. Other factors were also at work.

Changing international norms as a result of the influences of global, regional, and national women's movements could be considered another contributing factor in influencing changes with respect to women's status. Most single-country case studies of the adoption of gender-related reforms in Africa only tangentially mention the international factors that have contributed to these changes, yet they have had considerable impact. These external influences were evident in the watershed United Nations conferences on women in Nairobi (1985) and Beijing (1995). These conferences, and the strategies and plans that came out of them, placed additional pressure on governments to respond to domestic and pan-African women's organizations. The merging of the development and human rights agenda in new rights-based approaches gave rise to a new normative consensus among governments and provided the conceptual basis for policies to advance women's status.

These new norms were diffused through (1) continental entities such as the African Union; (2) subregional organizations such as the Southern African

Development Community (SADC), which have in turn pressured national governments for gender-related policy changes; (3) multilateral bodies like the United Nations agencies, the World Bank, the Commonwealth, and the UN Conferences on Women; and (4) foreign donors, including bilateral agencies, international NGOs, foundations, and other such actors. SADC, for example, played a catalytic role in advancing women's representation in southern Africa. It set targets for its fourteen member states in 1997 and again in 2005 to improve women's political representation and to adopt policies to advance women's status in the region. Thus SADC countries have on average higher rates of female representation in their legislatures compared to non-SADC countries. Specific gender-related policies such as gender budgeting initiatives were also the result of diffusion among former British colonies, not just in Africa but also worldwide. This was because of contemporary networking among women's organizations in former British colonies, especially through the Commonwealth organization. Other effects of diffusion could be seen among left-leaning parties in power, which were also more inclined to promote key woman-friendly policies.

Similarly, the African Centre for Gender and Development of the United Nations Economic Commission for Africa (UNECA), the Gender Directorate of the African Union (AU), and its predecessor, the Organisation of African Unity (OAU), were instrumental in advancing women's rights on the continent. The OAU and UNECA helped organize regional and continentwide conferences in preparation for the Fourth World Conference on Women in Beijing (1995). The OAU and its successor, AU, periodically organized joint meetings of governments and NGOs together to discuss women's rights (Adams and Kang 2007).[1] African women's movements have influenced the work of these regional institutions while they, in turn, have helped bring African perspectives into international fora.

Why do governments succumb to pressures from such external actors? In this book, we explore possible explanations that range from the instrumental desire for foreign assistance (Mama 1995; Okeke-Ihejirika and Franceschet 2002) to the desire not to fall out of step with one's neighbors and to be able to present one's country as "modernizing" (Htun 2003).

Countries with greater economic resources (measured by per capita gross domestic product [GDP]) were more inclined to adopt some

---

[1] As of 16 July 2008, Angola, Benin, Burkina Faso, Cape Verde, The Comoros, Djibouti, the Gambia, Ghana, Lesotho, Liberia, Libya, Malawi, Mali, Mauritania, Mozambique, Namibia, Nigeria, Rwanda, Senegal, Seychelles, South Africa, Tanzania, Togo, and Zambia had ratified the Protocol to the African Charter on Human and Peoples' Rights on the Rights of Women in Africa (adopted by the Second Ordinary Session of the Assembly of the Union, Maputo, CAB/LEG/66.6 13 September, 2000; it went into force 25 November 2005).

woman-friendly policies, such as Universal Primary Education and gender budgeting initiatives, in part because of the availability of resources required to implement such policies. Donor support has also made a difference in the capacity of national women's machineries, for example, to implement various gender-mainstreaming initiatives. However, financial capacity is irrelevant if there is no political will or commitment. The limited resources committed by the relatively wealthier South Africa to its gender budgeting initiative resulted in its demise, while some of the poorest countries in Africa have continued to pursue such initiatives. Gender budgeting involves the analysis of budgets to determine how government spending impacts women and men differently and making recommendations for future budgets to equalize the way in which funds are allocated. Similarly, some of the poorest countries in Africa, such as Rwanda and Mozambique, have some of the highest rates of female legislative representation due to the commitments they have made in this area while some wealthier countries have less to show in this regard. Thus, the provision of resources must be matched by a commitment to gender equality.

Regime change or administrative transition has opened up political spaces for women activists to advance their causes (Accampo and Fuchs 1995; Gilmartin 1995). However, in Africa, it was more than regime change or administrative change that accounted for these changes: it was the end of conflict or major upheaval in society that became yet another important factor contributing to the adoption of female-friendly policies. There is already evidence that the end of conflict affects rates of female representation globally (Hughes 2004). The end of major civil conflicts since the 1990s from South Africa to Namibia, Mozambique, Rwanda, Burundi, Liberia, and Sierra Leone opened up new opportunities for women activists. Georgina Waylen (2007b) suggests that in South Africa it was critical that there were formal opportunities in the reconstitution of the polity in which women could participate during the transition from apartheid to democracy.

The postconflict period leveled the playing field and the process of rewriting constitutions and reconstituting the political order afforded women new opportunities to insert themselves in new ways into the polity. The disruptions of war dislodged traditional gender roles, opening up new possibilities for women. In some cases, it also disrupted potential opponents of gender-based reform and disorganized them. Women seized such opportunities in almost all constitution-making processes throughout Africa that came about as a result of the end of conflict.

To be clear, these observations are not in any way a normative prescription for or glorification of civil conflict and all its horrors, but rather an analysis of the opportunities that such disruptions may have presented to women's movements. Since 1990, thirty-eight African constitutions have been rewritten and six had major revisions. Some of these new constitutions were adopted in the aftermath of major conflict, whereas others were introduced in the context of shifts toward multipartyism and political opening. For women's rights activists, the big innovation in many of these new constitutions was the stipulation that the constitution and statutory law override customary law, a provision that is generally understood to have clear implications for women's rights. Ten out of fourteen postconflict countries have such clauses, and two refer specifically to gender in this context, whereas only eleven out of thirty-two non-postconflict countries have such a provision. Similarly, thirteen out of fourteen postconflict countries have banned discrimination based on sex, whereas only twenty-five out of thirty-two non-postconflict countries have such a provision (see Table 5.1). Of the countries that have passed land legislation in recent years to address women's right to land, five out of seven were postconflict countries. Similarly, with the exception of Tanzania, all the countries with the highest rates of female legislative representation in Africa (where 30 percent or more the legislative seats are held by women) had come out of conflicts after 1986, such as Burundi, Mozambique, Namibia, Rwanda, South Africa, and Uganda. Thus, the most significant changes in Africa with respect to women's rights have occurred when there were opportunities to rewrite "the rules" of the political order, which generally occurred after major civil conflict.

In sum, countries that were most likely to adopt female-friendly policies had stronger women's movements than those without. They were also likely to be more influenced by transnational women's movements and changing international norms, mediated by the United Nations as well as regional and subregional organizations of states. They tended to be relatively wealthier countries or countries with access to donor resources with which to implement various policy changes. Paradoxically, they often were countries that had experienced serious disruptions, where the social and political order underwent upheaval as a result of conflict. As they emerged out of years of civil conflict, new constitutions were written and the rules ordering the policy were recrafted. This presented women's movements with opportunities to assert themselves.

## NEW GENERATION OF GENDER LEGISLATION AND POLICIES

The 1990s saw the passage of legislation, the adoption of new constitutions, and the signing of international treaties addressing a new range of issues in Africa, some of which were path breaking even by world standards. The

2003 Protocol to the African Charter on the Rights of Women, for example, is more radical than the Convention on the Elimination of All Forms of Discrimination against Women (CEDAW), which has been signed by virtually all countries of the world and ratified by all but Iran, Oman, Qatar, Sudan, and the United States. The 2003 Protocol to the African Charter on the rights of women includes a provision that is the first recognition of a limited right to abortion in international law. It recognizes the right of a woman to self-protection and to be protected against sexually transmitted diseases, including HIV/AIDS. It also mentions women's rights to live in a positive cultural context and is the first international treaty to mention female genital cutting. The protocol provides for the rights of widows, the disabled, and elderly women, which are innovations in international law. Other examples of ground-breaking changes can be found in South Africa, which has the only constitution in the world that outlaws discrimination based on sexual orientation and recognizes the right of people in same-sex relationships to marry. In 2006, legislation was passed in accordance with the South African constitution to allow for same-sex marriages. This occurred on a continent where open homosexuality is still generally considered taboo and is illegal in Ghana, Kenya, Nigeria, Tanzania, Uganda, Zimbabwe, and many other African countries.

The vast majority of sub-Saharan African countries have signed CEDAW; the International Covenant on Economic, Social, and Cultural Rights; the African Charter; and the 2003 African Union Women's Protocol. This fact suggests that there is general acceptance of these norms regarding women's rights in Africa at the governmental level, even if implementation falls short. Opponents of gender-related reform have sometimes argued that the pursuit of women's rights is the product of Western feminist influences in Africa. In light of the aforementioned agreements, these objections to change ring increasingly hollow, given that it is primarily African women's organizations and networks that have spearheaded initiatives to build support for these treaties and protocols (Banda 2005).

The post-1990s policies reflect a new rights-based approach that incorporates both human rights and development concerns. These are distinct from earlier purely developmental approaches in several important ways: (1) The new post-1990 policies seek equal gender representation in political and other institutions, including legislatures, executive branches, judiciaries, nongovernmental associations, religious institutions, and other bodies. (2) New legislation and constitutional reforms challenge customary practices affecting familial relations and gender relations within the private sphere of the home, kinship group, and clan. (3) The new generation of policies seeks to protect women's bodily integrity through legislation around female genital cutting, abortion, domestic violence, and other such concerns. (4) New policies have emerged to address women's rights to a livelihood through access to land, property, credit, agricultural inputs, and other resources. (5) And finally, these policies have sought equal rights for women as adult citizens and the abolition of women's status as minors in a few remaining countries (e.g., Lesotho and Swaziland).

Although it is beyond the purview of this book to evaluate the impact of these policies, it is important to recognize that in spite of the difficulty of implementing and enforcing them, the effects of the policies are being slowly but surely felt on the ground, where they matter. As a result of land legislation in Uganda, for example, increasing numbers of women are taking their disputed claims to magistrate's courts, especially in areas where land pressures are great, such as Kigezi (Khadiagala 2001). No longer can men sell land without the consent of their wife. Even in rural areas, lawyers who oversee such transactions will often strictly adhere to this requirement. The impacts are evident in girls' education levels, women's ability to access credit, women's leadership capacities, and the increasing presence of women leaders in a wide variety of nongovernmental arenas. Today in Uganda's universities, it is no longer only women who demand gender balance on committees and in leadership positions: Male faculty and administrators are requiring greater female representation. Thus, in a country such as Uganda, there is evidence of real changes as a result of the adoption of female-friendly legislation, constitutional changes, and policy reforms, even if there remains a long way to go.

## DOES DEMOCRATIZATION MATTER?

It is not evident that the democratizing trends experienced continentwide after the 1990s directly contributed to the adoption of all of the female-friendly policies described in this book. The number of democracies in Africa doubled between 1980 and 2007, whereas the number of authoritarian states decreased from roughly one-half to one-third in this period. However, the largest number of countries remained neither fully democratic nor authoritarian. Democratization coincided with and shaped many of the changes with respect to women's status. Women's rights activists participated in movements of political liberalization as described in Chapter 4. Democratization certainly facilitated the growth of women's organizations. But one finds many nondemocratic countries that adopted woman-friendly policies, including Ethiopia, Rwanda, Uganda, and Zimbabwe. How they actually implemented these policies and framed them is another matter and one that needs to be determined empirically.

Democratization in Africa in the 1990s not only included an expansion of political rights and civil liberties, it included a shift away from military rule toward civilian rule, the introduction of multiparty systems (away from single-party rule), the emergence of a freer press and greater freedoms of expression, and an opening up of political space for nonstate associations, including women's organizations. The freedoms of press and association were particularly important to women's organizations. But it is not clear that these changes directly affected the adoption of policies advancing women's status when looked at comparatively. Undoubtedly, democratization affects the substance of the changes and their implementation.

This book asks, in part, why do some authoritarian and semi-authoritarian regimes adopt pro-women policies? To date, there is a growing comparative literature on potential linkages between democratization and the adoption of women's rights policies. Ronald Inglehart, Pippa Norris, and Chris Welzel (2002), for example, in their study of seventy countries, find a global trend toward greater gender equality that is strongly linked with democratization and cultural change. They argue that economic development results in social and economic transformations that become the key to democratization. Simultaneous cultural shifts are reflected in increases in gender equality. According to them, democratic countries have higher rates of female representation, not directly because of democracy but rather because democratization causes cultural shifts that result in these changes. One change that occurs with democratization is the change in the perception that men make better leaders than women. The authors' evidence for this link between gender equality and democracy is their claim that democratic societies have higher rates of female parliamentary representation.

Inglehart et al. (2002) included only five sub-Saharan African countries in their study and drew on survey data looking at multiple waves from 1981 to 1997. The introduction of electoral quotas for women in Africa began in earnest around 1995 and expanded dramatically after 2000, resulting in sharp increases in the numbers of women legislative representatives. Thus the findings of Inglehart and his colleagues do not capture many of these more recent changes that we are describing in Africa, nor do they predict them.

In Africa today, there is no correlation between democracy and women's representation. Of the countries where women claim over 20 percent of all legislative seats, six countries, or 38 percent, of all authoritarian states fall in this group, 40 percent (eight) of all semi-authoritarian states are represented in this group, whereas only 20 percent (two) of democratic states have higher rates of female representation. These findings are borne out in a global crossnational multivariate study using 2006 data (Tripp and Kang 2008).

Many countries that democratized in Africa were left in a holding pattern of illiberal democracy. In these semi-authoritarian states, violations of civil and political liberties continue. Indeed, what distinguishes semi-authoritarian regimes from democratic regimes is their lack of consistency in guaranteeing civil and political liberties. At the same time, it is their regard for some of these liberties that sets them apart from full-blown authoritarian regimes. They often manifest patterns of personal clientelistic-based rule reminiscent of African authoritarian regimes, with the executive holding a preponderance of power. Even within these systems, women's rights activists have been able to make modest gains on the policy front.

Nevertheless, in the literature, democratization is in one way or another implicated in many explanations for improvements in women's status in Africa, especially in the area of political representation, where the scholarship has been most extensive. Some, such as Kathleen Fallon, have argued that the transition to democracy opened up new possibilities for women to fight for political rights in Ghana and elsewhere in Africa (Fallon 2003). Staffan Lindberg (2004) suggests that women's chances for being elected into the legislature improve incrementally in all regime types with each consecutive election, but especially in democratic systems. Mi Yung Yoon (2004) looks at women's representation in African countries that held democratic elections between 1990 and 2001 and points to quotas and proportional representation to be important explanatory factors in enhancing women's representation in African legislatures, while culture acts as a constraint. Moreover, she argues that "the recent transition toward democracy in sub-Saharan Africa has significantly increased the number of female candidates for parliamentary seats..." (p. 458). Gretchen Bauer and Hannah Britton (2006: 1–30) find that "the diffusion of multiparty politics has paved the way for women's greater political gains." They also point to quotas as being often the "most immediate and successful tools for increasing the number of women in national office." They too see the postconflict influences, availability of women candidates, electoral systems, role of political parties, and influences from global women's movements as additional factors facilitating women's legislative representation in addition to the effects of multipartyism.

Clearly, democracy shapes the ways in which policies are adopted and framed. However, as indicated previously, the empirical data do not suggest a correlation between democracy and women's descriptive legislative representation and the adoption of quota policies. Moreover, when taken in a broader comparative perspective, Georgina Waylen (2007a, 2007b) concludes that many democratic transitions from Latin America to East Europe have been fairly disappointing in terms of their gender outcomes. Her finding is supported by much of the literature on transitions in Latin America (Franceschet 2005; Htun 2003; Tobar 2003; Waylen 1994) and East Europe (Buckley 1997; Einhorn 1993; Gal and Kligman 2000a, 2000b; Jaquette and Wolchik 1998; True 2003).

Some have argued that there are exceptions, with democratization opening up possibilities for Taiwanese women to gain greater political representation and South Korean women activists to make strides in the area of legislation affecting women (Clark and Lee 2000; Lee 2000a, 2000b). However, even in East and Southeast Asia, nondemocratic countries such as Malaysia, the People's Republic of China, and Singapore have adopted more pro-women policies relative to democratic states in the region (Hipsher and Darcy 2000), underscoring the need to look at the relationship between democracy and women's rights crossnationally rather than simply on a country-by-country basis.

Waylen (2007b) sees South Africa as an exception to the overall pattern in which democratization has not resulted in significant gains for women. In particular, Waylen details the conditions that facilitated the advances made in South Africa, where there had been a long history of women's mobilization as part of the apartheid movements. She argues that women activists were able to intervene because (1) there were relatively favorable political opportunity structures (in particular, the pacted transition created opportunities for intervention in the negotiations for change); (2) there was a triple alliance of women academics, politicians, and activists who were able to act strategically in articulating women's interests at critical junctures during the transition; and finally (3) there were mechanisms not just to get issues onto the policy agenda but to translate them into "positive policy outcomes" (p. 524).

Our overall comparative findings in Africa correspond well to Waylen's findings, but we would suggest at least one modification: It was not only democratization that accounted for the adoption of women's rights policies in South Africa, but rather the fact that there was a major rupture with the apartheid past necessitating a negotiated transition that women activists sought to influence. In this regard, South Africa is like other African post-conflict countries that have established new constitutions in which women's rights are enshrined. The women's movement was critical to these changes, as were international influences and the fact that the government committed resources, at least initially, to these changes.

Our study suggests that more attention should be given to the types of changes that occur, the circumstances under which they take place, and how those reforms substantively affect women. A central question of this book, then, is not only why was there a sudden upsurge in adopting woman-friendly policies in Africa after the 1990s, but more specifically, why did nondemocracies adopt woman-friendly policies? The reasons appear to be the same regardless of the level of democracy, as previously mentioned: the role of women's movements, changing international norms and pressures, major societal upheaval that created opportunities for women's rights activists to advance their agendas, and the allocation of resources to carry out these reforms.

However, it is especially curious when a country such as Zimbabwe, which is facing serious political and economic turmoil, adopts some of the most progressive legislation regarding domestic violence anywhere in the world. Although one may wonder whether any aspect of the legislation will actually be implemented, one equally wonders why it was passed at the very moment that Zimbabwe had fallen into deep political and economic crisis. The law carries with it the visible imprint of feminists in Zimbabwe. Its passage is replete with irony. Prior to the passage of the bill, the nonpartisan Women's Coalition, an umbrella body for thirty-five women's organizations led demonstrations to protest the comments of an opposition parliamentarian who railed against the bill.[2] Over two hundred protestors, including the ruling party Zimbabwe African National Union–Patriotic Front's (ZANU-PF) Women's League, joined a demonstration in front of parliament at a time when the government had been loath to permit any demonstrations and had been ruthlessly suppressing them. The Domestic Violence Prevention and Protection of Victims Act of 2007 provides both protection and relief to victims of domestic violence. It defines domestic violence in broad terms to include physical, sexual, emotional, verbal, psychological and economic abuse, harassment, stalking, damage to property, and breaking and entering into the complainant's residence.[3]

---

[2] Parliamentarian Timothy Mubhawu of the Movement for Democratic Change (MDC) drew the ire of women's rights activists when he told parliament: "I stand here representing God the Almighty. Women are not equal to men. This is a dangerous bill, and let it be known in Zimbabwe that the rights, privileges and status of men are gone" ("Gender Activists Protest...." 2006).

[3] It also includes depriving or preventing the complainant access to his or her place of residence. Included in violence is abuse arising from any cultural or customary rites or practices

Nondemocratic African states are not unusual in their capacity for such legislative reforms. Nondemocratic and even democratic states have historically harnessed women's rights to serve a variety of political and economic goals, some of which have little to do with the improvement of the status of women. Socialist states in Eastern Europe and the former Soviet Union passed laws that advanced women's rights, from property to labor, marriage, and divorce laws. They provided maternity leave, day care, and other benefits that supported women's role as laborers. Their intention with such policies, which varied over time, was to enlist women primarily to serve the goals of economic growth.

The introduction of female-friendly policies has also been a way in which various states have sought to establish themselves as modernizers, often placing women's rights at the crucible of broader societal change. In Morocco, Tunisia, Turkey, and other predominantly Islamic countries, efforts to promote women's emancipation have often come to symbolize a major fault line between the secularists and Islamicists (Brand 1998; Murphy 2003: 193). In Africa and elsewhere, the desire to be seen as compliant with donor objectives influences many of the decisions to adopt woman-friendly policies.

Thus, the fact that countries adopt woman-friendly policies needs to be seen in light of these other objectives, because they shape the way in which policies are adopted. For example, under the semi-authoritarian rule of President Alberto Fujimori in Peru, the state adopted a birth control program. Fujimori was the only president to speak at the 1995 Fourth International World Conference on Women in Beijing, and this encouraged Peruvian feminists to ally with the government in its reproductive policies. The state, however, ended up advocating only sterilization as the primary method of birth control. Between 1995 and 1998, about 250,000 mostly poor Peruvian women were sterilized, many without their consent, as part of an antipoverty program of the government that was tied to the clientelistic distribution of food to Mothers Clubs and emergency social programs involving women (Barrig 1999). Although in this book we do not explore in great detail the ways in which states implement women's rights policies and their intended and unintended consequences, these are clearly matters of serious concern to women's rights advocates. The passage of legislation or adoption of a policy may be only a first step.

that discriminate against or degrade women, such as forced virginity testing, female genital mutilation, and pledging of women and girls for purposes of appeasing spirits. Abduction, child marriages, forced marriages, and forced wife inheritances are also addressed by the Act. Abuse against an individual because of his or her age or physical or mental capacity is also considered domestic violence.

DEFINING WOMEN'S MOVEMENTS

The women's movements discussed in this book are movements that have named women as the primary constituency that they are mobilizing. They have built organizational and/or political strategies around the concerns of women. The improvement of women's economic standing, political representation, cultural status, and legal rights are the central goals of these movements.

The heterogeneity of the new organizations has been striking. At the national level, women have formed a wide variety of organizations, including professional associations of women doctors, lawyers, engineers, and so on; advocacy groups and networks focused on rape, domestic violence, reproductive rights, disability, and other such concerns; organizations involved with the provision of services to women (e.g., legal aid and family planning); women's business and credit associations; and associations that provide training in health care, literacy, safe motherhood, leadership skills, and other such areas.

Although some of the activists described in this book might call themselves feminists, most women's rights activists do not self-identify in this way even though they may share the same objectives as those calling themselves feminists. In Africa, the term "feminism" has often had carried with it the baggage of being regarded a Western and foreign construct. However, this is rapidly changing, as feminism itself is being redefined through global and African dialogues that are no longer primarily Western.

There are several reasons that the term "feminism" has been embraced with some reluctance in African countries. There has been a worry that it would compromise the project of national development. Since the 1960s, feminism was often regarded as a Western ideology of individual women fighting against men, with men as the main enemy of women. Although this always was only one of many interpretations of feminism, it was this stereotypical perception of feminism that was promoted by politicians and the media in Africa. Until the 1990s, even governments that were generally disposed toward women's advancement saw the concerns of women's rights advocates as being only incidental to the broader project of development.

In Mozambique, for example, from the 1970s until today, the ruling Frente de Libertação de Moçambique (FRELIMO) party has been critical of feminist movement, although it has been supportive of women's advancement on many fronts. FRELIMO was influenced by the Marxist view of woman's liberation: that women would be liberated together with the liberation of the society as a whole. The party-affiliated Mozambican Woman's

Organization (OMM) was linked to the socialist International Federation of Women (FEDIM) that espoused this same view. FRELIMO's criticism of feminism has resulted in most women activists today avoiding use of the term. Instead, they use "gender" as an analytical tool, a descriptor of organizations, and as a substitute for the term "feminism."

Self-identifying feminists, however, take a different approach. Organizers of the first African Feminist Forum, held in Ghana in 2006, argued that in Africa today, some women's organizations focus on reforms that will improve the conditions under which women live and work, but do not challenge discriminatory structures and institutions that might bring about major transformations in gender relations. Feminists, in contrast, challenge the legitimacy and the basic underpinnings of patriarchal institutions, values, and norms. The Forum came up with a Charter of Feminist Principles that articulates this latter view:

We define and name ourselves publicly as Feminists because we celebrate our feminist identities and politics. We recognize that the work of fighting for women's rights is deeply political, and the process of naming is political too. Choosing to name ourselves Feminist places us in a clear ideological position. By naming ourselves as Feminists we politicise the struggle for women's rights, we question the legitimacy of the structures that keep women subjugated, and we develop tools for transformatory analysis and action. We have multiple and varied identities as African Feminists. We are African women – we live here in Africa and even when we live elsewhere, our focus is on the lives of African women on the continent. Our feminist identity is not qualified with "*Ifs*", "*Buts*", or "*Howevers*". We are Feminists. Full stop.

What is remarkable about this charter, which was drafted by many of the leaders of women's movements throughout Africa, is that it in many ways indicates a deliberate departure from some of the ambivalence and defensiveness about using the term "feminism" in Africa and openly embraces the transformative goals of feminists worldwide. There is a general recognition that there is a plurality of views within both women's and feminist movements regarding strategy, ideology, and priorities and that these differences are markers of the vitality and breadth of these movements. Generally speaking, however, as the Feminist Forum organizers pointed out, there is consensus on the need to address issues like "poverty, illiteracy, health and reproductive rights, political participation and peace."[4]

What unites most of these organizations, both those calling themselves feminist and those that do not, is their goal of improving women's status to

[4] http://www.africafeministforum.org/v1/?menuId=23310&linkId=23312, accessed 27 January 2007.

gain equality with men, which is in essence the main feminist objective. As Myra Marx Ferree (2006: 6) puts it: "Feminism is a *goal*, a target for social change, a purpose informing activism, not a constituency or a strategy. Feminist mobilizations are informed by feminist theory, beliefs and practices, but they may take place in a variety of organizational contexts, from women's movements, to positions within governments."

At the same time, the debates that came out of the Feminist Forum provided a glimpse into the sophistication of current feminist debates in Africa. The participants challenged the "hypocritical" and "sexist" defense of "African culture and tradition" to justify discrimination against women; the tokenism in which one out of twenty of those in decision-making positions is a woman; patriarchal and sexist attitudes in interpersonal relations "with particular reference to sexual and reproductive health and rights"; the use of notions of motherhood in state policies to minimize women's contributions; policy makers' misuse of the idea of "gender mainstreaming," which ought to address the gap between opportunities for men and women; the linkages between educational opportunities and socioeconomic and environmental challenges as a result of globalization and the introduction of structural adjustment policies; and the feminization of HIV/AIDS and poverty. The emergence of this type of critique and agenda gives an idea of how women's movements have evolved since the first newly autonomous organizations emerged in the late 1980s.[5]

MEASURING WOMEN'S MOVEMENTS

For the purposes of this book, we measure the strength of women's movements in a number of ways. Because there are multiple ways of evaluating strength, we looked at a composite of measures. The strongest movements in Africa are found in Cameroon, Kenya, Mali, Senegal, Tanzania, Uganda, and to a lesser degree Ghana, South Africa, and Zimbabwe. Movement strength is determined, in part, by measures that contrast the numerical strength of the women's organizations relative to other types of organizations. These include (1) the ratio of women's human rights organizations relative to the overall figure for human rights organizations in a country[6] and (2) the ratio of women's organizations in the UN Economic and Social Council (ECOSOC) relative to the overall number of organizations from a country represented in ECOSOC. We also looked at (3) the number of women's

---

[5] http://www.africafeministforum.org/vi/, accessed 22 July 2007.
[6] http://www.hri.ca/organizations, accessed 16 July 2007.

organizations in a country relative to the number of women's organizations in other countries by comparing the per capita number of NGOs from each country attending the 1995 UN Conference on Women held in Beijing.[7] Finally, we examined the impact of women's organizations by looking at (4) the proportion of coverage of women's issues relative to general articles in each country in the news service AllAfrica.com over six months from 16 February to 16 July 2007 (accessed from LexisNexis). This includes coverage in both French and English and covers the whole of Africa, including the Lusophone countries. The articles are about the activities of women's organizations as well as about key issues being taken up by the women's movements in various countries, including issues of political representation. This measure captures the relative influence of women's movements on public discourse and the media. The second and fourth variables provide additional information on the extent to which women's organizations are engaged in international fora.

Although admittedly these are not precise measures, when taken together, they provide some comparative sense of the strength and visibility of women's movements in Africa.

## THE CASES OF CAMEROON, MOZAMBIQUE, AND UGANDA

This book draws on the expertise of its authors to examine the cases of Cameroon, Mozambique, and Uganda within the broader context of change in Africa. The cases reflect much of the variance that we are examining and, when combined, the cases are fairly representative of sub-Saharan African states today.

Relatively more has been written about women's mobilization in South Africa than in other parts of Africa (Albertyn 2005; Britton 2005; Goetz and Hassim 2003; Hassim 2006; McEwan 2000; Waylen 2007a). Therefore, it behooves us to explain why we are not focusing on this area, even though there is considerable reference to South Africa throughout the book. In a short period of time after the transition to democracy in 1996, South Africa was able to pass a significant amount of legislation affecting women. Women parliamentarians, through the Joint Committee on Improving the Quality of Life and Status of Women, had a positive effect on many key pieces of legislation, including laws impacting women, such as the 1996 Choice on the Termination of Pregnancy Act allowing women the right to abortion; the

---

[7] http://www.un.org/documents/ga/conf177/ngo/fwcw1995-ngoattendees.htm, accessed 22 July 2007.

1996 Films and Publications Act, which protects against the degradation of women and children; and the 1998 Domestic Violence Act, which increases the legal and institutional protection for victims of domestic abuse. The Labour Relations Act recognizes maternity rights and women's rights against sexual harassment in the workplace, whereas the Employment Equity Act requires employers to hire fairly across race, gender, and disability (Britton 2002). Moreover, women activists together with the parliamentarians were able to put in place a Commission on Gender Equality through the 1996 Commission for Gender Equality Act with the aim of ensuring that such laws were fully implemented. South Africa presents all the elements that help explain these policy changes, such as major upheaval in society, an active women's movement, membership in SADC, and greater economic wealth than that of the other African countries. South Africa has certainly had an impact on other countries, which is addressed in the book.

However, South Africa is somewhat of an anomaly for comparative purposes because it is considerably more urbanized, industrialized, and wealthier than its neighbors; it gained majority rule recently; it has a large white settler population; and it contends with the legacy of an apartheid state. Because it is not representative for the subset of countries that we are examining, we have left it out of the narrower selection of cases, even though it almost proves our arguments "too well."

The cases include former colonies of the United Kingdom (Cameroon and Uganda), Portugal (Mozambique), France (Cameroon), and, prior to World War I, Germany (Cameroon). The legacy of former colonial powers is evident primarily with respect to the adoption particular policies, such as the Family Code that is found in Francophone countries and gender budgeting policies primarily in the Commonwealth countries.

Cameroon is situated in Central Africa, whereas Uganda is in East Africa and Mozambique in southern Africa. This affects the kinds of regional alliances with which the countries are involved. Mozambique, for example, is involved with SADC, which has put pressures on member states to adopt woman-friendly policies.

All three countries have vibrant women's movements. Mozambique and Uganda have enjoyed especially autonomous women's movements. This autonomy is characteristic of movements emerging after the 1990s in much of Africa and has afforded women's organizations greater freedom than in the past to choose their own leaders, set their own agendas, and pursue their own sources of funding. Associational autonomy has allowed organizations to shift beyond the focus on income generation and handicrafts that typified women's organizations of the 1980s to an additional focus on political engagement and advocacy around issues that profoundly affect the status and welfare of women.

The three countries are fairly comparable in terms of GDP. Mozambique and Uganda fall squarely in the middle of African nations when it comes to measures of economic growth. The median per capita GDP for Africa is $1,536,[8] Uganda stands at $1,487 per capita GDP purchasing power parity (PPP) (medium human development), Mozambique has $1,237 GDP PPP (low human development), whereas Cameroon has a slightly higher $2,174 GDP PPP but falls between Mozambique and Uganda in terms of human development rankings.

Of the three countries, Mozambique has democratized the most, whereas Uganda has experienced some political opening but operates as a de facto semi-authoritarian state. Cameroon, which became a multiparty state in 1990 with an active civil society and women's movement, has nevertheless remained basically authoritarian. According to opposition leaders, its elections are fraught with manipulation and fraud, and the media are tightly controlled as media workers regularly complain of harassment. The strongest opposition is based in the Anglophone part of this country, which was a German colony until World War I, after which it was divided between Britain and France as a mandated territory under the League of Nations. Thus it retains both Francophone and Anglophone legacies to this day. With the exception of a few incidents, such as the 2007 protests against the lifting of presidential term limits, the country has largely been stable and peaceful since independence. Although the human rights situation has improved somewhat, human rights activists note that the judiciary is corrupt, freedom of association is limited, and members of the political opposition face repression and can be held without charges. They report torture, extrajudicial executions, and the disappearance of prisoners in custody. Ethnicity factors into appointments within the civil service, the military, and the parastatals (Fonchingong 2004; Mbaku 2002; Nkwi and Socpa 1997).

Uganda today is neither the dictatorship of Idi Amin (1971–9) nor of Milton Obote II (1980–5), nor is it democratic, even though it has held regular multiparty elections. Its introduction of multipartyism in 2005 took place at time when the executive was expanding its powers by lifting the constitutional presidential two-term limit. Extralegal repressive tactics continue to be used against opposition leaders, compromising the integrity of elections and creating an untenable human rights situation. Since the current constitution was adopted in 1995, Uganda has slid precipitously backward

---

[8] United Nations Development Programme, http://www.hdr.org/, accessed 10 July 2007.

in terms of respect for civil and political liberties. The government increasingly has harassed and intimidated opposition members, media workers, and even members of the judiciary. All these groups have vigorously sought to protect their autonomy. Associational life and the independent media are thriving, although subject to state monitoring and intermittent harassment and intimidation.

In Mozambique, elections are generally free and fair. The constitution guarantees freedom of the press, and the media operate freely, as do NGOs and human rights organizations. The judicial system has improved since the country moved to a multiparty system; however, it is crippled by lack of resources, widespread corruption, and the excessive influence of the executive. There are state tendencies to control civil society. Nevertheless, compared to the other two countries, it is considerably more democratic and mindful of political and civil liberties.

With respect to conflict, Mozambique and Uganda represent most dimensions of postconflict situations found in postindependent Africa and particularly after the 1990s: Mozambique won independence from Portugal in 1975 after a protracted decade of armed struggle; Uganda's five-year civil war ended in 1986 and marked the beginning of a new trend in postconflict advocacy for women's political representation and legislative reform. Mozambique's conflict between *Resistência Nacional Moçambicana* (RENAMO) and FRELIMO-led government forces ended in 1992, at a time when throughout Africa women were beginning to get involved in peacemaking activities in ways not seen in the past. The conflict in northern Uganda came to an end in 2006 after lasting nineteen years. In this last conflict, as in civil strife in Burundi, the Democratic Republic of Congo, Liberia, and Sierra Leone, women's organizations demanded to be included in the peace talks. Cameroon represents a country with no armed conflict.

## Comparison of Cases

The comparison of Cameroon, Mozambique, and Uganda illustrates the importance of all four explanatory factors that we have identified as crucial in explaining change in women's status: Mozambique has a relatively small but nevertheless autonomous women's movement that has made considerable gains, perhaps more than in our other cases of Uganda and Cameroon. Because Mozambique is a postconflict country and is influenced by SADC's women's rights agenda regionally, it has most of the factors that have helped explain the rapid adoption of a woman-friendly agenda. It has also benefited from donor support for gender-related reforms. Moreover, the ruling party

FRELIMO is committed to women's advancement, which stems in part from its socialist leanings.

Uganda has advanced in women's rights more than many other countries because of the relative strength of its women's movement, which is autonomous from parties and the state. Uganda has been influenced by the spread of gender-related international norms, as have the other two countries. It has also benefited from an influx of donor funds in the 1990s that supported the advocacy of women's organizations. Moreover, it is a postconflict country that underwent a fundamental transformation with the takeover by Yoweri Museveni's National Resistance Movement in 1986, after which many of the changes regarding women were evident. A 1995 constitution further institutionalized these new norms of gender equality. However, the failure to pass a key gender-related clause in the amendments to the 1998 Land Act and the languishing Domestic Relations Bill have also revealed the limits of this progress to women activists.

Cameroon has an active women's movement, and women's organizations are involved in activities that benefit the daily lives of women. Nevertheless, it has made little progress in advancing women's legal rights since independence. It does not share with Mozambique and Uganda a postconflict legacy, which is perhaps the most important difference between Cameroon and these two countries. Although Cameroon belongs to the subregional organization Economic Community of Central African States (ECCAS), this organization has only recently begun to advocate for women's rights and has yet to establish a record like that of SADC when it comes to female legislative representation in its member states. Cameroon has faced the same external pressures for reform as the other two countries, but has been slower than them, for example, in ratifying the AU Protocol on Women's Rights.

Cameroon has relatively low female representation, as 14 percent of the seats of the lower house are held by women whereas Mozambique has 35 percent of its parliamentary seats held by women and Uganda has 30 percent. Cameroon is similar to countries such as Kenya and Mali, where there have been strong pressures by women's movements to advance women's rights regarding representation in government and parliament, but little to show for such pressures.

Women's organizations in Cameroon, for example, mobilized with limited success around a number of legal provisions considered as discriminatory against women. These include Article 7 of the trade code, which permits a husband to put an end to his wife's gainful activity through notification of his opposition to the Trade Tribunal; Articles 1421 and 1428 of the Civil Code, which limit women's use and disposal of a couple's property;

and Article 1421, which grants the husband the right to manage a couple's jointly owned property and the right to sell or mortgage such property without the wife's consent. Furthermore, Articles 108 and 215 of the Civil Code grant the husband the exclusive right to determine the family residence, and Article 361 of the Penal Code defines the crimes of adultery in terms that are favorable to men.

In spite of pressure from women's groups to increase representation of women in decision-making positions, the revised 1996 Constitution of Cameroon provides for affirmative action for historically marginalized groups, but does not include women in these provisions.

The fact that Cameroon, Kenya, and Mali have trailed countries such as Burundi, Mozambique, Rwanda, and Uganda when it comes to female representation says much about the postconflict impact on women's representation. In 2007, after vigorous lobbying, women activists in Kenya failed to get legislation passed establishing a quota system in the country's parliament that would have added fifty special seats for which only women could compete. This book suggests that the existence of a vigorous women's movement alone is insufficient for reforms to be introduced. What needs to be explained is not why so little has happened in Cameroon, Kenya, or Mali, but rather why gender-related reforms occurred at all in countries such as Mozambique and Uganda. Major disruptions such as civil war or the collapse of an apartheid regime created new opportunities for women's movements to push for change in the latter group of countries. However, disruptions in and of themselves are also insufficient for change to occur. There needs to be a conjuncture of developments, including the rise of autonomous women's movements, the end of societal upheaval, the targeting of new resources to advance women's rights, and the presence of international influences and pressures for change. If the continuities with the past are too great, as in Angola and Eritrea, where an independent women's movement has been less evident, progress in women's rights has been slower in coming.

Nevertheless, it should be pointed out that women are advancing their circumstances in multiple ways, and sometimes the most meaningful changes come through women's extensive activities in organizations that seek to improve the lives of women and their communities at the local level. Women frequently belong to a wide range of organizations simultaneously. These organizations can also be intensely political in the local context. Women are involved in a mosaic of organizations, coalitions, and networks. In Cameroon, for example, these include faith-based organizations in their own churches as well as in ecumenical contexts; professional and common-interest sectoral groups both at home and in the diaspora; and women's rotating credit schemes and mutual support groups known as the *njangi* and *tontines*. Additionally, there are women's branches of development-oriented village or hometown development associations, common initiative groups, and the alumni organizations of the various single-sex or all-girl educational establishments, to name a few examples. Women to this day may serve as primary custodians of customary practices affecting women within the various chiefdoms, kingdoms, lamidats, and clans, which is a major source of authority at the local level.

Women's self-help organizations have often emerged as key actors for the socioeconomic development at the local level. They have their own internal rules and regulations governing their activities, violations of which sometimes draw fines. These women's groups generally concern themselves with the improvement of their families and communities but also the empowerment and improvement of the livelihood of women and girls. Because of these functions, they have often attracted external support. The Gatsby Charitable Foundation, the Mutual Financing Association for African Women, the National Employment Fund, the Private Enterprises Credit Agency, SOS Women, the Women Promoters' Savings and Credit Cooperatives, and other such organizations have also contributed to the mobilization of women in the micro-credit and income generation areas.

Although the aforementioned descriptions are based in the Cameroonian context, they reflect general patterns found throughout the continent. And although the focus of this book is primarily on national-level mobilization of women for women's rights, these local organizations generally are the most salient forms of organization in transforming the daily lives of women in the most immediate sense.

CONCLUSIONS

Women's organizations increased exponentially throughout Africa since the early 1990s, as have the arenas in which women have been able to assert new and varied concerns. Today, women activists are organizing locally and nationally and are networking across the continent on an unprecedented scale to advance their goals of promoting woman-friendly policies. They have been actively using the media to demand their rights in ways not as evident in the early 1980s. In some countries, they are taking their claims to land, inheritance, and associational autonomy to court. Women are challenging laws and constitutions that do not uphold gender equality. In addition, they are moving into government, legislative, party, NGO, and other leadership positions previously the exclusive domain of men. They are fighting for a female presence in areas where women were previously marginalized, such as the leadership of religious institutions, sports clubs, and boards of private and public institutions.

In these and other ways, women have taken advantage of the new political openings that occurred in the 1990s in the contexts of the end of major civil conflicts and the onset of political liberalization. While political liberalization has allowed for the expansion of women's organizations and associational life more generally, the changes we are witnessing have occurred in countries regardless of the level of democratization. Therefore, what explains these changes is not democratization per se, but rather the occurrence of major transformation, offering women's movements political opportunities that they could take advantage of to advance their goals.

The international women's movement and, in particular, the 1985 and 1995 UN women's conferences in Nairobi and Beijing, respectively, gave added impetus to women's mobilization. Pressures from multilateral organizations such as the United Nations agencies and from regional organizations such as SADC pressured governments to take steps to improve the status of women domestically. Donors increasingly allocated funds to support these efforts, while improving economic conditions facilitated the adoption of woman-friendly policies in some countries.

## 2

# Historic Influences on Contemporary Women's Movements

The contemporary women's movements in Africa draw on multiple historic traditions of resistance. They draw some of their tactics from indigenous women's strategies that were part of African societies before colonization. They have also been influenced by experiences of anticolonial resistance and by national liberation movements that thrust women into new roles beyond motherhood, being a wife or an obedient daughter. And finally, and perhaps most directly, they grew in response to the postcolonial party/state-directed women's organizations in the era of single parties and military rule. This chapter traces the historic origins of some of these forms of protest and collective action. It also discusses some of the historical factors, and the impact of colonial policies on civil society and in the area of education that influenced these earlier forms of mobilization.

## PRECOLONIAL AND INDIGENOUS FRAMES AND FORMS OF COLLECTIVE ACTION

Contemporary women's movements have drawn on a wealth of historical traditions of collective resistance, some of which predate colonialism. They have been transformed from more localized forms of resistance into broader anticolonial protests, and some tactics have found their way into contemporary protest movements.

### Political Motherhood

One older frame for political action that is frequently drawn on in contemporary protest movements is an essentialized notion of "motherhood"

(Tibbetts 1994). Motherhood is generally the basis on which women often say they sacrifice for their families, love and rear their children, oppose violence, take selfless action, and carry out many other duties and obligations. In a variety of contemporary contexts, women have at times transformed the trope of "motherhood" into a political resource, while at other times it has served as an obstacle to women's advancement. Due to the historical and cultural separation between women and men's mobilization, women have often used their position as mothers as a basis of moral authority from which to argue for their inclusion in politics. They have used it as a resource with which to demand changes in political culture, demanding that the values of nurturing, sacrifice, and justice be included in political practice and that corruption, violence, and sectarianism be rejected.

Iina Soiri calls this "radical motherhood" in the Namibian context, where during the liberation struggle, motherhood was seen, not as a silent passive, domestic activity, but rather as a revered and valued position from which to fight against injustice (1996: 91).

For some it is a rhetorical device. As Winnie Byanyima, former Ugandan member of parliament and leader of the women's rights group Forum for Women in Development, explained in a reference to "eating" (a metaphor with multiple meanings but often connoting personal appropriation of state resources):

Values which we women care about such as caring, serving, building, reconciling, healing and sheer decency are becoming absent from our political culture. This eating is crude, self-centered, egoistic, shallow, narrow and ignorant. We should ban eating from our political language. Madam Chairman,...it is a culture which we must denounce and do away with if we are to start a new nation. (Proceedings of the Constituent Assembly 1994: 1490)

Asha Ahmed Abdalla ran for president of Somalia in 2003 using the slogan "Give Somalia a Mother's Nurturing!" Abdalla was a representative in the fifteen-member parliament in Somalia's Transitional National Government after 2000 and served as the minister of demobilization, disarmament and reintegration (Packard 2003). One Botswanan women's rights organization, Emang Basadi, even has had as its slogan: "Vote a Woman! Suckle the Nation!" Women sometimes draw on their domestic experiences to create a new kind of political imagery that defies the paternal one that evolved with the colonial state and has remained in the postcolonial context. For example, in Kenya during the 1992 elections, one delegate argued at a meeting of the National Committee on the Status of Women that since women carry the responsibility for the security and stability of the family and community, "let it be understood that women are already minister of culture in their own homes" and now they want to take charge of key portfolios ("Kenyan Women..." 1992).

The motherhood trope has particular resonance in postconflict contexts; in Liberia, for example, Ellen Johnson-Sirleaf is often referred to as the mother of the nation who "heals the nation" from the wounds of war. One time she was greeted by hundreds of supporters singing "Sweet Mother, Liberia Needs You" ("Liberia Politics..." 2006).

The use of motherhood is not the only basis for women's political authority, nor is it the only resource used by women. Nevertheless, is it not considered as controversial or problematic in the way that it is regarded by many feminists in the West.

Judith Van Allen (2000) has shown that the public/private divide in Tswana society in Botswana, but even more generally in Africa, does not correspond to Western perceptions, which draw a sharp divide between domestic/household/child-rearing activities and work/politics/warfare. In Africa, women's labor, whether it is in the fields, in a factory, or as a professional, is generally seen as an extension of her reproductive activities, as part of caring for her children and feeding and clothing them. In politics, as in other "public spaces," women's movements demand equality but they generally do not want to be considered the same as men. As Van Allen explains:

Women's rights discourse itself reflects the continuing construction of "woman" as "mother," and the assertion of the nurturing, provisioning, suckling mother as a model of female leadership, both in its goals and in its language....In campaign slogans and campaign discourse in general, this assumption is carried into a positive statement about women: they are better fitted than men to be in government because it is in their "nature" to be caretakers. (Van Allen 2000: 8)

Feminists in Africa and elsewhere often criticize the use of motherhood as a basis for political authority because excludes those who are not mothers. It reinforces a stereotype about women that their roles may limit them to that of mother. It also associates women's participation with what many consider a natural role rather than agency and choice. It may prevent women from entering into politics on an equal basis with men if the focus is on their roles as mothers. Moreover, if women are seen as "peaceloving" or "good political leaders" because they are mothers, then if they turn out to be violent or poor leaders, does that mean that we reject them because they are mothers? It has implications for equally stereotyped notions of men and women without children.

In 1994, Mary Karooro Okurut ran as a delegate in Bushenyi District for a seat in Uganda's Constituent Assembly in Uganda, the body elected to debate and complete the Draft Constitution. She found herself defeated, in part, because her opponent – and voters – questioned her capacity to lead and be empathetic since she had not experienced motherhood. She later went on to win two legislative races in the same district, but found the initial experience demoralizing.[1] Okurut was not the only woman politician confronting such beliefs about motherhood. The aforementioned Winnie Byanyima, who also won a legislative seat in Mbarara, did so in spite of the fact that the Mothers Union of Mbarara explicitly told her that its members could not vote for her because she was not married at the time and that they were not sure that she as a single woman could represent their interests. She managed to convince most of them to support her by explaining that each individual has different talents and opportunities and while they were blessed as wives and mothers, she had other talents that enabled her to represent them in parliament effectively. But even she was forced at one point to produce her partner to prove that she was a "normal woman."

In spite of such serious limitations of the essentialized motherhood trope, the idea of a political mother whose purview extends into the public realm is nevertheless one that is drawn on in contemporary contexts and one that resonates deeply in most African societies.

## Continuities in Forms of Mobilization

Apart from ideologies of motherhood, a variety of precolonial tactics have carried over to the present and were marshaled from time to time in the struggle against colonialism, with some continuing to this day. A word of caution is warranted since some of these tactics are fairly uncommon forms of protest today and should not be perceived as dominant forms of collective action.

Secret cults are one form of collective action that has precolonial origins. For example, in the post-electoral violence that broke out following the 1992 presidential elections in Cameroon, unarmed elderly women of Cameroon's Social Democratic Front (SDF) belonging to a secret cult known as Takembeng took guard at the entrance of the residence of Ni John Fru

[1] Personal communication with Joy Kwesiga, January 2008.

Ndi, a presidential candidate and founder and chair of Cameroon's SDF who was contesting the election in which Paul Biya of the Cameroon Peoples Democratic Movement (CPDM) was declared the victor. There they chanted and invoked their much feared supernatural powers in protests supporting the SDF party. Unarmed, Takembeng members held silent morning marches across the Bamenda city, during which they exposed their breasts and brandished peace symbols. The Takembeng women were responding to allegations of Ndi's imminent arrest in Bamenda, in the North West Province of Cameroon (Awasom 2002). It is widely believed that these women played a key role in the peaceful restoration of order and tranquility in this part of Cameroon during that crucial period. There were rumors of casualties within the ranks of the government forces following their encounters with Takembeng, thus deterring officers from attempting to arrest Ndi (Mbunwe 2007).

Takembeng was an indigenous women's organization with historic antecedents, whose members were believed to possess mystical powers derived from their "sacred reproductive organs" (that is, the source of life). The women's militancy was seen as a spiritual antidote to disaster. Any number of misfortunes might befall someone who set eyes on their nakedness, including impotency, infertility, and death. According to a Feminia (2002) report, Takembeng was a mutual-support group that counterbalanced the male-dominated village governance structure, Kwifon, and protected the weak within the community against the powerful members. Takembeng's members would let the Kwifon know whether they disagreed with decisions it had taken. Part of the attraction of this mode of women's mobilization is its appeal to the human conscience and its tolerant, pacifist, and nonviolent character, which resonates with some of the key attributes associated with women's participation in the political arena.

Older organizational forms have sometimes been revived or modified, including location-based development associations and dual-sex organizations. There has been a revival of the dual-sex governance structures in Igbo (Nigeria) as well as other West African societies. A dual-sex political system is one in which representatives of each gender govern their own members through a council. In much of former Eastern Nigeria, most communities historically had a broad-based Women's Governing Council that had sole jurisdiction over wide-ranging political, economic, and cultural affairs of women, from market issues, to relations with men and to morality. These organizations were autonomous of the state, yet their decisions were binding regardless of social status, education, or income level. Moreover, the local councils could represent women living as far apart as Lagos or New York.

Their leaders serviced a wide range of associations and therefore were multifaceted in their approach, since they were concerned with social, cultural, religious, economic, and political issues simultaneously (Nzegwu 1995).

These are but a few examples of older forms of mobilization that have been modified and adapted to modern circumstances. Others include rotating credit associations, farming groups, dance groups, and other cultural groups (for example, *lelemama* women's dance groups in Kenya and Tanzania), age-sets, mutual assistance groups, market associations, and beer brewer's associations. Some, such as the *lelemama* groups in coastal East Africa, played important roles in the independence movements; others were established to meet the daily needs of women, their families, and communities; and still other groups served political functions at the local level.

## Continuities in Collective Action Tactics

Some of the more dramatic precolonial tactics were evident in the struggles for independence. In British Cameroon during the colonial era, Kom women drew on their earlier tradition of Anlu and Fombuen to ridicule and shame colonial male authorities in the late 1950s in a three-year rebellion involving seven thousand women against rising taxes and laws regulating farming techniques (Diduk 1989). The practice involved women dressing as if they were engaged in battle: They wore men's torn trousers and vines and smeared their faces with charcoal. The women would let out shrill cries and start taunting the man who had offended a woman. They might shout and sing insults, expose their private parts, or urinate and defecate in the surrounding area in order to shame the man into repenting by wearing the vines. After this, the man would be forgiven, bathed, and the matter would be dropped.

In Guinea, similarly, women invoked the spirit guardian of women and children, Bassikolo, in the struggle for independence. They drew on precolonial practices associated with shaming men who had beaten their wives, donning male clothes (trousers), brandishing sharp knives called "penis cutters," and pounding on the building of the offending male (Schmidt 2005a).

In some of the most vehement protests against colonial rule in Zambia, leaders of the Women's Brigade of the pro-independence party United National Independence Party (UNIP) mobilized women to expose their breasts to various colonial officials. One such leader was a financially independent widow, Julia "Chikanomeka" Mulenga, who came to be known as "Mama UNIP" and mounted protests against colonial leaders, including the British foreign secretary, Ian Mcleod (Geisler 2004).

These types of shaming and cursing tactics have been incorporated into modern-day struggles across the continent, even though they have to be understood within the contexts of their particular societies. Similar strategies involving female nakedness were incorporated into contemporary struggles from South Africa's shanty towns against the regime during apartheid, to Kenya's democracy movement in the 1990s, and into protests starting in the 1990s against foreign oil companies in Nigeria's delta region. In 1992, in Uhuru Park at the center of Nairobi, Kenya, women found themselves in a violent confrontation with police when they went on a hunger strike in support of political prisoners. Older women stripped themselves naked to heap the most vehement of curses on the military police who tried to break the strike. This tactic was a powerful statement of condemnation also aimed at government authorities and their repression.

Similarly, in other contemporary contexts, women protested the allegedly rigged elections in Zambia in 2002 by demonstrating half naked. This time, the protesters were not UNIP women, as they had been during the struggle for independence, but rather women of an opposition party, the United Party for National Development (UPND), who were protesting the Movement for Multiparty Democracy (MMD)–led government. They felt that women had borne the brunt of MMD rule by paying expensive school fees and costly maize meal prices and by dealing with poor health services ("We're Capable of Fighting..." 2002).

In East Africa, the exposure of breasts in protest has been used not to shame as in West Africa, but rather as an expression of opposition through mourning and grief. One of the most dramatic examples of this kind of resistance was mounted by women in the northern Gulu District in Uganda in an April 1989 march for peace. Over 1,500 women walked through the streets of Gulu for five hours protesting the "bitterness of the war." They wore their mourning dresses, tied scarves around their heads, and carried baskets as they wept, chanted funeral songs, and blew funeral horns, bringing almost the whole town to tears. Many of the women were half naked, lifting up their breasts to denounce the fighting. Their protest was aimed at highlighting the ways in which women had borne much suffering as a result of the unrest in the north. It was as much an expression of resistance to the actions of their own menfolk as it was against the government troops (Tripp 2000).

These strategies involving transgressions of gender – for example, women wearing trousers and engaging in warlike behavior – and transgressions of gender norms – in which women expose their private parts in public – are responses to intense societal disruptions in which gender relations are under strain. As in the collective shaming of individual men who have violated a social norm, the shaming of colonial authorities reflected the fact that women were under duress. As Meredith Terretta (forthcoming) explains, women expressed themselves historically through this type of protest when they faced increased political and economic marginalization due to the introduction of new taxes or cash crop farming, increased workloads as men became laborers, or new demands on their labor, land, time, and resources. The use of these shaming and grieving strategies in contemporary contexts has been employed to underscore women's outrage with authoritarianism, war, apartheid, and undemocratic practices of various governments, but it has also served to highlight the gendered nature of these phenomena and the ways in which women have experienced them.

## Colonial Rule and the Emergence of Women Nationalists

Another inspiration of contemporary women's mobilization arises from the anticolonial movements in which women were actively involved. Anticolonial resistance was one of the few ways for women to enter into public life during the rise of nationalism. Women played key roles in the independence movements, participating as nationalists, freedom fighters, and as members of political parties, trade unions, and civil society organizations. Before looking at the ways that women engaged the nationalist movements, it is worth examining the broader context of colonial policy toward civil society mobilization in general and toward women's mobilization in particular.

### COLONIAL POLICY TOWARD CIVIL SOCIETY

One of reasons for today's weak civil societies in Africa is the fact that colonialists permitted only limited forms of mobilization and purposefully curtailed the development of civil society, even very benign forms of mobilization. Some colonial powers were more restrictive than others and this, in turn, had an impact on the evolution of women's organizations and movements in later years. The Portuguese, for example, generally did not allow Mozambicans to have their own associations. There were some local associations of small producers – traders, carpenters, washers, hairdressers, painters, tailors – but none were officially recognized. The Portuguese in Mozambique had their own associations guided by corporate principles representing the interests of entrepreneurs, laborers, agriculturalists, and other professionals. The colonial state, in other words, defined and controlled associational life (Cahen 1984).

Thus the majority of the Mozambican population relied on informal urban and rural networks, organizations, and mutual-interest associations to assist with funerals, marriages, unemployment, imprisonment, and the support of immigrants from neighboring countries. The lack of opportunities for mobilization affected women's organizations in Mozambique, which even to this day are less varied and numerous than those found in neighboring Tanzania, where mobilization was also restricted by the British colonial administration and by post-independence governments.

## COLONIAL EDUCATION POLICY

Colonial education policies and opportunities for the professionalization of women also had an impact on contemporary women's movements. Access to education created a small cadre of elite women who were active in leading women's movements prior to independence. Some had studied abroad, others were economically independent. They were involved in a wide variety of women's organizations, generally oriented around religious, professional, welfare, and development concerns (Amadiume 2000; Jirira 1995; McFadden 1997). Thus, colonial and mission education, in spite of its discrimination against girls and women and its focus on creating "suitable" wives for educated African men, nevertheless opened up opportunities for a limited few. This was uneven across the colonies, which had implications for future mobilization.

By 1980, the legacy of different colonial patterns of education was evident: In former British colonies, the ratio of girls to boys enrolled in primary schools was 90 percent, while the ratio stood at 74 percent in former Belgian colonies, 61 percent for former French colonies, and 56 percent for former Portuguese colonies (Robertson 1986). These colonial legacy gaps are still detected a quarter of a century later in differences in female representation in tertiary education. By 2007, the percentage of females who made up the student body in universities of former British colonies reached 40 percent on average, while in Francophone countries they barely constituted 29 percent. In the former Portuguese colonies, women made up 35 percent of the student body, which has less to do with their colonial legacy and more to do with the political objectives of contemporary ruling parties.[2] Of the former Belgian colonies, Rwandan women made up 39 percent of the students and Burundian women 28 percent. These educated women form the bulk of the leadership of the national women's movements, which may help explain, in part, why former British colonies – with larger numbers of

---

[2] Department of Economic and Social Affairs, United Nations Statistical Division. *Tertiary Education. Statistical and Indicators on Women and Men*, Table 4d. Updated June 2007. http://unstats.un.org/unsd/demographic/sconcerns/education/, accessed 19 August 2007.

university-educated women – have more active women's movements when compared with some of the other former colonies.

Missionary and colonial education often had the goal of making African women into better wives of "Westernized" or educated African men. Much of the education of girls in schools and in women's clubs was focused on child-rearing practices, hygiene, housekeeping, nutrition, and other domestic activities. Education of girls imposed on African societies Western notions of gender, domesticity, morality, and household divisions of labor, regardless of women's own realities, needs, or priorities (Callan and Ardener 1984; Hunt 1990, 1999; Masemann 1974; Mianda 2002; Predelli 2000; Strobel 1991; Summers 1991; Yates 1982). Although some of this education served to keep women domesticated and depoliticized, women often used their education to broaden their horizons, participate in and lead women's organizations, engage in political activities, seek employment, and start businesses.

Those women who were able to gain secondary and higher education early on frequently became involved in national women's organizations, where they exchanged ideas with other women. Some entered leadership positions. For example, in 1955 Eunice Lubega of Uganda became the first African woman to gain a university degree in East Africa. She went on to become the first African woman to head the Uganda Association of Women, one of the first organizations advocating women's rights in that country. Education enabled women to provide leadership in other fora as well. Women were elected, for example, into mainstream church leadership but also into community-related development associations.

Educated women in the pre-independence period organized to demand changes in laws, particularly family law. In Uganda, for instance, educated women used the Uganda Council of Women to push for the Kalema Commission, a government commission on marriage, divorce, and the status of women. The Commission traveled throughout the country to solicit views from individuals and organizations on the subject. Its 1964 report laid the foundation for an amendment to the statutory Succession Act, which allowed the wife and children to receive a large enough portion of the deceased husband's estate, enabling them to maintain themselves. Nascent women's movements during the colonial period also advocated girls' education and, in several cases, were able to convince government to increase opportunities for girls' education.

Education was the key to political leadership as well. In 1954, Sarah Ntiro of Uganda became the first woman in East Africa to obtain a degree from Oxford University. Ntiro later become one of the first African women members of Uganda's Legislative Council, where she served from 1958 to

1961 and was a member of three Ugandan delegations to the United Nations General Assembly.

Some educated women were selected to head institutions, such as schools. Such positions opened up opportunities for women to be appointed to policy-making bodies, such as the board of directors of parastatals or private firms.

During colonial rule, some community development departments or ministries offered select women leadership roles in which they could influence society. This was useful in linking elite women to grassroots women through childcare, health education, literacy, and other such services.

Some educated women traveled abroad and acquired new perspectives as they sought further education or served as representatives of their organizations. The Young Women's Christian Association (YWCA), for example, sponsored two Ugandan women to the United States for several months of training in 1952–3. There they met Harry Truman, Lucille Ball, and Marilyn Monroe. Rebecca Mulira recounted the impact the trip had on her:

I saw how active each woman was.... And I said to myself, in Uganda we are sleeping, we are leaving everything in the hands of men. When I get back I'm going to do something about it.... My intention was to see that women also take part in politics, instead of leaving it in the hands of men only. (Tripp 2000)

The expansion of girls' education in the 1940s and 1950s in Nigeria, for example, made it possible for many women eventually to become teachers, education officers, and other civil servants. In particular, training in domestic science permitted women to become involved in many new small-scale businesses as seamstresses, bakers, caterers, or restaurant, café, or hotel operators. The daughters and sons of these independent women entrepreneurs later became quite influential (Denzer 1992).

Formal education also enabled women to become role models for others. Many parents, both fathers and mothers, encouraged their daughters to go to school because of those who had already gained an education and succeeded in the various professions as teachers, nurses, and civil servants. However, the lack of education for large numbers of women had profound effects on the ways in which they engaged in the nationalist movements, as we will see in the following section.

## WOMEN IN NATIONALIST MOVEMENTS

Women were integral to nationalist movements throughout Africa. Women had different goals within the nationalist movements. We now turn to four ways in which nationalist movements engaged women: (1) As we see in the case of Algeria and Tanganyika, women were part of the struggle for independence, but their particular concerns were not articulated or addressed by the nationalist movement. (2) In other cases, such as Mozambique, women's rights issues were addressed, but were set aside to be taken up after liberation. (3) In the cases of Guinea and Mali, women's concerns were seen as part and parcel of the process of independence. (4) Finally, in some contexts such as in Cameroon, women themselves became involved in nationalist movements to advance their own gender-specific and other agendas. In Cameroon, women activists engaged the colonial administration regarding issues such as the taxation of women, market prices, and labor disputes. These issues often affected women more than men because of their extensive market involvement. Yet in other contexts, as in Uganda, the nationalist movement provided an opening for women to mobilize to expand women's rights to run for office, to vote, and to be represented politically. They fought for expanded employment opportunities for women, the expansion of girl's education, and women's literacy initiatives. The extent to which women succeeded in achieving their objectives after independence varied considerably from country to country.

An additional distinction needs to be made between the educated Christian women nationalists – who were few in number – and those who made up the bulk of the nationalist movements, who often had little formal schooling and had little contact with Westerners. Elizabeth Schmidt (2002) argues that in this respect the movements in Guinea, Nigeria, and other parts of West Africa resembled East African women's nationalist mobilization. However, unlike in Guinea, Kenya, and Tanganyika, elite women were fairly visible and active in nationalist movements in Nigeria, Sierra Leone, and South Africa.

## WOMEN NATIONALISTS WITHOUT WOMEN'S RIGHTS

In some nationalist movements, women became involved to further the goal of attaining independence, but their own specific gender-based goals were either subsumed or ignored within the more general nationalist movement. This influenced the way in which women's policies were addressed in the post-independence period. Nevertheless, women's commitment to independence often made them loyal supporters of the liberation movements, even when their own demands as women were forced onto the backburner or denied altogether.

Although women's involvement in the Algerian war for independence from France (1954–62) has often been thought of as the catalyst for future women's involvement in armed struggles in other African liberation wars, women had in fact fought in nationalist struggles much earlier. As early as 1916, they fought in battles near Tangier against the Spanish, taking up places in the firing line after men were killed. Women continued to fight on the frontline against the Spanish colonialists in Morocco into the 1920s. In 1921, women were reported to have ambushed a Spanish patrol in Jibala while their men were away and had fought against the first Italian incursions into Libya in 1911–12 (Pennell 1987).

In Tanganyika, which in 1964 merged with Zanzibar to become Tanzania, women were part and parcel of the nationalist movement, which willingly incorporated women as participants and leaders but did not address their gender-specific concerns. Susan Geiger (1987) has shown that Tanganyikan women formed the backbone of the nationalist movement and were critical to the success of the Tanganyika African National Union (TANU) and its women's wing in leading the country to independence. In the pre-independence period, Bibi Titi was as well known as Julius Nyerere in leading the independence movement. As a fiery orator, she was able to rally and inspire the crowds who came to hear Nyerere and herself (Geiger 1987, 1990; Meena 1992). One British observer who in 1957 traveled throughout Tanganyika to study the nationalist movement found that women made up a "considerable proportion of the audience" at TANU rallies. She observed "many of them still draw their veils across their faces when being personally addressed by the male members, but the leaders of the women's organization in the capital were every bit the equal of the other members of the Central Committee [of TANU]." She noted Bibi Titi's "jovial" and "dynamic enthusiasm" to be "contagious in its optimism and determination" (Wicken 1958). Nevertheless, although women were central to the independence movement, women's concerns were not of paramount importance at this time in Tanzania.

Women's experiences in the Algerian revolution were similar in this respect. Women participated as combatants (*mujahidat*), spies, and porters, as well as in supporting roles as nurses, cooks, and launderers. Conservative estimates indicate that women accounted for about eleven thousand (3 percent) of the fighters and many more participated in the revolution in other ways. However, after the war, many women felt that rather than being rewarded for their multiple roles in the revolution, they were instead deprived of their rights as women. Although many were ready to return to normal family life, they had not anticipated this sharp reversal. As Madame Houria Imache Rami, a *mujahida* fighter, put it, "[in the *maquis*] (guerilla bands) we were all equal in the war – it was afterward that our citizenship was taken away from us" (Turshen 2002). These setbacks were enshrined in a 1984 Family Code that classified all women as minors when it came to education, work, travel, marriage and divorce, and inheritance. Although women petitioned and got some of the worst clauses retracted from the law, many felt the Code was an affront after all the sacrifices that women had made during the revolution. The quid pro quo they were expecting did not materialize. Only recently have women begun to advance, making up 70 percent of the country's lawyers, 60 percent of its judges, 60 percent of its university students, and the majority of doctors. Women are also increasingly contributing a greater share of the household income than men (Slackman 2007).

## WOMEN'S LIBERATION POSTPONED

Unlike the independence movements in Algeria or Zimbabwe, where women participated in the movements strictly as nationalists, in countries such as Guinea-Bissau and Mozambique, women's liberation was considered integral to the liberation of the countries from colonial rule (Ranchod-Nilsson 2006; Urdang 1978). FRELIMO (Liberation Front of Mozambique, or *Frente de Libertação de Moçambique*) was formed in 1962 out of several nationalist organizations to fight for independence from the Portuguese fascist and colonial regime. Many women shared these goals and participated in the armed struggle. But they also saw these movements as a way to defend their interests as women (Arnfred 1988).

FRELIMO leaders had a vision of building a new type of non-patriarchal society in which women's liberation was an integral part of a post-colonial order. As Mozambique's first president, Samora Machel, said at the First Conference of the Mozambican Woman's Organization in Tanzania in 1975: "Woman's liberation is a necessity of the revolution, a condition of its triumph, and guarantee of its continuity" (Urdang 1978).

In the liberated zones in 1965, some women created their own military contingent as they confronted the necessity of defending newly liberated zones. By 1966, the FRELIMO leadership officially incorporated these women into its army, naming them the Feminine Detachment (*Destacamento Feminino*). This decision was met with resistance from both women and men in FRELIMO who were unprepared for this challenge to gender power relations and feared the consequences of women's military involvement in the struggle (Casimiro 1986, 1999). This was an important turning point in the armed struggle. Up until that time, men had made most decisions regarding the liberation movement. When women sought a greater role within the movement, they were challenged and shunned. It was not until 1973 that the Organização da Mulher Moçambicana (Mozambican Woman Organization) was created in exile in Tanzania (Casimiro 1999).

Due to influence from communist parties in Eastern Europe and the Soviet Union, FRELIMO did not incorporate the domestic sphere and the invisible work of women in its analysis. There was never a discussion within FRELIMO about the division of labor within the household, as women were considered simultaneously mothers, wives, and freedom fighters without regard for their domestic contributions. For FRELIMO, women's liberation could only take place by their participation in the labor force, which discounted their work as cultivators and homemakers in a country where 85 percent of the population lives in the rural areas and where women were the main agricultural producers in a country where smallholder production was predominant. Large numbers of men were contracted to work in the South African mines, farms, and plantations.

Thus, the women's movement in Mozambique was created and shaped by the nationalist movement, with a narrow socialist vision and a political policy toward modernization that did not account for the multiple challenges that women faced. The movement was characterized by an uneasy relationship with the nationalist movement and its leaders, complicated by loyalties that originated during the armed struggle. Some women leaders were strongly attached to the FRELIMO party ideology and seldom dared to speak out against its gender policies because they felt that they owed FRELIMO their positions and had great respect for the party (Arnfred 1988; Casimiro 1986, 1999).

After independence in 1975, the emerging sensibilities of women became even more apparent, especially as women sought to assert themselves as political and social actors and to transform the personal into the political. If women tried to talk about women and gender specificities, they might be considered hostile to African culture and acting against the FRELIMO party or the state.

Some liberation movements, such as the one in Mozambique, were explicit about their intent to liberate women after liberating the country, yet they rarely lived up to this goal, even after independence. Women's agency and capacity to act autonomously of the liberation movement were circumscribed due to the armed struggle, which made it difficult if not impossible to challenge the discipline imposed by those in power. Only when and where women mobilized autonomously after the liberation struggle was over, in countries such as Mozambique, Namibia, and South Africa, were changes in women's status apparent.

## WOMEN'S LIBERATION AS PART OF NATIONALIST MOVEMENTS

Women were drawn to some nationalist movements because the movements themselves incorporated demands for gender equality and a greater public role for women. In contrast to Mozambique, where women's demands were postponed until the country was liberated, in Guinea and Mali, women's emancipation was considered integral to the independence movement in the 1940s up to independence in 1958 and 1960, respectively.

The nationalist movement appealed to many Guinean women in part because the leader of Party Démocratique de Guinée, Sékou Touré, offered them a greater public role. Touré had made women's political participation one of the four guiding principles of the party. Led by women such as Mafory Bangoura and Camara M'Balia, women created cultures of anti-colonial resistance through their songs, dress, performance, dance, and rallies (Schmidt 2005b). Women contributed significantly to Touré's success. Guinean women participated actively in the 1947–8 railway workers' strike and the 1953 general strike; they opposed French appointed chiefs in 1955; and women voted against Guinea's membership in the West African French Community, which helped pave the way for the country's independence (Geiger 1990).

In French Sudan (Mali), women's roles did not permit public political action. Nevertheless, the Women's Bureau of the Union Démocratique des Peuple Maliens (Democratic Union of the Malian People) was formed in 1958 and engaged women in the independence movement, demanding a role for women in the liberation and socioeconomic development of the country. They called for literacy and improvement of health services for women, as documented in 1975 in *Femme d'Afrique*, written by Aoua Kéeita, a Malian nationalist and feminist leader (Turrittin 1993).

## WOMEN'S ECONOMIC AND POLITICAL CONCERNS WITHIN THE NATIONALIST AGENDA

Finally, there were many instances where women did not wait for the independence movements to take up their demands. They engaged in nationalist struggles in order to defend their own interests as economic and political actors. They fought their own battles for gender equality, which were integral to the independence struggles.

Economic issues affecting women's livelihood, such as taxation, galvanized women in many of the African colonies. In former East Cameroon, a mandate territory of France, women's political activities can be traced back to 1946, when the Association of Cameroonian Women (Association Pour L'Emancipation de la Femme Camerounaise) was formed under the leadership of Dieng neé Eteki Maladie Laurence in Douala. In 1948, the nationalist party, the Union des Populations du Cameroun (UPC) was created. It focused on women's mobilization and channeling women's energies into social centers for nonpolitical action. In 1952, women militants in the UPC formed an exclusively female party, the Union Democratique des Femmes Camerounaise (UDEFEC), under the leadership of Emma Mbom in Koumassi Douala. Its activities contributed to the fight for the independence and reunification of Cameroon. In 1955, the UPC launched an armed struggle for independence and was subsequently banned. At the same time, the UDEFEC was dissolved but continued its activities in hiding until 1960, when it was relegalized. By 1962, the party had disappeared altogether.

A second women's political party, the Union of Cameroonian Women (UFC) was formed in 1949. It was affiliated with the conservative party Evolution Sociale Camerounaise (ESOCAM), which was backed by the French administration to resist popular demands for the reunification of the British and French parts of Cameroon. The UFC gave rise to leaders such as Marie-Irène Ngapeth, Julienne Niat, and Marthe Ouandié, who were united in their view that women's rights and equality were integral to democracy. Ngapeth and Ouandié eventually joined the UDEFEC, but with the banning of the party, Ouandié was forced into exile in 1956 and Ngapeth went into hiding. Niat, who remained with UFC, became the sole female member of parliament after independence in 1960 (Adams 2004b; Terretta forthcoming).

Cameroonian women also engaged the international arena in their struggle for independence. An astounding one thousand of the six thousand recorded petitions sent to the United Nations Trusteeship Council came from women nationalists, according to Meredith Terretta (forthcoming). They called for independence, the reunification of the Cameroonian territories under French and British control, the withdrawal of foreign troops, and the lifting of economic restrictions on the Cameroonian business sector. Women petitioned the Trusteeship Council regarding land rights, the licensing of home-based self-employed workers, restrictions on food and beverages vending points, and other such issues affecting the livelihood of women and their families.

Female political militancy continued within associations such as the powerful Conseil National des Femmes Camerounaise (CNFC) under the leadership of Madeleine Mbono Samba, whose extensive capacity to mobilize women was viewed as a threat by what was then the country's single party, the Cameroon National Union (CNU). With independence and the reunification of the country in 1960, the activities of the CNFC were checked. Subsequent machinations by national government authorities in the ruling party led to its absorption into the CNU's women's wing, the Women's Cameroon National Union (WCNU).

In Nigeria, one of the first women's groups to mobilize was the Lagos Market Women's Association (LMWA), founded in the mid-1920s by Madame Alimotu Pelewura, a fish trader and head of market women in Ereko market. The LMWA actively protested market taxes imposed by the colonial administration along with price controls and poor trading conditions. The Association was particularly opposed to efforts by European companies and various chiefs who used such tax laws to monopolize trade. Although members of the LMWA such as Pelewura joined political parties, the organization remained an independent interest group (Johnson 1982).

In southeastern Nigeria, thousands of Igbo women from several provinces launched a women's war in 1929 against threats that colonial authorities would tax women's property. The war involved demonstrations, burning buildings, looting factories, breaking jails, and attacking European stores and trading centers (Ifeka-Moller 1973; Leith-Ross 1965; Van Allen 1972, 1976).

Underlying these tensions was a deeper change in male–female relations in which women were being sidelined. Women had lost political and other powers that they had previously held when the colonial administration banned almost all institutions outside of the Native Administration. For example, the colonial authorities banned the political functions of the women's *mikiri* or consultative meetings that were held to discuss and regulate market activity. Moreover, the introduction of Christianity instituted a religion that was embedded in Victorian notions of gender, thus further marginalizing Igbo women (Van Allen 1972).

In the 1940s, the Abeokuta Women's Union (AWU), led by the Nigerian Yoruba woman Funmilayo Ransome Kuti, represented over one hundred thousand women who organized demonstrations, petitions, and boycotts to oppose the taxation of women. They even sent a representative to London to present their case. The Union succeeded in getting female taxation suspended and, in 1948, women gained a seat on the transition council that would replace the government. Suspicious of corruption, the women hired an accountant to audit the local administration accounts and proposed their own alternative budget. They filed a number of court cases, charging the local authorities with corruption. The AWU was later was transformed into a national Nigerian Women's Union, with branches across the country.

Around the same time in 1944, Lady Oyinkan Morenike Abayomi had formed the Women's Party in Lagos to campaign for women's rights. The founders were motivated by the fact that a large number of women owned homes and paid taxes, yet had no political representation. Moreover, girls had no opportunities to study in the United Kingdom because government scholarships were reserved for boys. The Women's Party lobbied for increased opportunities for girls' education and literacy for adult women, more employment of women in the civil service, the right of female minors to trade in Lagos, and the protection of the rights of market women. The women were drawn together by their common interest in nationalism, remaining firm in their conviction of seeking unity across ethnic and religious lines (i.e., Christian and Muslim) – a theme that reoccurs in women's mobilization in Nigeria and elsewhere from the pre-independence period to the present. The party sought political office for women and succeeded in getting women onto the Lagos Town Council. The party eventually was blended into the National Council of Women's societies in 1956 (Johnson 1982; Parpart 1988).

In Sierra Leone, the struggle for women's rights emerged from the nationalist movement in which market women played a major role. Although women's protests focused on economic concerns, they soon incorporated broader issues relating to equality. Initially, ten thousand women led by Mabel Dove Danquah and Hannah Benka-Coker had protested the rising cost of food in Freetown in 1951. They petitioned the colonial administrative offices to allow market women to regain their monopoly of the trade in palm oil and rice, which had been usurped by Lebanese traders and large foreign trading establishments (Steady 2006).

The women succeeded in achieving many of their goals. In the process, they formed the Sierra Leone Women's Movement (WLWM) in 1951. The WLWM was made up of women of various ethnicities and from all walks of life, from nurses to teachers, businesswomen, and market women. Seeking a common Sierra Leonean identity, the organization played a major role in Sierra Leone's nationalist movement and had as its aim the improvement of the status of women; protecting the rights of market women; and ensuring female representation in government bodies with jurisdiction over policies regarding education, social welfare, and the economy. This was in stark contrast to the political parties at the time, which had been established along ethnic lines and were sharply divided.

One of the SLMWM leaders, Mabel Dove, became the first woman in West Africa to be elected to the legislature in 1954. Constance Cummings-John, a Krio, helped galvanize the movement, which was largely made up of non-Krios. She went on to win a seat in parliament in 1957 with the Sierra

Leone's Peoples Party. A decade later in 1967, she was elected mayor of
Freetown (Steady 2006: 64). The SLMWM was eventually overshadowed
by the National Congress of Sierra Leone Women (NCSLW), the women's
wing of the All Peoples' Congress Party led by Siaka Stevens, which came to
power in 1967. The NCSLW had little independence from the party and did
not work with other women's groups. At its height, it claimed a membership
of 35,000 (Denzer 1995).

Economic-related protests were organized in East Africa as well. Women
rioted against colonial procedures for assessment and collection of taxes in
Pare District, Tanganyika, in the 1940s (O'Barr 1976). In 1945, five hundred
Usangi women marched on the Pare District headquarters to protest a new
graduated tax arrangement. When the officials refused to meet with the
women, they stoned their cars and detained one chief and a police officer.
This outbreak provoked a battle with thirty police officers in which sixty-
four women were injured (Rogers 1980). In the 1950s, Muslim women
of Bujumbura, Burundi, similarly opposed colonial taxes for single women
(Hunt 1989).

In all these cases, women's concerns that pertained to their central role
as economic actors and as providers and household caretakers were framed
as part and parcel of the nationalist cause. This included demands relating
to the taxation of women, licensing of women's businesses, restrictions on
the operation of women's businesses, access to land, employment, women's
literacy, girls' education, and health services.

In Uganda, women leaders mounted protests against colonial officials
when they deported the king of Buganda in the years leading up to independence. At the same time, women anticipated a greater political role for
themselves as independence drew closer in 1962 and so the Ugandan Council
of Women (UCW) started preparing women to influence policies affecting
women by promoting literacy, formal education for girls, leadership skills,
and civic education for women. The UCW launched a Citizenship Education Committee in 1961 to encourage women to take part in community
affairs. It spearheaded a voter education drive with the Uganda Association
of University Women in 1961 and 1962 in preparation for parliamentary
elections. The council's Citizenship Education Committee ran leadership
training courses for officers of the UCW throughout Uganda. It held workshops on the responsibilities of office holders; organization of committees as
well as membership and fundraising drives; and program organization and
operation (White 1973). Women's organizations such as UCW also challenged the parties for their lack of commitment to promoting women leaders.
As early as 1954, there were two (British) women serving on the Legislative

Council in Uganda, both of whom were UCW leaders. In 1956, the first African woman, Pumla Kisosonkole, was brought on the council, and by independence in 1961, nine women had served on the council (Tripp 2000).

## WOMEN'S PARTICIPATION IN THE POSTCOLONIAL SINGLE-PARTY REGIMES

After independence, women found their organizational efforts curtailed once again, only this time the constraints came not from colonial powers but from the newly independent single-party and military regimes, which increasingly limited autonomous associational activity. National women's activities were to be channeled through a single women's organization, usually linked to the ruling party, which used it as a source of funds, votes, and entertainment (Staudt 1985; Steady 1975). Moreover, even though these organizations claimed to represent the interests of all women in their respective countries, especially rural women, they often served as more of a mechanism of generating votes and support for the country's single party.

## PARTY CONTROL OF WOMEN'S ORGANIZATIONS

Ruling parties and regimes sought to bring women into state-related clientelism by controlling women's associations through various strategies, including the creation of women's wings tied to the ruling party; suppressing or controlling independent associations by banning, coopting, and absorbing them; mandating registration of autonomous associations in state-run umbrella organizations; and infiltrating associations with patronage networks. These forms of control parallel attempts to control other forms of associational life, including trade unions, cooperatives, student and youth organizations, market traders, and other societal interests that could potentially threaten the state (Wallerstein 1964; Wunsch 1991).

In some cases, the women's wing had belonged to the party from its inception. In other instances, women's organizations were created by the party/regime. The Women's Union in Tanzania, for example, had always been affiliated with the ruling party. Prior to independence, it had been the women's section of Tanganyika African National Union (TANU). With independence in 1961, it was renamed the Women's Union (Umoja wa Wanawake wa Tanzania) and was formally affiliated with TANU in 1962 (Rogers 1983).

In the Ghanaian case, the 31st December Women's Movement (31DWM) was formed by the Provisional National Defence Council (PNCDC) regime in 1981 and grew to become the largest women's organization in Ghana. It worked closely with the National Democratic Congress (NDC) and spread the NDC's patronage networks throughout the country, expanding its female constituency. It absorbed grassroots women's organizations and kept them from challenging Ghana's leadership on its performance in the areas of women's welfare and rights (Dei 1994; Mikell 1984).

The relationship of ruling party/regime to independent women's organizations was somewhat more complex than these parties/regimes' ties to organizations of their own creation. Different strategies were adopted in dealing with these organizations. In the most extreme cases, independent women's organizations, especially at the national level, were abolished or discouraged from forming. Uganda's military ruler Idi Amin banned all independent women's organizations and established in 1978 the National Council of Women by presidential decree to serve as an umbrella organization in order to control existing women's associations. According to the decree, "No women's or girls' voluntary associations shall continue to exist or be formed except in accordance with the provisions of this decree."

In some cases, existing organizations were coopted into serving as a de facto women's wing. In Kenya, for example, the ruling party, Kenya African National Union (KANU), gradually coopted the large women's organization Maendeleo ya Wanawake (MYW) so that by 1987 it was fully under KANU's control. This was a time of economic decline and loss of political legitimacy for the ruling party. By expanding its control over MYW's twenty thousand member groups, KANU hoped to spread its influence and give it the necessary ties to grassroots organizations to shore up its plummeting popular support. Access to MYW funds and donor money that had been diverted away from government initiatives made the takeover of MYW all the more attractive (Kanyinga 1993; Nzomo 1994; Wipper 1975).

In contrast to the overt cooptation of women's organizations, in other contexts the regime simply infused local organizations with patron–client relations. The well-known *harambee* self-help movement in Kenya increasingly fell subject to various clientelistic manipulations. The *harambee* movement, which involved large numbers of women, led community initiatives to build schools, clinics, wells, cattle dips, and other similar projects. Although local resources supported local projects, which leaders claimed to their credit, the leaders themselves also provided the *harambee* groups with resources of their own in exchange for votes and political backing. Sponsored by top party leaders and the president himself, the movement was a critical source of voter support for KANU. It facilitated the initiation of costly large-scale projects that did not necessarily serve the interests of the community but were intended to reflect positively on the patron. Competition among patrons sometimes resulted in a duplication of efforts. And stalled projects were common if patrons and clients experienced a falling out. Moreover, politicians often did not deliver the money they had pledged (Kanyinga 1993: 72; Tripp 2001b).

The relationship between the ruling party and women's organization was sometimes solidified by placing the association under the control of the wife of the head of state or under the leadership of other female relatives of party/state leaders, a phenomenon described as a "femocracy" by Amina Mama (Ibrahim 2004; Mama 1995). First ladies frequently headed the larger national women's organizations: Nana Ageman Rawlings chaired the 31st December Women's Movement in Ghana; Maryam Babangida headed the Better Life for Rural Women Programme; Mariam Traoré was president of the Union Nationale des Femmes du Mali; whereas Betty Kaunda was affiliated with Women's League in Zambia.

Interestingly, in the 1990s first ladies started to patronize the new independent NGOs as the large party-led organizations lost their appeal. For example, Janet Museveni, wife of Uganda's president Yoweri Museveni, is patron of the popular Uganda Women's Effort to Save Orphans. Anna Mkapa (former first lady in Tanzania) formed the Equal Opportunities for All Trust Fund. However, even these NGOs have been used politically as in the Zambian case, where Vera Chiluba used her Hope Foundation to attack the political opposition when her husband was president.

POLITICAL IMPACT OF COOPTATION OF WOMEN'S ORGANIZATIONS

Party cooptation of key women's organizations effectively marginalized women's leadership and channeled women into mobilizing around a narrow set of issues. In some cases, the regime has been involved in strategies of dividing the women's movement and exacerbating or creating tensions. Much of the emphasis of the state's efforts has been on form and image rather than on substantive change (Geisler 1987; Wipper 1975). The focus often was on top-down strategies that benefited only a small group of privileged urban elite women at the expense of the majority of rural and poor urban women, often leading to disenchantment with women's organizations (Geiger 1982; Munachonga 1989).

The Women's Cameroon National Union (WCNU) was an annex organization of the ruling party, the Cameroon National Union Party, and the organs of the WCNU were placed under the tutelage of the respective organs of the party at each level. In the 1960s, the government of President Ahmadu

Ahidjo banned all independent women's associations in the process of eliminating remnants of the political opposition and under the pretext of building national unity and abolishing tribalism. He sought to bring all women's
organizations under the rubric of the WCNU. Cultural and religious groups –
such as the Mamfe Glee Club, the Catholic Women's Association, and the
Bamenda Women's Cultural Association – that remained outside the WCNU
were pressured to join the Union. By remaining outside the umbrella of the
WCNU, they risked being linked to former opposition parties and as such
being considered political enemies of the state (Adams 2004b).

Although about 45 percent of the party membership was in the WCNU
and 23 percent in the youth wing, women had only minimal chances to take
meaningful action in their own interests. The party constitution forbade
WCNU members from holding political meetings and effectively barred
them from raising their own issues within the party. The WCNU's own
constitution similarly stipulated that the organization was to remain nonpolitical and exclusively social. Seminar discussions, for example, focused
on family planning, juvenile delinquency, prostitution and rural exodus,
housekeeping and being a good mother, etiquette, and body and household hygiene (Adams 2004b). Throughout the 1970s and 1980s, Women's
Houses were created throughout the country to teach girls domestic skills.
The WCNU encouraged women to form cooperatives and farming groups.
WCNU women provided the entertainment at party-organized parades and
rallies and catered political events and celebrations.

CNU's successor party, the Cameroon People's Democratic Movement
(CPDM), was formed by Ahidjo's successor, Paul Biya, in 1985. The
CPDM formed a women's wing, the Women's Cameroon People's Democratic Movement (WCPDM), and the party declared its commitment to the
advancement of women. The party allowed the WCPDM to engage in political activities, unlike the WCNU, but the organization nevertheless remained
under the supervision of the party. Male party leaders in Cameroon, thus,
have enjoyed an almost unchallenged status of defining politics, turning to
women only to legitimate their powers in state institutions, where women
remain underrepresented. In Cameroon, as elsewhere, women's wings of parties were assigned limited roles and, as might be expected, required clearance
from the main party structures for any significant innovation or even to exercise their basic functions. The CPDM was associated with men, whereas the
WCPDM was seen as the women's organization, which meant that women
running for office through the CPDM were seen as moving onto male turf.
In fact, men would openly ask the women why they did not remain within
the confines of their own WCPDM (Adams 2004b).

In Ghana, the 31st December Women's Movement of President Jerry Rawling's Provincial National Defence Council dominated the political landscape of women's organizations for a long time. Women's rights activist and University of Ghana sociologist Dzodzi Tsikata explained in an interview:

Depending on the circumstances, it would present itself as a revolutionary organ, or as an NGO, or any number of things. But it had taken up all the space and stifled and constrained women's independent organizing. It also controlled the national machinery for women, the National Council for Women and Development, so very few organizations were able to function at all (Mama 2005).

The close relationship between women's organizations and the state served to strengthen patronage ties. As former Zimbabwean parliamentarian Margaret Dongo explained in reference to the Women's League of President Robert Mugabe's ruling party, Zimbabwe African National Union–Patriotic Front (ZANU-PF): "The fee is allegiance. Once someone pulls you up, you have to pay for it. This kind of women's advancement means that women who benefit in this way are accountable to the men who put them there. Because you have the position and you want to maintain it, you are more likely to let down your supposed constituency." Or as another former politician ZANU-PF politician, Sarah Kachingwe, put it: "Whatever they [the Women's League members] do, they do on the understanding that they are doing it for the party [ZANU-PF]. When they are told to sing and make it sound like an army, they will do so. When that has been done, the question will be, how do we share the benefits of that singing?" (Mumba 1997, 5).

By tempting women's organization leaders with patronage, the state was able to keep them focused on personal gain rather than addressing real issues or the broader interests of the membership. For example, the National Council of Women's Societies (NCWS) was the only umbrella NGO recognized by the Nigerian government until Olusegun Obasanjo came to power in February 1999. It had been plagued by south–north and Christian–Muslim conflicts over state patronage that took the form of ministerial and parastatal appointments, overseas travel, and funds, while the organization was diverted from challenging the regime's record on advancing women (Abdullah 1995). Moreover, unlike independent organizations in Nigeria, it adopted pro-regime policies that independent women's organizations such as Women in Nigeria (WIN) perceived as undermining women's status – for example, supporting the Austerity Programme of 1982–3 and government harassment of poor urban street vendors, large numbers of whom were women (Imam 1996).

While built by drawing on a wide base of support from grassroots women, these patronage-based women's organizations often ended up benefiting only a few individual elite women with personal ties and connections to the national leadership. The leaders frequently elicited apathy on the part of women because they were often unqualified for their positions, patronizing, and out of touch with the realities of their poor rural women constituents. Nigeria's military regime, for example, launched a Better Life for Rural Women Programme (BLP) in 1987 to promote literacy, vocational training, social welfare and health programs, and income-generating projects throughout the country. Popularly referred to as the "bitter life program for rural women," the BLP was led by Maryam Babangida, wife of Ibrahim Babangida, Nigeria's military ruler at the time. Wives of civil service chiefs and professional academic women assisted her. At regional levels, wives of state governors and wives of chairmen of local governments were selected to head up local BLP branches with no consideration of these women's merit. Such nepotism contributed to poor organizational leadership, but it also ensured that what resources were made available to the organization remained at the top.

Between 1987 and 1992, the BLP received $18 million, of which little remained for rural women's groups after office buildings, vehicles, staff salaries, and overseas travel were covered. In 1989, a lawyer, Gani Fawehinmi, sought a court injunction to restrain the military government from authorizing additional public funds to Maryam Babangida because she had no duties assigned to her in the organization. Later a government-appointed National Commission for Women also sought greater accountability from the BLP, but the Commission was dissolved by a 1992 military decree before any of its recommendations could be implemented (Abdullah 1995; Okonjo 1994).

These party-affiliated organizations became gatekeepers of women's admission into politics. In the past – and even today in some cases – the ruling party typically had to approve nominees for leadership in these mass organizations. Their funding generally came from the party or government. Their party-dictated agendas were limited and basically did not challenge the status quo when it came to pushing for women's advancement. This is not to say there were no instances of political mobilization around women's issues, but generally it was limited. For example, NCWS in Nigeria lobbied the government to amend its discriminatory population control policies that targeted only women and not men. It also got the state commissions for women upgraded into a full-fledged Ministry of Women Affairs and Social Development. But for the most part, these structures did not tackle the difficult laws, policies, and practices that discriminated against women.

They got women to attend party rallies and meetings and to sing, dance, and cook for visiting dignitaries and basically tried to keep women apolitical. In Zimbabwe, the government not only wanted the women to sing and dance patriotic songs at official functions, they also wanted women to wear the national dress at these functions. This prompted Zimbabwean activist Kwanele Jirira (1995: 12) to ask: "Why are women viewed as the transmitters of social values and the custodians of patriotism, while men can choose what to wear and as such are not expected to wear the yoke of patriotism?" Former Zimbabwean member of parliament (MP) Margaret Dongo, in fact, helped end the practice of women being forced to kneel at the airport out of respect to visiting dignitaries and the president. The practice was borrowed from Malawi, where "president for life" Hastings Banda had started the practice. "How, after putting on my pantyhose could I kneel down on the tarmac?!!! If this is a state occasion then men have to kneel also. Why is it that only women have to kneel?" asked Dongo (Jenje-Makwenda 1998).

One of the consequences of the entertainment functions of women's wings was the discrediting of the women's wing in parties altogether in many countries, even in a multiparty context. For example, in Malawi, new parties were reluctant to start women's wings because of the historic relationship between *mbumbas* and the Malawi Congress Party. *Mbumbas* were Women's League women who danced at former president Hastings Banda's rallies and were seen as entertainers rather than as credible political participants. By the time that Malawi democratized, the Women's League of the MCP was virtually defunct (Kathleen Mulligan Hansel personal communication, 28 October 1998; Semu 2002).

Under one party rule, women's political activities were to be contained within their designated women's organizations, which meant that few women ever worked outside the bounds of these organizations to involve themselves in the parties themselves (Geisler 1995). This further reinforced women's political marginalization.

## DEVELOPMENTAL AND WELFARE FOCUS OF GROUPS

In the early post-independence period, women's organizations tended to be focused around religious, welfare, and domestic concerns. Local handicrafts, savings, farming, income-generating, religious, and cultural clubs dominated the associational landscape of women, especially at the local level. The discourse was primarily one of "developmentalism" (Ngugi c. 2001). Women's organizations adopted a "women in development" approach, which was divorced from political concerns and in line with the focus of the educational curriculum in many countries. They focused on research into discriminatory practices and laws and on consciousness raising, referred to in English-speaking Africa as "gender sensitization" or "conscientization" (Geisler 1995).

Ruling parties and governments were able to keep the women's organizations depoliticized, conservative, and focused on narrowly defined "development" objectives such as generating income instead of advocating women's rights. Parties tended to narrow the organizations' agendas so that, for example, the Women's League in Zambia had as one of its main functions the regulation of women's morality as did the Union des Femmes du Niger in the 1960s. Moreover, in many countries, women's activities were monitored and directed to ensure that they would support various party/regime campaigns and initiatives (Cooper 1995; Geisler 1987; Hirschmann 1991). Although some of these state-led movements did from time to time genuinely defend women's rights, the overall pattern with women's leagues was one of depoliticization, especially when one contrasts their activities with those of independent organizations.

For example, Maendeleo Ya Wanawake (MYW), which has had the largest membership of any organization in Kenya, was confined to improving childcare, domestic care, handicrafts, agricultural techniques, and literacy, and engaging in sports (Wipper 1975). The conservative stance of this organization is reflected in the thinking of its president at the time, Jane Kiano, who optimistically claimed in 1972 that "women in this country do not need a liberation movement because all doors are open to us" (Sahle 1998: 178).

Hussaina Abdullah (1993) has argued that the key state-sponsored women's institutions in Nigeria, such as Better Life for Rural Women Programme, National Commission for Women, and National Council of Women's Societies, were primarily concerned with keeping women in their roles as mothers. Mumbi Ngugi (c. 2001) says of the National Council of Women's Societies, which was formed in 1959: "Unlike the human rights organizations like FIDA [Women Lawyers], it has not ruffled the feathers of the male dominated state by taking up issues on women's rights vis-à-vis men, such as equality and equal representation."

PARTY WOMEN'S WINGS AFTER 1990S

Although the era of single umbrella women's organizations and women's wings has receded as innumerable independent women's associations have emerged, in some countries a single party still dominates in a multiparty context. This creates particular challenges for the newly emerging women's movements. Even in Botswana, which has been a multiparty democracy since independence in 1966, the umbrella Association of Botswana Women's Organizations was financially dependent on the government and promoted nonpolitical behavior of NGOs (Holm 1989; Zaffiro 2000). In some cases, women's organizations such as Maendeleo ya Wanawake, which has thousands of affiliates throughout Kenya, remains de facto linked to the dominant party, the Kenya African National Union, but is technically an independent organization. In other countries such as Mali, the women's wing of the ruling party under Moussa Traoré dissolved with the fall of his party (Wing 2002).

There are still countries where the old model persists, where they have not embraced new autonomous organizations. For example, in Eritrea today, there is basically only one national women's organization, the National Union of Eritrea Women (NUEW), which was founded by the Eritrean Peoples Liberation Front in 1979 when it was fighting for Eritrean independence from Ethiopia. After independence was achieved in 1991, the two hundred thousand–member organization became semi-autonomous and shifted to educate women for involvement in service provision and project management, but did little in the way of advocacy. It did succeed in making a few modest changes in the old Ethiopian civil code. For example, marriage contracts had to be made with the full consent of both parties; the eligible age for marriage for girls was raised from fifteen to eighteen to match that of men; and the sentence for rape was extended to fifteen years imprisonment. They also allowed women to initiate divorce and placed limits on bride wealth while banning a form of genital cutting called infibulation, although cliterodectomy was still permitted.

But NUEW did little to address concretely the backlash against women that occurred after independence. For example, a disproportionately larger number of women were demobilized from the military only to find that employers were reluctant to hire them (McKinley 1996). Many felt that there was a need for a multiplicity of organizations to work on the most pressing issues, but the few organizations that attempted to work autonomously were closed down by the government on various pretexts (Connell 1998; Wilson 1993). NUEW is charged with implementing government policy regarding women's rights, and thus its lack of autonomy from the government has created divisions within the organization (Kwesiga et al. 2003: 26; Pool 2001).

In other countries, independent women's movements coexist with the older models. The Organization of Mozambican Women (OMM) was delinked from FRELIMO as were other mass organizations in 1990 at the time that multipartyism was enshrined in the new constitution. It was to be an independent registered umbrella organization. However, OMM's affiliation to FRELIMO was reestablished six years later as its leaders were unable and unwilling to exist as an autonomous entity. Some OMM leaders felt that the timing of the decision to delink the two organizations was inopportune. Other independent organizations had already sprung up and were competing for donor funds for which OMM was not competitive. Moreover, earlier in 1984, OMM had launched an ambitious and costly program involving thirty-five interest groups (*Circulos de Interesse*) of women throughout the country organized around education, health education, and income-generating activities. OMM was unable to sustain these groups without continued party support.

Then, quite unexpectedly in 1996, the OMM reversed its 1990 decision and decided to affiliate formally once again with FRELIMO. Without warning at the OMM's congress, a delegate from Nampula (ironically an area that had strong allegiance to the opposition party, Resistência Nacional Moçambicana [RENAMO]) asked that the congress clarify that OMM is indeed "the fruit of Frelimo." The delegates responded with applause and pro-FRELIMO chants, after which, according to an article in Mozambique-file: "It was then simply declared that the congress had decided unanimously to 'return to Frelimo'. No debate took place, nor was there any vote. The singing and dancing in the aisles, however, had made it abundantly clear that the majority of delegates did indeed want to retie the umbelical [sic] cord between the OMM and Frelimo." OMM elected a new leader, a FRELIMO veteran, who was quoted as saying that OMM was wrong to dissociate from FRELIMO in 1990 ("OMM Returns to Frelimo..." 1996). Another reason for relinking OMM and FRELIMO may have been that FRELIMO also wanted to make sure that it maintained its female constituents through OMM.[3]

Those who advocated for OMM's return to FRELIMO argued that its independence had not resulted in an increase in membership and that it had remained a de facto organization of FRELIMO women. They were concerned that the historical relationship between the party and OMM was being forgotten, and about the fact that some OMM members were not pleased with the organization's autonomy. Although to date OMM is the only woman's organization operating throughout the country, it has little capacity to defend women's interests nor to challenge the party on its decisions that hurt women (Casimiro 2004).

In Tanzania, the Women's Union (Umoja wa Wanawake wa Tanzania [UWT]) had been similarly conflicted about its future as new autonomous

---

[3] Personal communication, Scott Kloeck-Jenson, 28 December 1998.

organizations emerged and were grabbing much of the donor funding. UWT sought to create an independent sister organization to access some of those funds, but soon found its success too threatening and sought to shut down the organization.

In most countries, Eritrea and Angola being two exceptions, the balance in influence between the party-led women's associations and the independent associations has changed so that the party-led groups, which once dominated women's mobilization, have been displaced by a plurality of associations and networks.

Both the Eritrean and Mozambican cases show the limits of relying solely on a single-party–affiliated women's organization to defend women's interests, even in parties that are keen to promote women's rights. The challenge for many women's movements has been to be sufficiently involved in political parties in order to influence their platforms regarding women's concerns and to ensure a good gender balance of party leaders and electoral candidates. At the same time, a lack of autonomy from a dominant party makes it difficult for women's organizations to select independent-minded leaders and set an agenda that prioritizes women's concerns.

## Emergence of New Women's Movements

One of the earliest debates regarding women's organizational independence from parties occurred at a 21–25 June 1982 meeting of the Association of African Women for Research and Development (AAWORD). At a seminar held in Dakar, Senegal, participants questioned whether it would be better to give priority to women's issues through autonomous women's associations or whether they should be integrated into the existing political parties and their structures. At this point, the debate was primarily about development: how to secure women's access to land; how to respond to state pricing policies for crops that held food prices artificially low for urban dwellers while hurting women agriculturalists who obtained poor prices on their crop sales; and women's lack of access to technological inputs, technical assistance, and agricultural extension services. At this meeting, feminism was seen as providing a basis for an alternative development model, and although participants advocated respect for national and ethnic traditions, they felt that "women must be mobilized politically for action" to challenge "aspects of our cultures which discriminate, restrict and devalue women's physical, psychological and political development" (Declaration 1982). In other words, the conference laid the basis for the shift that was to come in the 1990s away from a strictly developmental approach to a political one that recognized the power and gender dimensions of what women were up against. Although the political strategies were unspecified and vague, a new course was being charted (Ahooja-Patel 1982).

By the mid-1980s, there already were signs of party/state loosening of restrictions on autonomous associations in some countries. As the economic crisis deepened in the 1980s, financially strapped governments in Africa began to allow for greater societal input through business and income-generating associations and NGOs. Professional organizations were also an important arena for mobilization, although some associations of journalists and lawyers appeared politically threatening and elicited government efforts to control them or create new government-controlled associations. The new women's associations increasingly had independent resources to employ in development initiatives, but, more importantly, they had the will to organize and devise self-help strategies at the local level.

Although the major proliferation of women's organizations occurred in the 1990s in the context of political liberalization, already in the 1980s many new NGOs were emerging in response to economic crisis, hardships brought on by economic restructuring, state retreat, and the subsequent opening up of new public spaces outside of the jurisdiction of the government and ruling party. In many cases, organizations sought alternative service-provisioning mechanisms where the state was no longer providing services. Greater donor emphasis on nongovernmental actors also contributed to the increase in formal associations. These developments were accompanied by changes in attitudes regarding the role of the government. As one leader of the Tanzania Media Women's Association (TAMWA) put it:

What changed was psychological.... Years of paternalistic state-led development had led to a prevalent attitude that if you want educational facilities, you wait for the government. If you want health services, you wait for the government. And then when that did not come, you blame the government. Economic crisis forced people to think for themselves. Economic crisis and political decontrol and loosening up stimulated people so much in terms of income-generation and in terms of real self-help efforts (Mtambalike 1994 interview with Tripp).

In Niger, the Association des Femmes du Niger formed in 1973 was virtually the only women's group to operate since independence. After the loosening of restrictions on associations in 1984, new women's groups emerged such as the Association des Femmes Commercants et Entrepreneurs du Niger, Union des Femmes Enseignants du Niger, and the Association des Femmes Juristes du Niger. In Tanzania, the opening came in the mid-to-late 1980s, after which groups such as the Tanzania Media Women's

Association, Medical Women Association of Tanzania, Tanzania Women Lawyers Association, and the Association of Women Artists in Tanzania emerged, although informal organizations linked to women's expanding role in income-generating activities had already been proliferating since the mid-1980s. By 1992, the national groups were so numerous that they were able to form a Tanzania Gender Networking Programme to coordinate strategies around legal reform, policy change, and public education.

Even in countries engaged in conflict, many of the same dynamics were felt. In Mozambique, the new women's movement emerged during the conflict, leading to a proliferation of humanitarian organizations and greater donor influence on women's mobilization. Until the late 1980s, very few international NGOs were operating in Mozambique. The few that had a presence were involved in emergency operations because of the 1977–92 war between RENAMO and FRELIMO. With the new global emphasis on neoliberalism and its focus on the retreat of the state, a new interest in NGOs emerged. Some of them increased as a result of the new availability of donor funds. Others were the result of local initiatives of autonomous groups that felt the need to resolve real questions of survival in order to provide effective and efficient means for development at the local level.

The break with the former one-party mode of operation did not come without contestation. The state proved resistant to the formation of one of the first independent associations in Cameroon in 1982, the Collectif des Femmes pour le Renouveau (CFR), which was made up of French and Cameroonian feminists and fought for women's increased political representation. Its founding president, Marie-Louise Eteki-Otabela, explained why CFR's members had moved away from the traditional developmental focus of women's organizations to a more intensely political one:

They [the women of the Collectif] base their analysis on a constant: women have always participated and worked in the development of their society, but they are excluded from important decisions concerning the organization and the future of their society. It is for this reason that the question of democracy precedes the question of development. How then can one resolve the question of development in a country where one single vision of problems is authorized, the official vision? (1992: 131 cited in Adams 2004b)[4]

---

[4] "Elles [des femmes du Collectif] fondent leur analyse sur un constat: les femmes ont toujours participé et travaillé au développement de leur société, mais elles sont exclues des décisions importantes concernant l'organisation et l'avenir de leur société. C'est pour cela que la question de la démocratie est un préalable à la question du développement. Comment alors peut-on résoudre la question du développement dans un pays où une seule vision des problèmes est autorisée, soit la vision officielle prônée par les pouvoirs publics?"

The Collectif leaders also objected to the claim that WCPDM, the women's wing of the ruling party, Cameroon People's Democratic Movement (CPDM), spoke for and represented all women in Cameroon, and put forward a new vision that departed from the limited goals of the WCPDM:

African feminists in contrast to the reformists who want to ameliorate the female condition advocate changes that aim to transform the social organization in its entirety. They not only attack the effects of this condition but above all its causes. (Eteki-Otabela cited in Adams 2004b)[5]

The CFR was eventually banned in 1991 along with several other organizations because, according to the Cameroonian Ministry of Territorial Administration, it threatened security, territorial integrity, and national unity. In other words, it had become too "political." Other independent organizations did emerge; however, their lack of full associational independence throughout the 1990s proved for a long time to be a constraint on the capacity of the women's movement to press for a more extensive agenda.

Today in Cameroon, laws governing civil society organizations provide for their full autonomy from the state and the ruling party. There are independent organizations such as Pauline Biyong's Ligue des droits de la femme et de l'enfant (League for Women and Child Education) that have been pushing for women's political leadership in Cameroon. Similarly, the independent Women's Political Caucus has begun making clear demands for improved access to community and political leadership positions for women.

CONCLUSIONS

In explaining the later policy impacts of women's movements in the 1990s, it is instructive to examine the past and the way in which it shaped later developments. The extent to which colonial powers educated females influenced their involvement in national-level women's organizations, employment opportunities, and leadership capacities in the postcolonial context. Thus, former Portuguese colonies such as Mozambique faced bigger challenges in cultivating women leaders who could influence and bring about policy changes when compared with former British colonies such as Uganda, which placed more emphasis on educating girls than did the other colonies. Similarly, all colonialists had restricted the scope of civil society, but the

---

[5] "Les féministes africaines, à la différence des réformistes qui veulent améliorer la condition féminine, préconisent des changements qui visent à transformer l'organisation sociale dans son ensemble. Elles ne s'attaquent pas seulement aux effets de cette condition mais surtout à ses causes."

Portuguese colonialists were even more inclined to regulate and curb the growth of civil society, which also placed particular constraints on the growth of independent women's organizations. Certainly the years of conflict prior to and after independence also significantly impeded the flourishing of civil society. For these reasons, Mozambique today has a weaker women's movement than countries such as Cameroon and Uganda.

Contemporary women's movements have been influenced by strategies and forms of mobilization deriving from precolonial collective action, from nationalist movements, and from postcolonial mass women's organizations that were tied to the ruling party and/or government. What is striking in our cases of Cameroon, Mozambique, and Uganda, as well as the other examples in this chapter, is the fact that the nationalist movements not only energized women politically, but also absorbed them in a cause that cut across ethnicities and party lines around common concerns. At the same time, they created a situation that was conducive for the cooptation of women's organizations to single-party–led women's associations and limited their autonomy and ultimately their agendas. Regardless of whether or not women participated in armed struggle for independence, and regardless of their associational autonomy within the nationalist movement, in the post-independence period, what little plurality of associational life had existed was virtually eliminated. Similarly, regardless of the extent to which the nationalist movements catered to women leaders, to women's demands, or to a platform that incorporated women's rights, women's associational autonomy was later curtailed.

Most nationalist movements incorporated women, and in fact, women were central to the creation of the popular base of support for nationalism in much of Africa. They not only attended rallies and organized pro-independence events, they also performed, sang, and mobilized supporters. However, not all nationalist movements incorporated women's rights as part of their independence struggles. Some deferred these concerns to the post-independence period with unspecified time frames and were often slow to deliver on those promises. Others, such as Sékou Touré's movement in Guinea, incorporated women's rights into the struggle for independence from the outset. With few exceptions, these sentiments were later to be channeled into party-led mass organizations.

This cooptation occurred even where women had acted independently of the nationalist movement, as in Cameroon. There women protested colonial policies, especially regarding taxation, access to land, market regulations, and other policies that had created new hardships for women. In the anticolonial struggles, women organized demonstrations, petitioned the

United Nations, formed their own political parties, and engaged in daily hidden forms of noncompliance with the colonial authorities.

Women's organizations became vulnerable to cooptation because there was often a common inclination, especially where women had an identifiable women's rights agenda, that, regardless of ethnic and party differences, the best way to build a unified nation *and* advance women's rights was to build organizations that could encompass all differences. In other words, the interest of women activists to forge a common agenda by building crosscutting ties dovetailed with the nationalist cause. However, this desire to build crosscutting linkages has been both an asset and a challenge to women's mobilization in the post-independence period. Women's organizations from the nationalist era until today have found that they can advance their broader goals around women's rights by linking up with other women across ethnic, party, and other lines to build as wide a coalition or organization as possible. However, this same unity during the single-party era became diverted to another cause: that of propping up the party/leaders in power regardless of their inclination to support women's rights and regardless of how repressive they were.

The extent to which new women's movements were able to extricate themselves from the ruling party in a multiparty context and exert leverage was reflected in their ability to select their own leaders, pursue independent funding, and set their own agendas. Those with the most autonomy were able to pursue the strongest women's rights agendas without having to accommodate other party priorities. This does not mean they did not build linkages and engage the parties, but they were free to adopt agendas that did not necessarily coincide with those of political parties.

Autonomous women's organizations began to play an increasingly important role after the 1990s in Cameroon, Mozambique, and Uganda. The level of organizational autonomy had implications for the types of demands that women's rights activists made and their capacity to forge a new agenda, which included new forms of legislation, constitutional reforms, and attempts to increase the numbers of women in decision-making positions.

Finally, even though the focus of our study is on the emergence of new associational autonomy, there are still large constraints impeding women's mobilization from changing the status quo. The dominant political culture holds enormous sway. Some activists can be quickly coopted or condone the gradual dilution of their positions and demands, leaving the status quo unchallenged. Women's organizations lack adequate channels through which their aspirations can be channeled in influencing policy, in spite of the creation of national women's machineries, which have rarely been at the forefront of changes in the status of women. Moreover, women's organizations face problems of financial austerity, uncertain mandates, the lack of coherent ideological clarity, and limited stable support constituencies (Biyong 1998: 32). Most women's organizations challenging gender discrimination often depend on the male-controlled media coverage for visibility and on government for resources and services. Both group leaders and members, therefore, often find themselves straddling their allegiance to their organizations and to government. Because they must also protect their source of livelihood and their organizations, allegiance to the government position often takes the upper hand. Thus, in the present-day context in which stakeholders may be leaning more toward collaborative processes seeking the same general outcomes, the perceived concerns of cooptation must be distinguished from women's informed, deliberate, and tactical responses to the strategic and operational realities of the political field.

# 3

# The Rise of the New Women's Movements

The women's movements that emerged in the 1990s were distinct from women's mobilization in the early post-independence period in several ways. First and foremost, they were generally autonomous of the ruling party and state. Women's organizations set new broader agendas and selected their own leaders. They obtained new sources of funding independent of state patronage networks, which women's organizations had depended on to a greater extent in the past. The new women's organizations took advantage of changes in donor funding patterns favoring nongovernment organizations (NGOs) after the 1990s, providing them the impetus to expand.

What then gave rise to these new movements in the late 1980s and especially in the 1990s? There is no single explanation for women's heightened activism in Africa, but three key factors are considered here. These include (1) international influences and the diffusion of ideas and tactics across Africa with respect to women's rights; (2) a changing resource base in which some women's associations had greater access to alternate sources of funding; and (3) in some countries the opening of political space for women's associations as a result of democratization and political liberalization. These factors are important because they shaped the ways in which the movements sought policy changes, the kinds of issues they took up, and their levels of success. This chapter discusses how these factors came into play.

All three of our cases experienced all three aforementioned dynamics to varying degrees. In terms of numbers of organizations (as distinct from impact), Uganda and Cameroon have the most active women's movements, whereas Mozambique has numerically the weakest movement in the triad, which is related, in part, to its colonial past (see Chapter 2). All three countries were influenced by international, regional, and subregional women's movements, and their women's organizations benefited from external funding. The opening of political space similarly benefited all three countries and allowed for the expansion of new forms of mobilization.

## TRANSNATIONAL AND REGIONAL INFLUENCES

Although the driving forces for women's increased mobilization were internal, global pressures and norms gave added impetus to these new movements. The global women's movement played a significant role in influencing women's mobilization and encouraging women in Africa to consider how their struggles related to an emerging worldwide concern for gender equality (Mbire-Barungi 1999: 435). The transnational impacts were global but were mediated through regional networks and organizations within Africa.

A new generation of autonomous organizations began to emerge after the 1985 UN Nairobi women's conference, although a few had been formed earlier. The conference in Nairobi was particularly important for African women's movements. Never before had so many women come together from around the world, and over half of the 13,504 registered attendees came from the global South, with large numbers from Africa (Antrobus 2004: 57). The conference provided an important impetus for many African participants, who were beginning to appreciate the importance of independent women's mobilization.

The earliest organizations that were part of the new generation of mobilization included Women in Nigeria, formed in 1982; Uganda's Action for Development, formed in 1985; the Association of Media Women in Kenya, established in 1982; and the Tanzania Media Women's Association (TAMWA), created in 1987. TAMWA leader Fatma Alloo described the galvanizing effect the Nairobi conference had in Tanzania in this way:

This conference emphasized the importance of women's mobilization in addressing the source of women's subjugation to patriarchal norms and in working towards transformation on this front. TAMWA came into existence through our own histories of pain, and the realization that unless we got together and did something, nothing would change in a patriarchal system. (quoted in Henry 2005: 140)

There have been three main organizational mechanisms through which gender-related transnational norms, practices, and ideas influenced African women's movements: (1) through coalitions and advocacy networks, which influenced policy at the international, national, subregional and continental levels; (2) through diffusion from regional and subregional organizations within Africa; and (3) from the United Nations and other multilateral institutions as well as foreign donors. As we show in our final chapter, African women leaders were not only on the receiving end of these ideas and influences, they were very much a part of shaping them.

Prior to the emergence of regional women's rights advocacy networks in the 1990s, African leaders frequently disparaged women's activism as a product of corrupting Western feminist influences. Today most of the impetus for promoting women's rights in Africa has come from within Africa and from regional-level networks, which serve as a conduit for global trends. This may explain the greater openness to these changing norms today, even as there remains continued resistance to advancing women's rights in specific areas. Africa, for example, has emerged as a world leader in promoting women's leadership in politics. The fact that the external influences on African governments today are primarily coming from the continent itself has contributed in no small measure to the willingness on the part of Africa's leaders to embrace these new norms.

Without a doubt, the 1979 the Convention on the Elimination of All Forms of Discrimination against Women (CEDAW) and other international treaties and conventions have been essential in shaping the norms driving the women's movements in Africa as have the various international conferences like the UN Conferences on Women in Mexico City (1975), Nairobi (1985), and Beijing (1995), and the UN conferences on population, the environment, education, human rights, and other such concerns. As in Latin America, the Beijing conference legitimized key elements of feminist discourse in African NGOs, parties, states, international development agencies, and other fora (Alvarez 1998: 295).

Other transnational influences came from feminist organizations in the global South such as Development Alternatives with Women for a New Era (DAWN), which started in 1984 prior to the Nairobi conference. The network, which includes women from Africa, Asia, Latin America, the Caribbean, and the Pacific, prepared a feminist critique of development, focusing on the impact of famine, debt, militarism, and religious fundamentalism on poor women for the UN Conference on Women in Nairobi in 1985. DAWN had an enormous impact on the Nairobi conference because it placed macroeconomic issues onto the feminist agenda and offered holistic analyses based on third world women's experiences and realities.

Nevertheless, much of the actual mobilization and diffusion of ideas, norms, and strategies occurred at the subregional and pan-African level, especially after the 1990s. The following subsections offer examples of multiple strategies that were employed in mobilizing to advance women.

## Direct Diffusion between NGOs and NGO Coalitions

Some influences came directly from women's networks and organizations in other African countries. The South African Women's Charter, developed by the Women's National Coalition of eighty-one groups, was replicated by women's manifestos of Botswana's Emang Basadi in 1994, the Uganda Women's Network in 1996, the National Women Lobby Group in Zambia in 2001, Liberia's National Women's Conference in 2004, and by Ghanaian women's organizations in 2004. For example, the Women's Manifesto for Ghana was developed to press the government to implement fully a comprehensive National Gender Policy by 2005 (Otu 2004; Selolwane 2004). In Ghana, the Manifesto was written and debated with input from a registered nurses association, a group of women with disabilities, several trade unions, many women's NGOs, over one hundred representatives from all 110 districts, representatives of several government departments, individuals from the Women and Juvenile Unit of the Ghana Police Service, a coalition for the Domestic Violence Bill, and the large coalition of women's organizations, NETRIGHT. The initiators themselves were surprised at the level of spontaneous interest and excitement that the process generated among women and women's groups throughout the country (Mama 2005: 130–8).

## Diffusion from Regional Advocacy Networks

There has been an explosion of Africa-wide as well as subregional advocacy and networking. The majority of such women's rights organizations and networks formed after 1990 and a large number were created after 2000. Only a handful of networks were established prior to 1990 and most of these were religious, academic, or focused on women in development. However, efforts to promote women's role in development and politics were not entirely absent at the time of independence. For example, the East African seminar, "East African Women Look Ahead," held 11–18 April 1964 at the Kenya Institute of Administration, was one of the first post-independence attempts to create a dialogue around redefining women's roles in public life. The UN Economic Commission for Africa (UNECA) sponsored five such seminars, out of which came its own program as it related to women in development (Snyder 2004). Since the 1990s, however, advocacy efforts have become far more widespread and the impetus for them comes from diverse sources.

The largest numbers of Africa-wide advocacy organizations are based in Kenya, Senegal, South Africa, Uganda, and the United Kingdom. Unlike the main transnational women's organizations during the colonial period (Young Women's Christian Association, Girl Guides, Mother's Union, International Council of Women, etc.), many of which are still functioning today, these new organizations are largely based in Africa and were founded by and run by African women. Their spatial distribution reflects a combination of factors, including stability of the country, strength of the women's movement, and development of communication facilities. Most of the British and U.S.-based organizations are run by Africans in the diaspora, creating stronger linkages between African and diaspora-based organizations, but also possible tensions between diaspora-driven agendas and those coming out of Africa itself. The diaspora-based associations increase the competition for donor resources and of the attention of key multilateral agencies.

Some diasporic groups have strengthened their ties with Africa by relocating. Akina Mama wa Afrika is a good example of a diaspora-based group that was formed in London and relocated its head office to Kampala, Uganda, in 2006. Because of increased activities on the continent, and specifically the visibility of the African women at the 1995 UN Beijing conference on women and the new importance of training young women as leaders, Akina Mama wa Afrika created the African Women Leaders' Institute and established a branch in Uganda to run a series of training workshops for young African women leaders below the age of forty. An annual leadership training program takes place each year, rotating around the region, and many young women have gained from this institute.

One of the very first Africa-wide networks of women was the Association of African Women for Research and Development (AAWORD), which was formed in 1977. According to Amina Mama, networks such as AAWORD

reaffirm intellectual traditions that challenge imperial legacies, encourage transdisciplinary research and value independent publication. As the established academic institutions deteriorated, these independent networks gained in importance, ensuring the survival of a vibrant intellectual culture closely attuned to the challenges facing Africans at all levels of their diverse and complex societies. (2004: 5)

One of the most important groups promoting peace-building activities, ISIS-WICCE, was established in Geneva, where it ran a Women's Resource Centre and an Exchange Programme for women in developing countries. It became clear that the objectives of the founders would be enhanced if regional offices were created, resulting in the opening of offices in Latin America, Asia (the Philippines), and Africa (Uganda) in 1993. ISIS-WICCE's insistence on relevance and "taking services nearer to the people" resulted in its "localized" focus, including conducting peace-building work in northern Uganda, Liberia, Sierra Leone, and other parts of Africa. Many argue that their efforts would not have been as effective had the organization not created a presence within Africa.

The new regional networks have focused on issues such as women's education, development, information communications technologies, media, peace, political participation, leadership, reproductive rights, and women's health. Women's peace-building efforts have become an increasingly important focus of subregional and regional advocacy networking. Women have been very active especially since the 1990s in peace-building initiatives throughout Africa, from Liberia to Sierra Leone, the Democratic Republic of Congo, Congo-Brazzaville, Mali, Senegal, Somalia, Uganda, Sudan, and other countries that have been wracked by civil war or conflict (see Chapter 8).

## Diffusion through International UN Influences

As mentioned earlier, the 1995 UN Beijing conference spurred considerable action in women's mobilization. One finds, for example, the majority of electoral quotas for women being adopted in countries after 1995, along with efforts for leadership training and promotion of greater political participation by women. The impetus for policy changes stemmed not so much from the actual event, but rather from the processes leading up to the conference. Much of the discussion around the expansion of women's roles in political decision making predated this conference as part of the subregional and regional conferences of women's organizations and government representatives that were held prior to the Beijing conference.

In East Africa, for example, a 1993 Kampala preparatory meeting brought together 120 leaders of women's organizations from Kenya, Tanzania, and Uganda to plan for the Africa-wide United Nations Women's Conference held in Dakar in 1994 and the subsequent international conference in Beijing in 1995. Women delegates placed access to power as their top priority on the agenda in all three countries when asked to rank their preferences to determine overall strategic goals in the region.

These agendas formed a preparatory process for the Dakar and Beijing conferences, becoming the blueprint for activism in the years leading up to the Beijing conference in all three countries. Even new subregional networks formed to advance these goals. For example, the Eastern African Sub-Regional Support Initiative (EASSI) was created explicitly to facilitate linkage, collaboration, networking, and information sharing between the different actors and stakeholders in the Fourth World Conference on

Women. One of its main goals was to promote the implementation, monitoring, and evaluation of the African and Global Platforms for Action within the East Africa subregion.

National plans were taken to the subregional conferences and to the 1994 All-Africa Dakar meeting to prepare for the 1995 Beijing meeting. It was out of these efforts that major networks were formed at the national level. In Uganda, the Uganda Women's Network (UWONET) was established in 1993 to promote networking and the formation of collective goals and action plans among women's organizations working for gender equity. The Tanzania Gender Networking Programme (TGNP), formed in 1992, played a similar role in Tanzania.

As important as the Beijing Platform of Action was for agenda setting for governments and NGOs, the parallel NGO Forum was especially invaluable to participants. Ugandan participants appreciated the action orientation of the NGO Forum, notably the minicourses and seminars they attended on fundraising, engaging and working with foundation representatives, lobbying, publishing, writing annual reports, using promotional materials for one's organization, and applying other strategies for publicizing an organization. At the same time, the sheer scale of the event, with fifty thousand NGO participants, offered a unique framework for an overview of the women's movements around the world.

Upon their return, delegates held sessions to report back to others on what happened in Beijing. Makerere University's Department of Women and Gender Studies devoted a full day to this type of reporting in Uganda. The Ministry of Gender organized a week-long seminar that included participants from around the country. Among the multiple outcomes from the conference, the most tangible one in the Ugandan context was the use of the media. While in some African countries women's media associations had been among the first independent associations created, in Uganda, as in many countries, the Beijing conference ushered in a new era of thinking strategically about their use of the media to influence public opinion.

## New Communications Strategies

One way in which the aforementioned diffusion of ideas occurred transnationally, regionally, and within countries was through the rapid expansion of new communications mechanisms. The Internet is still largely a luxury, and connectivity is affordable only to a marginal percentage of the population in academia, the professions, and civil society, most of whom live in urbanized areas. However, Internet usage is increasing: currently twelve in one thousand are Internet users in Africa, compared to zero in 1990 (UNDP 2005). The rates of women's usage are even lower than that of men. A disproportionately large percentage of users in Africa are found in South Africa. Factors limiting the use of the Internet are widely documented and include low telephone connectivity, sparse availability of computers, weak user skills, illiteracy, and language barriers due to the predominance of the English language on the Internet.

At the 1995 UN Beijing Conference on Women, the issue of Information and Communication Technologies (ICTs) was highlighted. However, only since 2000 has the issue attracted significantly greater attention in Africa. There has been more emphasis on women's use of ICTs after the formation of the WomenAction 2000 Project[1] sponsored by WomenWatch, the UN interagency gateway for the advancement and empowerment of women coordinated by UN Division for the Advancement of Women, the United Nations Development Fund for Women (UNIFEM), and the International Research and Training Institute for the Advancement of Women (INSTRAW). WomenAction, for example, established a global network of regional and subregional gender-based ICT focal points. Flame[2] has been one such online network of women activists that promotes the use of ICTs to carry out advocacy around the post-1995 UN Beijing conference on women agenda both within Africa and globally.

There are a wide variety of gender-based ICT initiatives in Africa. The Association for Progressive Communication's APC-Africa-Women (AAW)[3] is a network of organizations and individuals that seeks to improve women's access and use of ICTs. Formed in 1996, it has helped raise awareness in Africa of the importance of ICTs for women in fighting for social justice. It provides information to women about ICTs and support to women's organizations by developing networking capacity. It lobbies and does advocacy work regarding gender and ICT policy at the regional and global level. The AAW provides ICT training to African women's organizations, carries out research on gender and ICTs, and hosts an e-newsletter, *Pula* (Radloff 2005: 92).

International Cross Cultural Exchange (ISIS-WICCE), based in Kampala, does much the same with rural women throughout Africa.[4] Other networks such as Sangonet in southern Africa promote ICT products and services to a

---

[1] http://www.womenaction.org/, accessed 22 July 2007.
[2] http://flamme.org/index.html, accessed 22 July 2007.
[3] http://www.apcafricawomen.org/home.html, accessed 22 July 2007.
[4] http://www.isis.or.ug/, accessed 22 July 2007.

broader audience, but place particular emphasis on women. Online gender networks such as Women of Uganda Network (WOUGNET)[5] promote the use of ICTs by women and women organizations in Uganda for sustainable development.

Other more specialized Internet networks have formed. Feminist academics have created virtual alternative universities online such as the Africa Gender Institute of the University of Cape Town, which has a Strengthening Gender and Women's Studies for Africa's Transformation (GWS-Africa) online listserv and an electronic journal, *Feminist Africa* (http://www.feministafrica.org). Some Web sites provide opportunities for similar online networking, such as the African Women's Communication and Development Network (FEMNET) in Kenya, Zimbabwe's Women's Resource Center and Network, Uganda's African Women's Economic Policy Network, and Cameroon's Association for Support to Women Entrepreneurs (Wilson 2007). Many of these networks have focused on issues of violence against women, women's access to land, business resources for women, and other concerns addressed by women's movements in Africa.

Another important way in which women are using the Internet is through telecenters, which can be found throughout Africa from Cameroon to Uganda, Senegal, and Mauritania. They provide Internet access and training to poor communities. Some cater specifically to women, such as the telecenter project promoted by the Informatics Centre at Eduardo Mondlane University and Fórum Mulher.[6] Telecenters have had a positive impact in the lives of women with access to them, assisting them with information on producer prices, marketing data, employment opportunities, and more. However, in Mozambique and many other countries, they are limited only to certain parts of the country and can serve only a small portion of the population.

The United Nations Educational, Science, and Cultural Organization (UNESCO) and other organizations promoting the use of ICTs among women have sought to make telecenters more useful and welcoming to women. They have realized that they need to consider the selection of times for training, hold women-only and women-led classes, and provide assistants to type messages on behalf of illiterate women. They also discovered the importance of teaching men about the merits of women's use of ICTs (Primo 2003: 71).

---

[5] http://www.wougnet.org/, accessed 22 July 2007.
[6] The Informatics/Computing Policy was approved by the Council of Ministers in December 2000 and includes a gender perspective in the communication and information technologies, special training programs for girls and women, and more.

The Internet is being used in a variety of ways today among women activists: In Sierra Leone, an electronic forum was used to hold discussions between women's groups and policy makers on the abuses that women experienced during the civil war. Diasporic communities are being linked via ICTs to communicate with women business entrepreneurs and associations in Uganda. Regional meetings across West Africa have brought individuals together in an electronic forum to discuss joint parenting rights. In some countries such as Senegal and Uganda, telephone companies are providing Internet connectivity to rural women farmers through Web Access Protocol or personal digital assistants (PDAs) to allow them to access agricultural price data or health data information directly while offering mobility not possible with computers (Primo 2003). However, limited access to the Internet remains the biggest constraint on women's adoption of ICTs.

Cell phones have also facilitated women's mobilization. The use of cell phones increased exponentially starting in the late 1990s within urban areas but also between rural and urban areas. Today, on average, sixty-nine of one thousand individuals subscribe to cell phones in Africa, which is up from zero in 1990 (the world average is 226:1,000). Nevertheless, even remote parts of Africa are connected these days. Mogadishu, Somalia, has the cheapest cell phone rates on the continent and one can find in the northern Somali city of Hargeysa markets selling the latest satellite phone technology (Pineau 2005).

Cell phone technologies have been especially important in lobbying campaigns. One year after adoption of the African Union's Protocol to the African Charter on Human and Peoples' Rights on the Rights of Women in Africa in 2003, women activists discovered that only one country (the Comoros) had ratified it. Women's regional networks, led by Solidarity for African Women's Rights (SOAWR), sought to pressure states to uphold their commitments to the Protocol. They established a rating system of the ratification status of each country and developed multimedia advocacy tools with which to engage their governments and the commission of the African Union. They launched a Short Message Service (SMS) text message campaign and sponsored a petition through the electronic newsletter Pambazuka News's parent organization, Fahamu. The petition gathered over 3,615 signatures, 468 of them SMS messages, calling on African states to ratify the Protocol. They followed up this SMS campaign with a conference on the Protocol sponsored by the SOAWR together with the Women, Gender and Development Directorate of the African Union in Addis Ababa, Ethiopia, in 2005. By the end of 2007, twenty-two countries had ratified the treaty, twenty-two had signed, whereas only five had not signed.

## Internal Diffusion: Media Strategies

An important part of the international and regional diffusion process involved internal diffusion strategies via the media. Women's media associations were among the first independent women's organizations that emerged in the mid-1980s in Africa as new spaces opened up for freedom of expression in many African countries.[7] These are mainly advocacy organizations that monitor the mainstream media and try to promote better informed, less stereotyped, and more balanced coverage of women in the media. The Media Monitoring Project, for example, based in South Africa but active throughout the continent, is a media watchdog that monitors coverage of women in the media. They have exposed the limited coverage of women's issues in the South African news media and the infrequent use of female sources in their stories. They point to the depoliticization of women, who are depicted primarily in stories relating to development and reconstruction rather than politics. They critique the stereotypical portrayal of women politicians and the infantilization of women in political cartooning (Media Monitoring Project 1999: 161–7).

Women's media organizations train journalists on gender issues and sensitize them to the ways in which they portray women in their stories. The organizations also train women media workers to improve their computer skills. The media associations lobby around the lack of women in media leadership roles and organize workshops and conferences for media workers to discuss gender-related issues. Some, such as the Ugandan Media Women's Association, sponsor their own radio station (e.g., Mama FM). Others have their own publications or sponsor pages within a mainstream newspaper to provide alternate coverage of women's concerns in order to counter the often demeaning and sexist portrayal of women in the media. The Uganda Media Association, for example, publishes a regular pullout in the newspaper *New Vision*, called *Other Voices*, which is written in an accessible way and deals with topical issues. Their provision of information on the activities

---

[7] Alliance of Female Journalists (Sierra Leone), Association of Media Women in Kenya (AMWIK), Association of Professional African Women in Communications (APAC), Botswana Media Women's Association (BOMWA), Ethiopian Media Women's Association (EMWA), Federation of African Media Women Zimbabwe (FAMWZ), Malawi Media Women's Association (MMWA), Namibian Media Women's Association (NAMWA), Sierra Leone Association of Women in the Media (SLAWIM), Réseau des Femmes Journalistes de Côte d'Ivoire (RFJCI), Tanzania Media Women's Association (TAMWA), Uganda Media Women's Association (UMWA), West African Media Network (WAMN), and Zambia Media Women's Association (ZMWA).

of women's organizations and their leaders has also helped publicize and give further impetus to women's movements (Ojiambo Ochieng 1998: 33).

Nevertheless, access to the media in Africa remains limited and is reinforced by widespread illiteracy and poverty, as well as various state-controlled mechanisms and manipulations that limit media freedoms. Radio is the main communications medium for most people in Africa, with television and the print media regarded as secondary in importance. Thus, greater attention is increasingly being paid to these media and other new communications technologies in the diffusion of ideas transnationally, transcontinentally, and locally.

## NEW RESOURCES AND DONOR INFLUENCES

In addition to diffusing ideas, women's movements have also taken advantage of the new availability of donor resources for gender-related activities, which has allowed women to mobilize in new ways. Increased donor funding of women's associations in the 1990s helped women break their ties with state patronage networks and form new organizations independent of the state. There is, however, evidence that bilateral and multilateral donors as well as foundations have been reducing such support since 2000 and are channeling more of their resources once again through governmental agencies (Clark, Sprenger, and VeneKlasen 2005: 2, 141). Nevertheless, new funding sources targeting independent women's organizations left a significant imprint on women's movements starting in the 1990s.

Overall, gender-based funding has been only a fraction of overall overseas development assistance (ODA). Of overall ODA in 2003, it is estimated that only 2.5 billion (3.6 percent) had gender equality as a major objective. That same year, 0.04 percent of European Commission aid supported women-specific programs, whereas U.S. foundations allocated 7.3 percent of their $3 billion spent outside the United States to women's initiatives. Since the 2000s, however, donors have increasingly perceived women's rights as being out of fashion. The funding of such concerns is also being challenged by forces of neoliberalism, conservative religious influences, and the rising cost of military expenditures (Clark et al. 2006: 11, 14).

Nevertheless, the influence of new donor funds – however limited – has had an impact on women's NGOs. There are a number of factors that explain the interest of donors in women's associations in the 1990s. Although only a handful of countries such as Benin, Mali, Mozambique, and South Africa democratized in the 1990s, most countries in Africa experienced some pressures to liberalize, bringing to an end some of the worst dictatorships and creating new political spaces for independent media, multiparty systems, and an expanded civil society. Thus, even in semi-authoritarian contexts, foreign donors were able to shift their funding strategies to support a broader range of activities related to strengthening "democracy and good governance," to use donor parlance. These included efforts to ensure free and fair elections and to support human rights initiatives, associations formed around particular advocacy causes, civic education, and leadership training. These strategies were part of a broader menu of initiatives that donors adopted in the 1990s to promote democratic reform, ranging from dialogue with African government leaders to overt pressure, often in the form of political conditionality on aid (Hauser 1999: 622; Ottaway and Carothers 2000: 303).

Donors' interest in NGOs was also spurred on by the retreat of the state in the 1980s and 1990s. States increasingly found themselves unable to balance their budgets and provide social services. By the late 1990s, almost 40 percent of the United States Agency for International Development (USAID) program funds in Africa were going to private voluntary associations and NGOs. There was a growing belief that it was easier to ensure accountability with NGOs, which were attractive also because of the role that they play as counterweights to the state, as monitors of the state, and as sources of pressure for social justice and democratization (Owiti 2000).

For women's organizations, the 1990s saw a shift in donor strategies from a sole emphasis on funding activities related to economic development, education, and health and welfare concerns to an added interest in advocacy for women's rights, as well as promoting women's political leadership and political participation. Donors, such as the Ford Foundation, began to fund organizations involved in advocacy for gender equality clauses in constitutions undergoing revision.[8] Donors supported nonpartisan activities for legislation regarding women's land ownership, marriage and inheritance (e.g., the Oxford Committee for Famine Relief [Oxfam] and ActionAid), female genital cutting (e.g., the United Nations Population Fund), rape, domestic violence, and many other such issues. They supported leadership and skills training of potential female electoral candidates and of those already holding elective office as well as training in specific areas such as gender budgeting

---

[8] This was particularly ironic in the case of USAID, which was supporting women's mobilization in countries to ensure gender equality within various African constitution-writing initiatives, as in Malawi, even though American women do not enjoy such rights under the U.S. Constitution.

and legal aid. Other donors helped support women's caucuses of parliamentarians or members of constituent assemblies (e.g., the Ford Foundation, the Danish International Development Agency [DANIDA], the Netherlands Government, and the SNV-Netherlands Development Organization). Funding for national and regional networking also increased. When it came to advocacy, multilateral donors played a significantly lesser role than bilateral donors and their international nongovernmental organization (INGO) partners (Owiti 2000).

In 2005, the Association for Women's Rights in Development (AWID) conducted a survey of 401 gender-based organizations around the world, including 94 from Africa. They found that the largest number (39 percent) in Africa had been formed between 1990 and 1999 and another 32 percent were formed between 2000 and 2005. In terms of issue areas, 72 percent of the respondents from Africa said that the easiest areas to obtain funding were health concerns related to AIDS (72 percent), gender-based violence (47 percent), and civic/political rights and participation (45 percent) (Clark et al. 2006: 135).

In ranking funding sources of the organizations, 38 percent of African respondents in women's organizations identified public foundations[9] as among their top three sources of funding, 34 percent said bilateral[10] or multilateral agencies[11] were at the top of their list of funders; 33 percent identified women's funds,[12] 26 percent membership dues, 22 percent large foundations,[13] 24 percent local government, 18 percent income generation,

---

[9] Such foundations included ActionAid; the Foundation for International Community Assistance (FINCA); the Humanist Institute for Cooperation with Developing Countries (HIVOS); Interchurch Organization for Development Cooperation (ICCO); and Oxfam, which now includes the Dutch NOVIB as well. Many of these international NGOs are almost entirely funded by international donors. HIVOS, for example, gets all its funding from the Dutch government, and NOVIB gets about 70 percent of its funding from the Dutch government.

[10] Bilateral donors included Canadian International Development Agency (CIDA), the Danish International Development Agency (DANIDA), the Japan International Cooperation Agency (JICA), the Norwegian Agency for Development Cooperation (NORAD), the Swedish International Development Agency (SIDA), and USAID.

[11] Multilateral donors included the European Development Fund, the United Nations Development Fund for Women (UNIFEM), the United Nations Development Programme (UNDP), the United Nations Population Fund (UNFPA), the World Bank, and the World Health Organization (WHO).

[12] Women's funds included the African Women's Development Fund and the Global Fund for Women.

[13] Foundations included the McKnight Foundation and the Rockefeller and Ford Foundations.

and 9 percent the corporate sector. In terms of types of activities, respondents indicated that it was easiest gaining funding for media, technology, and communications activities (41 percent); advocacy and policy (35 percent); networking (33 percent); public education (32 percent); and organizational capacity building (31 percent). They felt it was harder to get support for employee salaries, administration, service provision, arts and sports-related activities, research and documentation, organizational capacity building, and training (Clark et al. 2006: 138, 141).

To a large extent, the national-level women's NGOs, much like human rights and environmental NGOs, came to depend on international donor funding for their advocacy around women's rights. On the one hand, this support helped open up new agendas for women in a context where financial support for such causes from elsewhere was not forthcoming. On the other hand, it often led to some rather harsh criticisms by observers that Western rather than local agendas were driving NGOs. Some even regarded donor funding of NGOs as providing a basis for the "second colonization of Africa" (Abdul-Raheem 2000).

Such characterizations of NGOs as donor driven do not apply as easily to women's advocacy organizations in Africa. It is the case that without donor support, many of the national-level women's organizations working around gender-related issues of legislative change and social transformation would have been significantly constrained in their capacity. Donors often, but not always, play an important role in supporting domestic women's movements to press governments to pass key women's rights legislation and to operate with greater transparency and accountability. African women's advocacy organizations are no different from such organizations in other parts of the world in their reliance on donor support. There is no doubt that reliance on donors gives them leverage; however, it is safe to say that the agendas of national-level women's organizations have for the most part been set within Africa. The impetus to advance women's rights and the strategizing and prioritizing of issues have come almost entirely from within women's movements in African countries, as will become evident in the chapters that follow.

## POLITICAL LIBERALIZATION AND WOMEN'S MOBILIZATION

The move toward multiparty systems in most African countries in the 1990s diminished the need for mass organizations linked and directed by the single ruling party. Where the state opened up political space for independent mobilization, new women's organizations flourished. Women and their organizations not only benefited from political liberalization, they were active in creating these political openings. Virtually every African country was affected in one way or another by these pressures for political liberalization, with varying degrees of democratization.

Nevertheless, women's movements vigorously sought to participate in the political reform movements of the 1990s because of the political space that they hoped to gain. They openly resisted corrupt and repressive regimes through public demonstrations and other militant action. Many were brave and fearless in their pursuit of democratic reforms.

In Mali, forces of President Moussa Traoré shot at two thousand demonstrating women and children when they marched in front the Ministry of Defense in 1991. The killing of women and children so incensed the public that Traoré was forced to make major concessions to the opposition before his fall in a military coup, which set in motion the political transition process.

Even in Niger, a country that had seen relatively little activism among women in its postcolonial history, several thousand women protested their exclusion from the preparatory committee for the 1991 national conference that would debate the introduction of a multiparty system in that country. Only one woman had been included among sixty-eight representatives to the conference. The women carried banners that read "National Conference without Women = Discrimination!" "Equal Rights!" and "No Conference without Women," and marched on the office where the preparatory meeting was being held. As a result, five additional women were appointed to the conference (Dunbar and Djibo 1992).

Like Niger, Chad was another country where women had not previously been visible in national politics. When the 2001 presidential elections in Chad were reportedly rigged, large numbers of women demonstrated twice in front of the French embassy, charging the French with complicity in the fraudulent election that resulted in the reelection of Idriss Deby. In one of the demonstrations on 11 June 2001, police hurdled grenades at the women, injuring fourteen ("Chadian Police..." 2001). One of the people injured in the attacks was Jacqueline Moudeina, a Chadian lawyer and human rights activist, who has represented the victims of the former president, Hissène Habré (from 1982 to 1990). He is alleged to have committed serious human rights abuses, including sponsoring torture of political opponents.

In Sierra Leone, women were the only group that openly defied soldiers as they demonstrated to demand that free elections be held when rumors began to circulate that the military might postpone the February 1996 elections (Bangura 1996).

In Togo in April 2005, according to press accounts, women, including many powerful businesswomen, were among the first out in the streets to protest, questioning the presidential electoral victory of Faure Gnassingbé, the son of Togo's late dictator, Gnassingbé Eyadéma. Even old women did not escape being beaten by soldiers in the deadly street clashes that ensued.

In Mauritania, police beat women protesters, injuring forty in a human rights demonstration in August 1991. Over 150 women had staged a sit-down strike outside a paramilitary police base in Nouakchott, demanding an independent inquiry into the fate of hundreds of Hal-Pulaar black Mauritanians who disappeared after being arrested following an alleged coup attempt in 1990.

In Conakry, Guinea, women organized a sit-in in front of the presidential palace in support of a 1990 general strike of workers and student demonstrations, and to protest the economic crisis, which they blamed on the country's leadership.[14]

In Kenya in the early 1990s, women were at the forefront of protests defending imprisoned human rights activists and found themselves in violent clashes with police. Wangari Maathai, the 2004 Nobel Peace Prize winner, led the Kenyan Greenbelt Movement (GBM) in one of the most successful environmental movements in Africa that became active in these pro-democacy protests. Formed in 1977, the GBM was made up of tens of thousands of women and some men who combined community development and environmental protection together with the promotion of democracy and human rights. Maathai's environmental activism led to numerous confrontations with Kenyan authorities in which Maathai and others were attacked by police, arrested, and imprisoned.

Sometimes women found themselves alone, the sole voice of opposition. Margaret Dongo was an outspoken opponent of the government of President Robert Mugabe in Zimbabwe long before the opposition Movement for Democratic Change came onto the scene. She had been a supporter of the Zimbabwe African National Union–Patriotic Front (ZANU-PF) since 1974 when she joined the liberation war and quickly rose through the ranks after independence, becoming a member of parliament and the party's central committee. She eventually left ZANU-PF and formed her own political party after years of being one of the only voices in parliament charging the government with corruption and state control of the media. When she ran for her seat representing Harare South in 1995, Dongo faced death

---

[14] Personal communication, Soriba Sylla, 1991.

threats and attacks on her home. When she lost, Dongo set a precedent when she contested the election results in court on the grounds of massive irregularities and fraud and won the case. She then ran successfully in a by-election (Jenje-Makwenda 1998).

Subsequently in Zimbabwe, women protesting violence against women linked their gender concerns to protest the broader political and economic crisis in that country. Over thirty riot police attacked a human rights and women's rights demonstration in Bulawayo of several hundred people in which several women were hospitalized with their babies on 29 November 2006. Women of Zimbabwe Arise had called on women to beat their pots and pans to mark the Sixteen Days of Activism against Gender Violence at that time.

Thus, women have been at the forefront of efforts to democratize in Africa. The demise of military regimes, the end of one-party rule, the institution of multiparty politics and competitive elections, and the greater freedoms enjoyed by the media and civil society opened up new possibilities for the mobilization of women. It is not evident that democratization directly led to changes in policy regarding women, especially when taken in comparative perspective, since one finds the adoption of pro-women policies as often within countries that did not democratize. Nevertheless, the changes that occurred were important in opening up political space for women's organizations to press for reforms.

CONCLUSIONS

In the previous chapter, we showed how women's collective action in precolonial, nationalist, and post-independence periods laid the basis for the newer forms of mobilization seen after the 1990s in Africa. We also described the importance of education in facilitating women's activism and leadership in years to come. This chapter laid the groundwork for understanding which factors influenced the emergence of new women's organizations in the late 1980s and 1990s as described in this chapter.

As we will see in Chapter 4, one of the major determinants of women's movements' capacity to influence policy was their level of autonomy from the dominant party and government. This autonomy gave women's movements the independence and distance to make new demands on the state. Without this autonomy, they easily remained beholden only to the interests of the state or the ruling parties, which often acted to suppress women's demands or relegated women to nonpolitical functions of the party and depoliticized their activities.

What accounts for this newfound autonomy in associational life? First, the diffusion of ideas from the international to regional and domestic levels contributed to the spread of a new brand of women's activism in new areas after the 1990s. At the same time, as we will see in Chapter 9, African women's organizations and networks, in turn, influenced these same global institutions and actors. Women's movements quickly embraced new communications technologies as they became available and creatively sought to make them accessible to larger numbers of women, especially those in rural and more remote regions. The use of these technologies was an important way in which new ideas were transmitted, as was the use of the media.

Second, African women's organizations had access to new resources after the 1990s, including their own funds from membership dues, but also external donor funds as a result of shifting donors strategies within the context of political liberalization. Although the influx of new resources may have plateaued by 2000, it played a role in galvanizing an important set of new actors. How well women's organizations can be sustained without continued support remains to be seen.

Finally, we have shown in this chapter how women's movements not only benefited from democratic openings but also actively participated in creating them. The political space that opened up in the 1990s created opportunities for new forms of women's mobilization.

# 4

# The Challenge of New Women's Movements

In contrast to the earlier postcolonial period when women's organizations tended to be closely associated with the ruling party and state, after the 1990s a new generation of independent women's organizations emerged with their own agendas, leadership, and sources of funding. Although the older welfare, domestic, and developmental agendas have persisted to this day, a new emphasis on political participation emerged, especially in the 1990s, that allowed women to press for the changes that we discuss in subsequent chapters, including constitutional and legislative reform and greater representation of women in legislatures, judiciaries, and the bureaucracy. New women's organizations formed to improve leadership skills, encourage women's political involvement on a nonpartisan basis, lobby for women's political representation, press for legislative changes, and conduct civic education.

This chapter looks at some of the characteristics of women's organizations and then examines some of the challenges that they face. It looks at the ways in which the authorities challenged women's associational autonomy. It shows how women's associations expanded their focus from developmental issues to the inclusion of more explicitly political concerns, to advocacy, and to demands for female leadership and representation. The chapter then identifies ways in which women's collective action is distinct from that of other interest groups. These differences lie not only in the goals of women activists but also in their inclusiveness across ethnic and party lines.

As discussed in the previous chapter, most organizations were formed after 1990, coinciding with the emergence of new democratic openings. The movements followed the 1985 Nairobi UN Conference on Women, which served as a catalyst for many women's organizations as did a growing number of international and regional women's rights networks and associations. The movements grew with the new availability of donor funds directed at nonstate actors, with the expansion of media freedom, and new possibilities for Internet communication, cheaper travel, and cell phone connections.

Even a country such as Mozambique, which had virtually no tradition of independent mobilization and had been fairly isolated from global trends as a result of years of conflict, saw the emergence of new organizations such as the Mozambican Association for the Development of the Family (1999), the Mozambican Association for Entrepreneur and Executive Women (1989), the Mozambican Association for Rural Development (1991), and the Mozambican Association for Housewives (1992). The first human rights group, Woman, Law and Development in Mozambique (MULEIDE), was created in 1991, initially linked to Women in Law and Development in Africa (WILDAF) (Casimiro 2004: 207–12). A decade later, the Democratic Republic of Congo, Liberia, and Sierra Leone similarly emerged from years of conflict with surprisingly active women's movements.

## CHARACTERISTICS OF NEW WOMEN'S MOBILIZATION

The formation of women's organizations in Africa in the late 1980s and early 1990s took place within the more general context of a proliferation of independent NGOs. However, women's organizations were among the first to emerge and were among the best organized, in part because women had longstanding experiences creating and maintaining grassroots and community-level organizations of various kinds, from savings clubs to religious, multipurpose, income-generating, cooperative, farming, social service, educational, cultural, handicrafts, and sports groups. Thus, they often found it easier to take advantage of new political spaces afforded by liberalizing regimes.

Similarly, in Tanzania, it is no accident that the main NGO networking body, Tanzania Association of Non-Governmental Organizations (TANGO), was started by women's organizations and had strong female representation in its leadership. Women in Mali brought their well-developed organizational skills, drawing on a long history of maintaining social and economic networks, to the newly formed NGOs in the 1990s. As a result, women claimed a strong presence in the NGO movement both in terms of making sure that development associations included programs that addressed women's issues and in terms of developing their own organizations, which ranged from legal to health, education, credit, and enterprise development associations (Kante and Hobgood 1994).

Women's mobilization, while sharing much in common with other civil society groups, has also stood apart from them in important ways. In a country such as Mozambique, the NGO scene was populated with development, humanitarian, human rights, youth and student, professional, religious, advocacy, and other international, provincial, and local groups and networks (KULIMA 1997). Women's groups have not only been interested in women's issues. They have linked their concerns to broader social movements.

Women's organizations account for a large proportion of NGOs in many African countries and perhaps the largest proportion in countries such as Kenya, Mali, Mozambique, and Tanzania, where they are the fastest growing sector of civil society. For example, a 2006 survey of civil society organizations in Uganda found that of their members, 77 percent were women (DENIVA 2006: 89). In at least twelve of the twenty-seven African countries with NGOs with consultative status in the United Nations Economic and Social Council (ECOSOC), over half the organizations are women's organizations.[1] Moreover, women's organizations make up around one-third of all human rights organizations in Angola, Eritrea, Gabon, Niger, Somalia, Sudan, Tanzania, and Uganda, and up to 40 percent in Mali and Swaziland.[2]

## Associational Autonomy

The new generation of organizations has tended to be independent of the regime and of ruling political parties in terms of their leadership, financing, and agendas. The new autonomous organizations have been financially independent of the state or ruling party. Women in Nigeria (WIN), one of the earliest of these new organizations, primarily funded its activities through membership fees, grants, and donations and from the sale of publications and T-shirts. Members also contributed their time and donated rooms in their homes for office space. Changing donor strategies to assist organizations were evident as WIN gained external donor support for specific projects after 1991 (Olojede 1999).

Financial independence has meant that the new organizations were outside the patronage networks that the ruling party and/or state had used to build loyalty. Their very existence has often challenged the legitimacy

[1] http://www.unpan.org/NGO-Africa-Directory/index.htm, accessed 22 July 2007.
[2] http://www.hri.ca/organizations/, accessed 22 July 2007.

of state patronage. This has made these autonomous associations potentially threatening to the state, especially if they have involved large numbers of rural women, as was the case with the tree planting Greenbelt Movement in Kenya, which came under increasing repression during the rule of President Daniel arap Moi. The ruling party's fight for the political loyalty of autonomous rural women's groups was particularly fierce as their numbers increased and economic resources grew. Kenya African National Union (KANU) politicians courted and manipulated local women's groups and made promises of patronage in order to win their votes (Sahle 1998: 175, 182–4). Some male politicians even formed women's groups through their female relatives in order to garner votes (Kabira and Nzioki 1993: 70). Thus, many Kenyan women concluded, as Wanjiku Mukabi Kabira and Elizabeth Akinyi Nzioki did, that the "first and most important issue to resolve" was "the question of autonomy" (1993: 73).

Associational autonomy has been critical to the success and legitimacy of this new generation of organizations. When the 1993 Nigerian presidential elections were annulled, Nigerians found themselves amidst a serious human rights crisis. WIN, together with other human rights and pro-democracy activists, launched a media campaign and demonstrated against the human rights abuses under the military regime and the disappearances of opposition politicians as well as human rights and pro-democracy activists (Olojede 1999). Such efforts by WIN and other civil society organizations eventually culminated in the restoration of an elected civilian government in May 1999, after which the most blatant human rights violations diminished considerably (Obiorah 2001). As one might expect, the organizations tied to the regime did not respond to the annulment of the elections in the same way as did the autonomous ones. Because the National Council of Women Societies (NCWS) had benefited from government largesse, it was "very unlikely for NCWS to pursue autonomous positions or present strong opposition to government on significant political issues such as political accountability and human rights," Iyabo Olojede (1999) argues.

Even in a democratic country such as South Africa, where the ruling African National Congress (ANC) has been an important advocate and ally of women's rights, the lack of autonomy of women's groups linked to the party has affected their capacity to defend women's rights consistently. The New Women's Movement, a grassroots organization of poor women allied with the better-resourced Black Sash activists, succeeded in increasing child support grants, while the ANC Women's League and ANC Minister of Welfare had proposed grant cutbacks (Hassim 2005: 17), thus highlighting the differences between the two types of organizations.

## Heterogeneity of Organizations

As political spaces opened up and new independent organizations were allowed to emerge, the heterogeneity of the new organizations was striking, especially when compared to the past. At the national level, women formed myriad organizations, including professional associations of women physicians, engineers, bankers, lawyers, accountants, market traders, entrepreneurs, and media workers. There have been national women's rights groups, organizations focusing on specific issues such as reproductive rights and violence against women and rape, as well as groups catering to particular sections of the population, including disabled women and widows.

Some organizations provide services to women in the areas of health, transportation, banking, protection, legal aid, publishing, and education to respond to the neglect of women in the mainstream institutions (Olojede 1999: 33). New forms of developmentally oriented organizations became especially popular in the 1990s, such as women's credit and finance associations as well as hometown and development associations. Women have also formed social and cultural organizations. Some occupational and political institutions such as trade unions and parties often have had a wing devoted to women. At the local level, there have been numerous multipurpose clubs that engaged in savings, farming, income-generating projects, handicrafts, sports, cultural events, and other functions, depending on the needs and priorities of members (Feldman 1983: 68; Mwaniki 1986: 215; Strobel 1979).

Most organizations, both at the local and national level, have been in some way concerned with advancing women's political, economic, legal, or social status. Women's advancement has been promoted even on many unexpected fronts. For instance, the Uganda Women Football Association successfully worked to introduce women's soccer throughout the country. The Association sought corporate and government sponsorship for games, equipment, training, and uniforms (Zziwa 1996: 15). Or to take another example, second wives in polygamous relationships have been mobilizing in Kenya, Tanzania, and Uganda on both a national and regional basis. A Single Mothers Association in the Upper East Region of Ghana promotes the welfare of unwed mothers by organizing consciousness-raising campaigns, promoting income-generating activities, and defending their rights ("Learning to Live . . . " 2005). Even women living in *purdah* (in seclusion and/or segregated from men) in Nigeria are demanding provisions to be able to vote. In 2006, the Jama'atu Ta'awumil Muslimeen Organisation of Nigeria called on the Independent National Electoral Commission to accommodate women in purdah and to enlist female officers to make sure that they were able to register to vote and also to vote (Kolawole 2006).

Women have begun to claim leadership of organizations that primarily have had a male-membership base, allowing them to introduce women's concerns into new arenas. There were many firsts in women's leadership after the 1990s. For example, Solomy Balungi Bossa was the first woman to head the Uganda Law Society in 1993; Constantia Pandeni was elected for the first time to head the Mineworkers Union of Namibia in 2001; Olive Zaitun Kigongo was the first woman elected president of Uganda National Chamber of Commerce and Industry in 2002; and Talitha Jario was elected the first woman president of the Namibian Basketball Federation in 2005. Increasingly women are leading Rotary Clubs, such as Dr. Burang Goree-Ndiaye, who became the first female head of Gambia's Rotary Club of Banjul in 2006.

Some organizations have branches throughout Africa, including the Forum for African Women's Educationalists (FAWE), which works on issues related to girls' education; the Women in Law and Development in Africa (WILDAF); the Society for Women and AIDS in Africa; Akina Mama wa Afrika; and many others. Others are regionally based, such as Women and Law in Southern Africa Research and Educational Trust (WLSA), Women and Law in East Africa and Southern Africa, and the Association de Lutte Contre les Violences Faites aux Femmes (Association against Violence against Women).

Still others are part of international associations, such as the International Federation of Women Lawyers (FIDA), Girl Guides, the Young Women's Christian Association (YWCA), and Zonta International. Most organizations in which women involved themselves were gender-specific, partly as an outgrowth of cultural divisions of labor and a historic preference for gender-specific organizations.

## Building Ties across Ethnic, Clan, and Religious Lines

One characteristic of women's mobilization that has set it apart from other forms of mobilization has been the keen interest in building ties across ethnic, clan, and religious lines, especially where relations in the broader society have been in conflict around such differences. Women's movements often sought to be as broad as possible because of their shared gender-based goals, which cut across differences. This often meant overlooking particularistic differences in order to build crosscutting links among all women.

In conflict-ridden areas, women organized across so-called "enemy" lines (that is, ethnic, clan, and religious lines) to find bases for peace. There were bold efforts of this kind in Burundi, the Democratic Republic of Congo, Liberia, Rwanda, Sierra Leone, Somalia, Sudan, and other countries. As detailed in Chapter 8, women often formed coalitions and networks for peace and/or collaborated in joint, mutually beneficial activities that helped build new bases for solidarity.

The inclusiveness of women's movements could be found along many dimensions. For example, women's organizations were usually preoccupied with how to build rural–urban linkages and bridge some of the gaps that isolated better educated women involved in national organizations from rural women in local groups. What is especially ironic is that urban male leaders of organizations are rarely questioned about their ties to rural constituencies, whereas women elite leaders often are charged with speaking on behalf of rural women without having sufficient links to them. This urban–rural gap is caricatured in Onwueme Osonye's 1997 play, *Tell It To Women: An Epic Drama for Women,* in which an activist organizes a conference attended by rural women who have no idea why they need to be "emancipated," and the organizer likewise does not understand why this is a problem. Although there is truth in the implicit critique in the play, generally urban women's organizations are quite attuned to the necessity of building such linkages and make efforts to do so in ways not always as apparent in non–gender-based NGOs. The lack of resources is often the biggest constraint on the building of these linkages.

Due to the limited resources of national-level NGOs and the monetary weakness of their constituent base, they have relied heavily on donors to fund their activities. This has resulted in what some have called the "NGOization" of feminism, which refers to the evolution of a feminist movement of professionals that since around 1995 has come to rely heavily on urban, educated women. In the Latin American context, these professionals were divorced from grassroots women's organizations (Alvarez 1998: 306–8).

Although there has developed an NGOization of feminism in Africa, the aim has been always explicitly to bridge the gaps with local groups and cooperate as much as resources and time permit. It has not been just national organizations that have sought these linkages. In Uganda, for example, even educated women in rural towns have sought to share their income-generating skills and know-how regarding nutrition, child-rearing, prenatal care, and preventative health measures with poorer rural women. Others have encouraged rural women to get into business or to save money. For instance, A Stitch in Time Women's Association was formed in Kabale in 1989 for women involved in tailoring, crocheting, and making carpets. But it also had as an objective to help poorer, less educated women's groups get involved in income-generating activities and savings clubs with the understanding that women's economic clout was a key to their empowerment (Tripp 2000).

### New Emphasis on Political Strategies

Although women had been politically active at the time of independence when they gained the right to vote and run for office, after independence they fell into more developmental and welfare-oriented activities. It was not until the 1990s that women became especially interested in politics as the single party gave way to multiple parties and a multiplicity of advocacy organizations. Although the older welfare and domestic agendas persisted into the 1990s in women's organizations, a new emphasis on political participation emerged. New women's organizations formed to improve leadership skills, encourage women's political involvement, promote women's political leadership, press for legislative changes, and conduct civic education. Advocacy groups mobilized around issues such as domestic violence, rape, reproductive rights, sex education in the school curriculum, female genital cutting, sexual harassment, the disparaging representation of women in the media, corruption, and other concerns that had rarely been addressed by the women's movements in the past and often were considered taboo by the government.

Kabira and Nzioki underscored the need for women to assert themselves politically in a 1993 statement that was indicative of the change in thinking that had occurred in the early 1990s, that is, a shift from a previous emphasis strictly on developmental approaches to a new adoption of political strategies. As they explained:

The state may criticize women's organisations as being elitist, ineffective, politically motivated, misguided or foreign. But women have to go where power and resources are by being powerful and resourceful themselves. Since groups know and express this desire, we suggest that women's organisations and political leaders focus their attention on long term changes that touch on the root causes of women's inequality and subordination in society. This approach will advance the women's cause towards meaningful transformation as opposed to individual advancement. (1993: 73)

As we show later in this chapter, although women's movements have embraced advocacy and political action, the focus on "the political" has not been unproblematic for women's organizations. This is partly because of the depoliticization of women's activities in the colonial and post-independence period, but also because of the way that politics has frequently been associated with corruption, violence, and ethnicity.

## Networks, Coalitions, and Alliances

Perhaps in reaction to the dominance of mass women's organizations under authoritarian rule, there was less interest in creating large overarching organizations that could speak for all women's interests than there had been in the past. The number of women's networks, coalitions, and ad hoc issue-oriented alliances multiplied throughout Africa, but there were few efforts to create organizations to represent all women in the country. Given the weakness of existing political parties, women's NGO coalitions and networks often represented a more stable coalescing of interests. They came together in coalitions and networked primarily around land issues, violence against women, women's political participation, and constitutional reform.

In a country such as Uganda, women's organizations have been leaders in all major coalitions and have taken up issues that go well beyond more narrowly defined "women's issues." They have brought women's perspectives and concerns to bear on a wide range of issues having to do with social justice. Ugandan women activists, for example, are in the leadership of important networks that have been created around land rights, hunger, debt, poverty, and corruption. At the same time, there are many networks that have formed around gender-specific issues such as domestic violence, rape, the common property amendment of the 1998 Land Act, the Domestic Relations Bill, and efforts to change the way in which women politicians are elected through an electoral college that is susceptible to manipulation.

In addition, more ad hoc and short-term coalitions formed in Uganda to address particular incidents. One ad hoc coalition was created to abolish the customary practice in which the Buganda king was to have had sexual relations with a virgin prior to his wedding ceremony in 1998; another coalition formed to protest the Italian court's ruling in 1999 that a woman wearing jeans could not be raped; and yet another coalesced to protest racist statements of a top United States Agency for International Development officer in 2001.

As mentioned earlier, some umbrella organizations were formed in the process leading to 1995 UN conference in Beijing, which provided the impetus to coalesce. Examples of such organizations include the Tanzania

Gender Networking Programme (TGNP) and Uganda Women's Network (UWONET).

In other countries, such as Mali, an umbrella organization of fifty associations (Coordination des Associations et ONG Féminines du Mali) was formed in 1994 to liaise with the women's national machinery (Wing 2002: 178). Coalitions were also formed to coordinate their activities with donors, who often helped support the creation of such networks in order to avoid duplication of activities.

In Uganda, for example, ActionAid and the Oxford Committee for Famine Relief (Oxfam) helped form the Land Alliance in which women's organizations played a leading role and many international NGOs played a key role in initiating the Uganda National NGO Forum. Similarly, in Mozambique, the Mozambican Women's Forum was created in 1990 as an initiative of UNICEF and United Nations Development Programme (UNDP) Women in Development program officers, who brought together other donors, NGOs, women's organizations, governmental agencies, and a research institution, the Centre of African Studies. The Forum was to share information, develop common projects and programs, and prevent the duplication of efforts.[3] In 1993, this group decided to establish an NGO network called Fórum Mulher (Women's Forum – Woman in Development Coordination). The Women's Forum is a network of various organizations – NGOs, state institutions, religious groups, unions, international organizations, international NGOs, party women's leagues, cooperatives, and peasant associations – that work for the emancipation of women. The main objectives are to create a communication network to share experiences; to train members of organizations on gender, leadership, and civic education; to influence constitutional changes; to lobby for women in leadership positions; and to press for gender perspectives in the government and in political parties. The coalition led the push to advance women's rights and the efforts of groups to revise, discuss, and disseminate information about laws, such as the Family Law, land laws, the civil and penal codes, labor laws, and laws pertaining to violence against women. The Women's Forum also networked

---

[3] The monthly Inter-Agency meeting included CIDA, CUSO-SUCO (Non Governmental Organization Canada-Mozambique), DANIDA, FAO, NORAD, Save the Children–UK, Save the Children–U.S. SIDA, USAID, UNDP, UNFPA, UNICEF, and the World Bank. Gradually this group included representatives from state organizations and Mozambican NGOs involved in WID, such as Mozambican Woman Organization (OMM), the Ministry for the Coordination of Women and Social Action (MMCAS), and the Women's and Gender Studies Department.

with other groups in Africa[4] as well as with other networks, NGOs, and government agencies within Mozambique.[5]

## Men's Support of Women's Causes

Finally, one of the main characteristics of the contemporary women's movements in Africa is the attention that they have paid to working with men and bringing men on board in their struggles, especially at the community level. One measure of the success of these efforts has been the extent to which men have supported women's causes.

Men have, for example, participated in many countries in initiatives relating to violence against women. In Botswana, men, women, and children marched through the streets of the capital Gaborone to parliament in 2001, holding banners that read, "Men against Rape" ("Batswana Stage Street Protests..." 2002). Similarly, in neighboring South Africa that same year, men held a demonstration through the streets of Cape Town against the abuse of children and women. The action was part of the worldwide Sixteen Days of Activism against Gender Violence campaign ("Cape Town Men..." 2002). In Mbarara, Uganda, men joined women in a demonstration against the rape of girls and women and against domestic violence. Government leaders, police, Red Cross staff, parents, and students demonstrated in March 2002, holding placards saying, "Unite against Defilement [rape of girls under the age of consent], Rape and Domestic Violence," "Avoid Nude Photographs," and "Stop Child Abuse..." ("Mbarara Stages Demo..." 2002).

In Kenya, Reverend Timothy Njoya leads a network called Men for Gender Equality Now (Kibwana 2001: 206). This movement has now spread, with the help of the African Women's Communication and Development Network (FEMNET), to other parts of Africa, including Ethiopia, Kenya,

---

4 Women's Forum networks with African Women Development and Communication Network (FEMNET); Forum of African Women Educationalist (FAWE); Nairobi Gender Network (GETNET), Cape Town; UNIFEM, Harare; Women in Law and Development in Africa (WILDAF), Harare; and the Zimbabwe Women's Resource Center and Network (ZWRCN), Harare.

5 In Mozambique, Women's Forum works with other networks, such as Link and NGO Forum; is a member of the governmental body Operative Group after Beijing; works with various commissions in parliament, including the Commission on Social Issues, Gender and Environment and the Commission on Juridical/Legal Issues, Human Rights and Legality; and is a member of the World Program for Food (PMA) Technical Committee and of the UNDP Steering Committee.

Malawi, Namibia, South Africa, Zambia, and Zimbabwe, to create awareness around gender equality, gender-based violence, and the relationship of
equality and violence to the HIV/AIDS crisis (Wanyeki 2005: 113). And
finally, in Mali, men have been integral to efforts by the Association des
jurists Maliennes (Malian Women Jurists Association) to persuade local
communities to end female genital cutting (Wing 2002: 181).

The reasons that men are embracing the cause of gender equality were well
articulated by the South African leader of EngenderHealth, Dean Peacock,
in his 2004 speech at a high-profile International Women's Day event on
women and HIV/AIDS at the United Nations headquarters, entitled "Mobilizing Men for Gender Equality: Supporting Women's Health and Rights."
As he explained:

I want to mention four reasons why it is in men's interest to change. First, it is in
men's interest to change because the same gender roles that leave women vulnerable
to HIV/AIDS also put men's own health at risk. Too often, men are encouraged
to equate masculinity with risk taking behaviour – such as the use of violence,
dominance over women, the pursuit of multiple sexual partners, use of alcohol
and the rejection of health seeking behaviours.... Second, it is in men's interest to
change because men often care deeply about the women in their lives – whether their
mothers, sisters, neighbors, co-workers or fellow congregants – and are frequently
devastated by violence perpetrated against them. Third, it is in men's interest to
change because pervasive domestic and sexual violence casts all men as potential
perpetrators and infuses fear and distrust into men's daily interactions with women.
Finally, it is in men's interest to change because relationships based on equality and
mutual respect are far more satisfying than those based on fear and domination.

### Gender Studies and Women's Movements

Gender/women's studies programs and departments have been among the
most important supports to women's mobilization in Africa. They are often
described as the "academic arm" of the women's movement and see their
linkages to the activist elements of the movement as vital to their existence.
Gender studies programs exist at twenty-seven universities; four universities
have a full department and five offer undergraduate degrees in this field.
The earliest teaching programs were started in 1988 at Eduardo Mondlane
University in Mozambique, in 1989 at Ahfad University in Sudan, the University of Ghana, and the University of Pretoria, South Africa, although as
early as the 1980s there had been a Women's Research and Documentation
Project at the University of Dar es Salaam, Tanzania.

In 1993, Cameroon established a Department of Women's and Gender
Studies (WGS) at the University of Buea in a context where – according

to the department's first chair, Professor Joyce Endeley – it benefited from the conducive atmosphere created by the United Nations conferences on women and women's responses to structural adjustment in Cameroon. The department was intended to train gender experts to work in the Ministry of Women's Affairs, in other national ministries and government units, and in NGOs. Within a decade of its establishment, the department's enrollments increased sevenfold to about 240 students in 2004, of which 10–20 percent were men (Endeley 2004). WGS is one of the most successful departments at the University of Buea, attracting foreign scholars, international linkages, and external support.

Formed in 1992, the Department of Women and Gender Studies at Makerere University gained international recognition in the field of gender studies when it hosted the 2002 Women's World Congress, one of the first major international academic conferences to be held in Uganda. Housed in an impressive three-story building, the department has seventeen faculty members, three of whom are men. It offers a two-year master of arts program and since 1999 has run a three-year undergraduate program; a five-week short evening course for decision makers in the public, private, and NGO sectors; and two short-term regional training programs that have attracted development practitioners from eastern and southern Africa. Recently it has begun to train Ph.D.s.

One central goal of the department from its inception, apart from training academics, was to train leaders in government, business, and NGOs so that they could become catalysts for the integration of gender concerns in policy making. The department developed outreach programs that were tailored to the needs of NGOs, government departments seeking to incorporate gender mainstreaming, and other university faculties and departments.

The Ugandan women activists who had attended the 1985 UN Nairobi conference returned convinced that Uganda needed a more long-term perspective on social transformation; it had to be autonomous of the government and it needed academic input. It was within this context that they formed an NGO, Action for Development (ACFODE). Simultaneously, those who were academics formed the department to help develop an intellectual and empirical research base as well as policy analysis for advocacy. It was a time of political upheaval, when a new government had come into power and there was a political openness to new initiatives for women, especially ones that linked academic research and teaching with practical concerns that would address problems of development, lack of rights in accessing basic resources, the gendered impacts of war and violence, and women's low rates of political participation.

A similar program can be found at Eduardo Mondlane University in Maputo, Mozambique. In 1988, the Center of African Studies created the Women's Studies Department with the support of the Ford Foundation. In 1990, this department was transformed into a Women's and Gender Studies Department. Its main activities have included producing scholarship on women in Mozambique, training gender specialists, maintaining a library on women and gender, and collaborating with state and nonstate associations. It has sponsored action and participatory research together with other university departments and organizations from outside the University as well as state agencies. As in Uganda, the department's faculty are founders of key women's rights organizations, including the Association of Mozambican Professional and Business Women (ACTIVA), MULEIDE, WILDAF, WLSA, and the Women's Forum. The department is part of the Operative Group for the Advancement of Woman in Mozambique, which directs the implementation of gender policy in Mozambique (see Chapter 7); it was a member of the NGO-directed Land Campaign; and it participates in the group known as the Women's Forum developing a Law against Domestic Violence program. Initially several of the department faculty were involved with the Frente de Libertação de Moçambique (FRELIMO) women's wing, Organização da Mulher Moçambicana (OMM), but today they work with various NGOs and as advisors to state bodies.

Because of the pressing need for practical gender expertise in policy, NGO, and grassroots contexts, gender studies faculty have wrestled with how to conceptualize gender and women's studies in an African context. Some have warned against the dangers of wholesale importation of Western models (Oyewumi 2003), while others have wondered whether women/gender studies constitutes a discipline in the traditional sense of defining a body of knowledge (Kwesiga and Ssendiwala forthcoming; Mama 1996). Some have focused on how to conceptualize gender mainstreaming within the African academy in a way that promotes gender equality (Sall 2000). Makerere University has been a pioneer globally in gender mainstreaming within institutions of higher learning and has developed a Gender Mainstreaming Division to take up these concerns within the university. It has produced a handbook to help departments tackle problems of gender mainstreaming and help create awareness of the problem.

In Africa, a key debate in women's studies has been the question of relevance. Academics ask, do gender/women's studies programs relate to what is important to contemporary African societies? Research and teaching have been generally tied to practical concerns, given the context in which the gender studies programs were initiated and the policy, advocacy, training, and other related constituencies that they serve. In other words, there has been emphasis on development concerns that are seen as urgent, with considerably less emphasis on subjects such as sexuality and identity (more commonly found in North American and European departments), although these interests are emerging, especially in southern Africa. Thus, research and teaching have focused on political, economic, and social concerns, given the urgency of high rates of maternal death, problems of landlessness, the AIDS epidemic, and other issues that weigh heavily on women and their communities.

## CHALLENGES FOR WOMEN'S MOBILIZATION

Women's movements have had measured successes in bringing about policy changes affecting women. They have faced particular challenges in their relationship to donors, in maintaining their autonomy, and in engaging in advocacy activities in countries with stronger authoritarian legacies, and they have faced these challenges with a deficit of internal institutional capacity. The next section tackles a few of these constraints.

### Relations with the State: The Problem of Autonomy

Maintaining that autonomy is a key challenge for organizations that are independent of the state, especially in semi-authoritarian contexts where the struggles to assert autonomy are the most vigorous. Many African governments have viewed NGOs as potentially disruptive to the polity and as a source of opposition to their rule, especially those NGOs that have lobbied for changes in policy. They have stressed the need for NGOs to align themselves with government policy. Some governments have accused NGOs of being self-serving rather than working in the interests of their intended beneficiaries; and because their funds are frequently externally derived, government leaders at times have charged NGOs with lacking in transparency or being a security risk. However, not all NGO–state relations are conflicted. Even in Uganda, where there have been tensions over the regulatory aspects of an NGO act, there have been many useful partnerships between the state and the women's movement in the area of HIV/AIDS activities and other health-related initiatives, for example.

With political liberalization, open repression and banning of organizations became less common. Such practices were replaced by a new repertoire of tactics to monitor, regulate, undermine, and, in some cases, destroy autonomous organizations that were perceived (usually quite erroneously) as having the desire and potential to undermine state authority. As a result, some organizations came under attack by their governments, which tried to revoke their registration, coopt or buy off their leadership, and harass and manipulate their members. One frequent strategy was to pass legislation to establish an oversight board that could monitor the activities of NGOs and deregister them if deemed necessary. In Kenya, there was a protracted battle between civil society and government as the government pressed forward with legislation to regulate NGOs. Civil society organizations became proactive and produced an alternative bill; they aggressively lobbied parliamentarians and thus managed to salvage reasonable space within which to operate. In contrast, in Uganda, despite five years of intense mobilization by civil society groups to stop a restrictive NGO bill from passing, the parliament voted it through in 2006.

Sometimes older politically oriented groups have come into direct competition with the newer NGOs in seeking supporters and donor funds. A case in point is a struggle that erupted after the 1995 formation of the Tanzanian Women's Council (BAWATA), which had been launched by the ruling party's women's wing, Umoja wa Wanawake wa Tanzania (UWT). Initially, elements within the leadership of the UWT had wanted to make the wing independent of the party, but the top party and the UWT leadership opposed this strategy. Instead, they decided to form an "independent" nongovernmental umbrella organization that could access donor funds, yet remain under UWT's thumb. One top official in the Ministry of Community Development, Gender and Children explained that women's NGOs did not feel "comfortable with the Ministry," and so the thinking was that the ministry would find it easier to "monitor, regulate and collaborate" with women's groups through a separate council.

BAWATA's leadership envisioned a broad-based autonomous organization that was to push for women's advancement on a number of fronts, including strengthening women's political leadership, advocating legislative change, and conducting civic education. BAWATA became involved in policy advocacy on issues such as violence against women, sexual abuse of children, improved social services delivery, inheritance laws, land ownership, and girls' access to education. BAWATA drew up a document evaluating each of the presidential candidates and their parties in the 1995 elections regarding women's issues. In doing so, they had overstepped their bounds in a society where the female electorate was critical to the ruling party's continued success. As Chris Maina Peter explained:

Every sensible State knows that women are faithful voters. They normally register and actually go to vote. Unlike men who talk a lot and do little [sic]. They might even register only to forget to vote on the elections [sic] day. Thus women are regarded as a safe and sure constituency and whoever controls them is guaranteed victory. By touching this sensitive area – BAWATA was seen as a mischievous lot. (1999: 11)

The Ministry of Home Affairs banned BAWATA on the grounds that it was operating as a political party and was not holding meetings or submitting annual financial accounts to the Registrar of Societies. The charges against BAWATA, which by all accounts were fabricated, indicated that the party and the government were not interested in permitting the formation of independent organizations with a bold agenda that might diverge from the ruling party's interests. One top UWT leader, who was also the minister of local government, ordered women district commissioners to discourage women from participating in BAWATA because women who were allegedly too "independent-minded" were managing it.

BAWATA took the matter to the High Court on the grounds that the government action was unconstitutional and in violation of international human rights conventions to which Tanzania is a signatory. The Court issued an injunction against the government, prohibiting it from deregistering BAWATA. In the meantime, members of BAWATA faced death threats, harassment, and intimidation. Husbands of BAWATA leaders were demoted or lost their government jobs, while members of the organization's branches faced coercion from local authorities. Local chapters found themselves unable to meet and run their nursery schools and day care centers. Although BAWATA eventually won its case against the government, in the process, the organization was destroyed and the intimidation of its leadership left local chapters in disarray.

The deregistration of BAWATA was widely condemned by other NGOs who were disturbed and demoralized by the implications of this action on the freedom of association. As one lawyer and journalist, Robert Rweyemamu put it:

Can an NGO geared to the development of the people be completely cut off from political life? It [the deregistration of BAWATA] is a test for those who claim to be devoted to uplifting the social, economic and cultural standards of Tanzanians. (1997: 9)

In Tanzania, which has been a multiparty state since 1992, the BAWATA case illustrates the limits of freedom of association and speech, even in a fairly tolerant country. The fate of BAWATA is indicative of the prevalent view that equates autonomous nongovernmental activities with an antigovernmental stance, making any kind of advocacy extremely difficult.

In Tanzania and elsewhere in semi-authoritarian and authoritarian African states, the most active women's organizations with the most far-reaching agendas often had difficulty registering or had their registration delayed indefinitely. They faced external manipulations and pressures to keep opposition party members from leadership of the organizations, even though their activities were nonpartisan in the context of the association.

Similar tensions between independent organizations and women's wings or branches of dominant parties have occurred even in democracies such as South Africa, where friction arose between the African National Congress and the Women's National Coalition after the women's charter campaign had united the broadest array of women's organizations in South Africa. In Namibia, another rift emerged between the Women's Council of the ruling South West African People's Organisation (SWAPO) and the Women's Manifesto Network (Geisler 2004: 211).

Nevertheless, the interest in preserving autonomy has also produced dilemmas for NGOs that, on the one hand, seek to preserve their nonpartisan character and, on the other hand, want to benefit from the leadership and input of women politicians and party leaders. When women party leaders and politicians lead women's NGOs, this creates both conflicts of interest as well as opportunities for women's groups to influence political parties. In Uganda, in 2001 the women's NGO ACFODE asked its executive director to step down when she announced that she was serving as the campaign manager for one of the opposition presidential candidates, Aggrey Awori. Because ACFODE was engaged in voter education, Awori's campaigning was seen as compromising the organization's activities. Although this decision agitated some, its consequences were not as serious as those of the decision taken by the Women's National Coalition (WNC) in South Africa in 1994 to bar women parliamentarians from being officers of the coalition. This decision meant that almost the entire leadership of WNC had to resign, resulting in a loss of continuity in leadership and contributing to the demise of the coalition (Geisler 2004: 85). Part of what motivated the decision to eliminate the party leadership from the coalition was the desire for greater autonomy from party influence. However, another element had to do with the view that women's concerns should be framed outside of politics.

Shireen Hassim (2006) has shown what a fine line women's organizations must tread in preserving autonomy yet engaging political parties and other political actors. Drawing on the distinctions made by Maxine Molyneux (1998) between independent, associational, and directed autonomy, Hassim argues that the women's movement in South Africa sought associational autonomy, but because of its roots in the anti-apartheid movement, it often found itself both energized and constrained by its allegiance to the broader nationalist project. This meant that the women's movement needed to maintain a strong bargaining position to avoid cooptation. It had to negotiate its relationship constantly with the broader anti-apartheid movement and with the African National Congress. The dilemma for the women's movement was how to navigate its alliances with broader political forces while maintaining autonomy to advance women's rights and a feminist agenda.

South Africa is somewhat unique in this regard because most women's movements in Africa went through similar struggles much earlier at the time of independence in the early 1960s and ended up largely being coopted by the ruling parties. The new movements we see today in Africa have generally already broken from these older types of relations with political parties and the state. Nevertheless, the tensions persist to this day, especially in countries with parties that have an overwhelming preponderance of parliamentary seats within a multiparty context. Autonomy and the ways in which women's organizations engage parties in a multiparty context are constantly being negotiated and renegotiated in new contexts.

## Redefining the Political

Related to the problem of autonomy from the state are debates over the extent to which women's organizations can legitimately advocate a greater political role for women and engage in advocacy around women's issues that would challenge government policies and authority. Women's organizations, especially those coming out of authoritarian contexts, have had an uneasy relationship with the notion of "the political." There are several reasons for this. One is the legacy of the single-party state and activists' experiences in an earlier era in which women's organizations were to be developmental and focused primarily on income-generating and social welfare–related activities.

After the introduction of multipartyism in Tanzania, the leadership feared that the new nongovernmental organizations would challenge the hegemony of the ruling party and its mass organizations. Organizations that posed such a threat were targeted, had difficulty registering, and were accused of being too "political." Organizations were often reminded that they needed to maintain their "developmental" focus rather than adopt political objectives. For example, the minister for minerals and energy told members of the Tanzanian Women Miners Association at their inaugural conference in 1997 to distance themselves from "politics" and concentrate on economic, technical, and commercial activities (Kivamwo 1997).

The authorities could interpret any manifestation of opposition to government policy, even benign advocacy, as a sign of adopting an antigovernmental position. The Tanzanian minister of home affairs warned in July 1997 that NGOs engaging in hostile exchanges of words with the government would risk losing their registration, as would NGOs that confronted the government through fora that created confusion and insecurity. This pattern is a common one found in many authoritarian and semi-authoritarian countries and has made NGOs, including women's NGOs, often hesitant to characterize their activities as political in any way, even when it is clear that they are engaged in lobbying, advocacy, or other forms of legitimate political action. Dzodzi Tsikata explained the dilemma in the Ghanaian context:

If you say something that is different to the government's agenda, then you are being subversive.... In many countries in Africa, gender activists are accepted as long as they focus on programmes such as credit for women, income generation projects and girls' education, and couch their struggles in terms of welfare or national development. Once they broach questions of power relations or injustices, they are accused of being elitist and influenced by foreign ideas that are alien to African culture. (quoted in Mama 2005: 129–30)

Another Ghanaian, Hamida Harrison, argues that for women activists, being political is unavoidable, given the nature of advocacy for women's rights:

NGOs are supposed to be politically neutral, non-partisan and so on. And I think that many NGOs are afraid of the word "political," many of them actually say, "we are not political," while we in the women's movement are saying, "This is politics." The minute you start talking about power and resources and so on, it is politics. This is something that makes people within the NGO setting very uncomfortable. (quoted in Mama 2005: 129)

But there are additional reasons that women's organizations sometimes hesitate to characterize their activities as political. In Uganda, for example, "politics" has been associated with the military, repression, civil war, and sectarian fighting, and so in rejecting the term "politics," women activists have signaled that they are rejecting these meanings of politics. As one Ugandan woman's rights leader put it:

We do not want these organizations to become terribly political. It would hurt too much. There would be too much pain, too much tension that we do not need right now. Everything has been so politicized along tribal, religious and party lines. Women through these organizations are rejecting that. We know the divisions exist among us, but it is more important right now to survive and to help each other out. (Tripp 2000)

However, for others, politics has been equated with corruption, nepotism, and patronage politics. For them, the struggle has been to redefine politics in a new way in order to allow women to seek political office. Several female politicians have taken up this challenge. In her memoir, Nobel Prize–winning Wangari Maathai comments on her bid for the presidency in 1997, saying that one of the reasons she ran was to

challenge the perception among some people, including Kenyans, that good people don't go into politics as if all politicians are tricksters and liars. Yet it was the politicians in Kenya who were making the policies that were repressing people and their aspirations and destroying the environment. It was their decisions that affected so much of our lives. To say that participating in politics is bad is to misunderstand the situation: Why leave your fate in the hands of liars or tricksters? (2006: 256)

Many of these negative attitudes about politics have contributed to rifts between women politicians and women's rights activists. Women's organizations sometimes accuse parliamentarians of not articulating issues of women, and women politicians often accuse women activists of being critics without providing sufficient support and assistance (Makanya 1999: 54). For this reason, WILDAF initiated a project to facilitate greater dialogue between the two groups in Malawi, Mozambique, Namibia, and Zimbabwe. Both groups are increasingly reaching out to one another to build mutually supportive ties.

### Relationships with Donors

As mentioned in Chapter 3, foreign donors have been one of the main influences on the growth of new women's organizations after the late 1980s and 1990s. The pullback of the state in the 1980s due to economic crisis, budget deficits, corruption, and pressures from international financial institutions and foreign donors meant that the donor community channeled more of their funds through NGOs, both national and international (Nyangoro 1999). Donors believed NGOs would be able to play a watchdog role with respect to the state, challenge state corruption and patronage, and promote good governance and democracy. They subsequently encouraged the formation of local and national NGOs through their funding strategies, leading to a rapid increase of NGOs, including women's organizations.

On the one hand, donors have benefited women's organizations in important ways. They have inculcated professionalism by insisting on accurate, timely, and regular accounting of funds, report writing, project management, monitoring, and evaluation in the interest of meeting transparenc requirements. They have often promoted capacity building through extensive training for staff and members. For example, in 1994, while delegates debated Uganda's Draft Constitution, the Ford Foundation supported the LINK program run by a leading women's organization, ACFODE, to collect views from the public and feed them into the parliamentary proceedings through various activities. Ford Foundation personnel assisted in proposal preparation by reviewing, questioning, and pointing to gaps in ACFODE's proposal, and subsequently they monitored the progress of LINK. The organization's leaders appreciated this role, which they felt helped strengthen the program rather than simply imposing views.

Donors have often encouraged checks and balances to ensure good practices, periodic change of the leadership to ensure democratic processes, generational transitions, and an influx of new ideas and input. Donors have generally demanded gender equity and inclusiveness in organizational membership and leadership. They have facilitated the networking of groups working in the same area to reduce duplication of efforts and share information and strategies.

Women activists (and other civil society actors) are often reluctant to talk about dilemmas that they confront with donors lest they be perceived as biting the hand that feeds them. On a continent where activists have few alternative domestic sources of funding, they can ill afford to jeopardize relations with donors. This is not to say that they are completely at the mercy of donors. The aforementioned ACFODE has on several occasions turned down funds from particular donors because its leaders felt that they were being pushed in directions not in keeping with their own goals. The same is true of the General Union of Cooperatives in Mozambique. But this is a luxury that only the most established organizations can afford.

Because of such donor dependence, the African Liaison Program Initiative, managed by InterAction, hosted a series of regional conferences starting in 2000 to allow U.S. private voluntary organizations, African NGOs, and USAID a space where they could talk openly about questions of programmatic, organizational, financial, and regulatory accountability. However, such efforts are rare and difficult and the outcomes ambiguous.

Facilitation by donors has sometimes put women's associations in a bad light. Some members of the public have interpreted the visible four-wheel drive vehicles, well-furnished office premises, and above-average salaries of some NGO professionals as a luxury and have questioned the NGOs' intent of serving the less privileged. The credibility of women's organizations is diminished by the (mis)perception that their leaders are more interested in material benefits than in serving the communities. Because of the general deprivation of society, this (mis)perception is more strongly felt in Africa than in other parts of the world.

## Excessive Donor Influence on NGOs

Although in general, women's organizations set their own agendas, at times there are donors that have excessive influence in shaping NGO operations. Such donors may, for example, provide consultants who recommend changes in organizational structure and programming. Although these may be well-intended interventions to improve efficiency, women's organizations often feel compelled to cut back or alter programs in ways that may go against the organization's own objectives in order to please a donor. Donors may place their own volunteers to work with the NGO even though the NGO did not request such assistance. This may lead to conflicts mainly because the volunteer is not familiar with the organization. It also potentially creates unnecessary mistrust, as the person is "seen" as a spy for the donor.

Donor assistance has sometimes, although not always, shaped NGO agendas around HIV/AIDS, children's rights, good governance, and conflict resolution by encouraging NGO activity and the emergence of NGOs in areas that they otherwise might not have been as interested. Although this is not necessarily a problem, it has sometimes hampered prioritizing activities that women activists themselves might find more pressing. For example, there may be inadequate funds for raising awareness of women in different areas of rights. Women's organizations often lack funding for conducting community needs assessments, yet they might find it easier to tap into donor funds for AIDS-related activities. Thus, international donors have their own agendas, which sometimes do not always intersect with the objectives of women's organizations. At the same time, however, not all NGOs have the capacity and the wherewithal to negotiate with donors effectively.

Governments and opponents of women's advocacy sometimes accuse women's NGOs of operating under foreign donor and Western feminist influences. These attempts to discredit the work of women's organizations have come up especially around struggles over female genital cutting, polygamy, women's inheritance rights, domestic violence, marital rape, sexual harassment, and challenges to particular customary practices. Even though such charges are, as Claude Welch puts it, "cheap criticisms," in most instances, the dependence on donor funding has sometimes made it difficult to counter them. Michael Bratton (1989) argues that some NGOs in Africa have found that such perceptions, however misguided, undermine their legitimacy and efficacy.

## Short-Term Funding

Donor-driven funding strategies often lack in long-term sustained support for women's rights advocacy. In spite of the fact that foreign donors and international NGOs have contributed to the new interest in women's advocacy in Africa, donors are generally hesitant to make a long-term commitment to such activities through, for example, supporting institution-building costs or research. Donors are frequently under pressure to support short-term activities that produce demonstrable results. Similar trends were evident in the funding of women's organizations in Latin America and elsewhere (Schild 1998). This funding imperative, focused on short-term projects with measurable outcomes, is often at odds with the goals of women activists, who see long-term activities leading to institutional change as critical if equality is to be achieved and as integral to sustainable political and economic development. Campaigns related to particular legislation can take years and the outcome may be far from certain, making donors, who operate on short-term timelines, hesitant to support sustained advocacy.

As the Uganda Land Alliance head put it:

From working with UWONET and working with the Land Alliance, we found it so much harder for networks doing advocacy work to get funding even though donors would tell us we should do advocacy. They still would rather give money to organizations that had quantifiable results at the end of the year. With advocacy you never know. We have been working around the Domestic Relations Bill forever.... I think even though they speak about it, they do not follow up with actual funding for advocacy at end of the day (Jacqueline Asiimwe 2001 Interview with Aili Tripp).

Activists find themselves having to engage in the provision of social and economic services in order to obtain donor funds that would sustain their advocacy work. But the donor emphasis on service provision, which is time consuming, detracts from work toward long-term goals regarding far-reaching legislation. This is a constant dilemma for women lawyers in Uganda, for example, who are torn between having to provide legal aid and legal information services to women to satisfy donors and pursuing their own priority of spending time working toward more far-reaching legislative change related to a domestic relations bill and women's rights to own land.

In the long run, encouraging NGOs to become training vehicles and service providers may produce immediate results, but it is not clear, as Michael Edwards and Davide Hulme (1996) have pointed out, that this is necessarily the best use of resources. Although women benefit from the training and legal services provided by the various women's organizations, in the long run, legislative change would have a far greater impact on the overall status of women and put them in an even better position to claim their rights.

This short-term approach to funding means that women's NGOs, including the advocacy NGOs, tend to be funded at the project rather than the program level so that long-term issues remain not tackled. Three-year, rather than ten-to-twenty-year programs, are encouraged, which has implications for sustained planning and advocacy. For instance, in the 1990s, ACFODE in Uganda set as its goal a long-term, integrated civic education program that would ensure that all citizens – men, women, and youth – were trained. Because of the limited project-oriented nature of funding, voter education was carried out each time that there was to be a general election. However, this did not provide adequate time to develop overall civic competence and awareness of political and civil rights.

### Accountability

Activists are more concerned about accountability to donors than to their own constituencies. Because organizational capacity is often weak, there is the sense that relatively too much valuable time is consumed by filling out paperwork, writing up financial accounts, activity reports, and grant renewals, especially in organizations that are already strapped by limited personnel and weak managerial capacity. Each donor has its own requirements and reporting format, which is burdensome for some organizations that would rather spend their time and resources doing the actual work that they are funded to carry out. A common complaint in the media is that women's organizations work for themselves. There is an element of truth in this, given the reporting requirements placed on them by donors.

Even though most activist agendas are not set by foreign donors, the terms under which women's organizations receive funding often lead to compromises in the way that they set their priorities. Such terms diminish the organizations' role as partners and suggest more of a contract-based relationship with donors. Part of the dynamic is perhaps unavoidable given the asymmetry of the donor–NGO relationship: one side of the "partnership" controls the purse strings, which means that the donor has more control over the recipient than vice versa (Elliott 1987; Lister 2000). The issue of "partnership" has not been resolved because women's organizations and other NGOs have less leverage than the donor, and thus negotiations are not carried out from an equal bargaining position. Women's organizations, like other NGOs, frequently lack capacity, exposure, and training (Tandon 1991).

## Internal Institutional Challenges

Finally, some of the challenges women's organizations face are related to their newness and lack of experience in the context of resource poor countries. Organizations may be overstretched and understaffed. Salaries are low, dividing women's energies among their activism, jobs, and families. Management skills are also important toward building and maintaining an efficient and effective organization. Many times those who become leaders do so because of their convictions and because they are able to convince their supporters to vote them into leadership positions. However, once they take over, it sometimes becomes clear that they themselves need skills in managing and running an organization: from organizational skills to professional knowledge regarding how to chair meetings, keep records, manage finances, produce reports and proposals, raise funds, carry out advocacy, and work with the media. They also need to be adept at working with people of varied backgrounds, from rural workers to teachers, lawyers, and health workers. The ability to analyze and articulate the challenges facing society is a core requirement of NGO leaders. Thus, institutional capacity and the caliber of the individuals who make up the organizations pose additional constraints on nascent women's movements.

CONCLUSIONS

The most important change that occurred in the late 1980s and 1990s was the creation of autonomous organizations that began to challenge the stranglehold that clientelism and state patronage had on women's mobilization in the post-independence period. Women's organizations were among the most organized sector of civil society in many if not most countries. The new autonomy allowed women to create organizations and forge alliances across ethnic, religious, clan, racial, rural–urban, generational, and other divides. Associational autonomy made it possible for women's organizations to challenge corruption, injustice, and their roots in clientelistic and patronage practices. It meant that they could freely select their own leaders, create their own agendas, and pursue their own sources of funding. It helped women's organizations to expand their agendas from a focus on income-generating and welfare concerns to a more politicized agenda. It permitted women to broaden their demands to challenge the fundamental laws, structures, and practices that constrained them. For the first time, many of them took on issues such as domestic violence, female genital cutting, and rape that had been considered taboo in the past.

This new generation of mobilization was characterized not only by its independence from established political institutions, but also by its heterogeneity in the types of organizations that had emerged. It received encouragement from male supporters, who mobilized to protest violence against women and demonstrate for and against other causes. It was made of loose networks, alliances, and coalitions of organizations that replaced the earlier single-party–affiliated mass women's organization or women's wing that was to represent all women. Moreover, unlike previous organizations that had focused on income generation and social concerns, these new organizations included nonpartisan political advocacy organizations and organizations that sought political representation for women.

In spite of important gains made in women's mobilization with this new generation of activism, key challenges remain. Of these, associational autonomy is critical. Because of the lack of civil and political liberties in semi-authoritarian states, there is an ever-present threat that political space will close, making the continued existence of advocacy organizations somewhat precarious.

Donors played a key role after the 1990s in supporting various advocacy initiatives of women's organizations in Africa. However, their support fell far short of the needs of women activists, especially of those seeking sustained support for advocacy. Although women's organizations were not driven by donor agendas per se, there is a sense in which the focus on short-term donor priorities placed certain limitations on their advocacy efforts. Due to a preoccupation with donor demands for accountability, women's organizations sometimes became less concerned with accountability to their constituents. Finally, there are the challenges of weak organizational capacity and skills. In spite of these obstacles, it is evident that women are in movement in Africa and they have set in motion unprecedented societal transformations.

# 5

# Women's Movements and Constitutional and Legislative Challenges

Since the 1990s, women's organizations have been pushing for and often succeeding in getting constitutional reforms and legislative changes. As a result of such efforts, today twenty-one out of forty-six African constitutions have provisions with customary law being overridden by statutory law and the constitution. Only three constitutions make specific mention of women or gender in this regard. Moreover, thirty-two countries have antidiscrimination clauses with particular reference to women. Gender equality is specifically mentioned in all but eight sub-Saharan Africa constitutions out of forty-six constitutions, further highlighting the importance of gender equality (see Table 5.1).

These are extremely profound challenges because they are more than attempts simply to improve legislation or add a few sentences in a constitution. They are, in effect, efforts to legitimize new legal-based sources of authority for rights governing relations between men and women and family relations. Prior to the 1990s, even when laws existed to regulate marriage, inheritance, custody, and other such practices, customary law coexisted and generally took precedence when it came to family and clan concerns. Today, women are challenging these norms through constitutional and legislative changes. This is no small matter, but one that will take time to realize even with legislative and constitutional reforms, because customary norms are so deeply entrenched and customary law is so widely practiced.

The constitutional changes have occurred in the context of reforms that were part of democratizing trends sweeping Africa. These aforementioned reforms with respect to customary law were found to one degree or another in the new constitutions in countries such as Mozambique (1990), Namibia (1990), Ethiopia (1994), Malawi (1994), Uganda (1995), South Africa (1996), Rwanda (2003), Burundi (2005), and Swaziland (2006). Many of

TABLE 5.1 *Key Constitutional Provisions Relating to Gender*

| Country | Latest Constitution | Constitution Makes Specific Mention of Gender Equality | Constitution Includes Antidiscrimination Clause Referring to Gender[a] | Constitution Can Override Customary Law; Reference to Gender[b] | Constitution Can Override Customary Law; No Reference to Gender[c] | Constitution Mentions Violence against Women |
|---|---|---|---|---|---|---|
| Angola | 1992 | Yes | Yes | No | No | No |
| Benin | 1990 | No | Yes | No | Yes | No |
| Botswana | 1965 | No | No | No | No | No |
| Burkina Faso | 1991 | Yes | Yes | No | Yes | No |
| Burundi | 2005 | Yes | Yes | No | No | No |
| Cameroon | 1972 | Yes | Yes | No | No | No |
| Cape Verde | 1992 | Yes | Yes | No | No | No |
| Central African Republic | 2004 | Yes | Yes | No | No | Yes[d] |
| Chad | 1996 | No[e] | Yes | No | Yes | No |
| Comoros | 2001 | Yes | No | No | No | No |
| Congo-Brazzaville | 2002 | Yes | Yes | No | Yes | No |
| Côte d'Ivoire | 2000 | Yes | Yes | No | Yes | No |
| Democratic Republic of Congo | 2006 | Yes | Yes | No | Yes | Yes[f] |
| Djibouti | 1992 | Yes | No | No | No | No |
| Equatorial Guinea | 1991 | Yes | Yes | No | No | No |
| Eritrea | 1997[g] | Yes | Yes | Yes | No | No |
| Ethiopia | 1994 | Yes | Yes | No | Yes | No |
| Gabon | 1991 | Yes | No | No | No | No |
| Gambia | 1996 | No | Yes | No | Yes | No |
| Ghana | 1992 | Yes | Yes | No | Yes | No |
| Guinea | 1990 | Yes | No | No | No | No |
| Guinea-Bissau | 1984 | Yes | No | No | No | No |
| Kenya | 1963[h] | Yes | Yes | No | Yes | No |
| Lesotho | 1993? | Yes | Yes | No | Yes | No |
| Liberia | 1986 | Yes | No | No | Yes | No |

*(continued)*

TABLE 5.1 *(continued)*

| Country | Latest Constitution | Constitution Makes Specific Mention of Gender Equality | Constitution Includes Antidiscrimination Clause Referring to Gender[a] | Constitution Can Override Customary Law; Reference to Gender[b] | Constitution Can Override Customary Law; No Reference to Gender[c] | Constitution Mentions Violence against Women |
|---|---|---|---|---|---|---|
| Madagascar | 1992 | Yes | No | No | No | No |
| Malawi | 1994 | Yes | Yes | Yes | Yes | Yes |
| Mali | 1992 | Yes | Yes | No | Yes | No |
| Mauritania | 1991 | Yes | No | No | No | No |
| Mauritius | 1968 | No | Yes | No | No | No |
| Mozambique | 1990 | Yes | Yes | No | Yes | No |
| Namibia | 1990 | Yes | Yes | No | Yes | No |
| Niger | 1999 | Yes | No | No | Yes | No |
| Nigeria | 1999 | No[i] | Yes | No | No | No |
| Rwanda | 2003 | Yes | Yes | No | Yes | No |
| Senegal | 2001 | Yes | No | No | No | No |
| Seychelles | 1993 | Yes | No | No | No | No |
| Sierra Leone | 1991 | Yes | Yes | No | Yes | No |
| South Africa | 1996 | Yes | Yes | No | Yes | No |
| Sudan | 2005 | Yes | Yes | No | No | No |
| Swaziland | 2005 | Yes | No[d] | No | Yes[j] | Yes |
| Tanzania | 1977 | Yes | Yes | No | Yes | No |
| Togo | 1992 | Yes | No | No | No | No |
| Uganda | 1995 | Yes | Yes | Yes | Yes | No |
| Zambia | 1991 | No | Yes | No | No | No |
| Zimbabwe | 1979 | No | Yes | No | No | No |

*Source:* African constitutions, Constitution Finder, University of Richmond, http://confinder.richmond.edu/index.php, accessed 27 May 2008.

*Notes:*

[a] Reference to gender here means specific reference to "women" or "sex."

[b] Reference to gender here means specific reference to "women" or "sex."

[c] Reference to gender here means that there is a provision to override customary law, but without any particular reference to "women" or "sex."

[d] Also mentions rape.

[e] General antidiscrimination provision.

[f] Antigender discrimination clause.

[g] Mentions domestic violence.

[h] Not implemented.

[i] Revised in 2005 but not adopted.

the most dramatic changes were found in countries where the end of conflict opened up new opportunities for changes in leadership and laws and for the creation of a new political order. The area where change has met the least resistance is that of political and economic rights that pertain to the state and the formal economy. Thus, it has been relatively easier to pass legislation regarding quotas for women-held seats in legislatures, laws regarding women's employment and labor, and citizenship laws than to pass laws challenging customary practices and laws pertaining to relations between men and women. Moreover, the implementation of family law has also been more challenging.

These pressures for legislative change have had to contend with some of the peculiarities of contemporary African legal systems, which are the product of a mix of legal traditions. African legal systems build on colonial common law traditions (e.g., in former British colonies) and civil law traditions (e.g., in former Belgian, French, German, Italian, Portuguese, and Spanish colonies). Both legal systems have coexisted at varied levels of comfort with customary law. These legal legacies, as we will see, have had important implications for the efforts of contemporary women's rights movements.

In the post-1990s period of women's rights activism, the hardest laws to change have had to do with customary law, especially laws that govern marriage, divorce, child custody, property rights, and inheritance. Some of the more controversial laws introduced in other parts of the world historically, such as the right to vote, the introduction of gender quotas, and antidiscrimination provisions, have met with relatively little and sometimes no resistance in Africa. At the same time, other laws relating to inheritance rights or age of marriage have been much more controversial. The fact that they have been resisted is an indication of just how contested the legal arena has become.

## THEORIZING LEGISLATIVE CONTESTATIONS

There have been numerous attempts to distinguish analytically between laws affecting women and the ways in which they have been framed in order to identify which types of legislation are most likely to be adopted and which frames are most successful. None of these frameworks seems especially applicable to the African context, where customary laws have tended to be the most controversial, while many of laws that have met with resistance elsewhere hardly raise an eyebrow.

It is worth noting some of these differences for the sake of comparison. Joyce Gelb and Marian Palley (1982: 9) distinguish between narrower "role-equity" legislation and more far-reaching "role-changing" legislation in the U.S. context. "Role-equity" issues are more likely to lead to success because they lead to more equitable treatment of women (equal credit opportunity, insurance, and pensions), whereas the "role-changing" legislation is harder to implement because it leads to more fundamental changes in women's roles (abortion, equal access to federal funds for athletics for both boys and girls in schools, legislation protecting pregnant women from being fired, etc.).

Maxine Molyneux (1985) distinguishes between "practical and strategic gender interests," where policies addressing practical interests improve women's conditions and are easier to realize but do not fundamentally change gender relations in the way that policies addressing strategic interests might. As with the distinction between role equity and role changing, it is not always clear where one would draw the line between strategic and practical interests. For example, providing affordable childcare, which addresses a practical need, may free women up to become employed, which has the potential to change gender relations.

The welfare state literature often distinguishes between "role-based legislation," which improves women's situation without challenging women's role within the family, and "rights-based frames," which expand women's individual rights. Merike Blofield and Liesl Haas (2005) apply this distinction to Chile and find that more rights-based than role-based legislation was introduced between 1990 and 2002; however, rights-based bills had lower rates of passage. Blofield and Haas go further to identify the determinants of the passage of a bill and argue that it had a greater chance of passage depending on the extent to which it was framed in ways that complemented the Catholic Church's teachings on women, sexuality, and family matters. Role-based legislation in Chile involved legislation to allow pregnant students to remain in school, the right to abortion in the event that a mother's life was at risk, and affordable day care. Rights-based legislation, according to Blofield and Haas, includes laws pertaining to equal rights over marital property, laws prohibiting sex discrimination and sexual assault, divorce bills, and electoral quotas for women.

Mala Htun identifies the locus of decision making as critical to the passage of woman-friendly legislation in the Latin American context. She distinguishes between "technical" and "absolutist" policies. Technical policies require legal expertise to understand (property rights, parental rights, etc.) and are decided by small commissions of experts, whereas absolutist policies involve moral issues (abortion, divorce) that are susceptible to resistance from the Catholic Church in the Latin American context. The latter were decided in legislatures (Htun 2003: 13). The technical policies were crafted by small expert groups and therefore were more easily adopted than absolutist policies, even under military dictatorships. Their normative nature makes them more challenging, especially because they often contend with oppositional forces, such as the Catholic Church, that take moral stances against gender-related policies.

Finally, others have simply looked at the types of legislation most likely to be passed. In a study of nineteen South and East Asian nations, Patty Hipsher and R. Darcy (2000: 119–21) found that the easiest laws to pass pertained first to political rights (e.g., right to vote and be elected), the second easiest were those related to economic rights (e.g., property rights, equal pay), the third easiest were abortion laws; and fourth and most difficult laws were in the area of rape, violence, and sexual harassment, with spousal rape being the most contentious.

## AFRICAN LEGISLATIVE CONTESTATIONS

Many of the aforementioned distinctions do not apply easily in African contexts because they do not correspond to the areas of greatest resistance and contestation one finds in Africa. In general, the customary/clan/familial versus public institution distinction would be the primary distinction in the African legal context when it comes to ease of passage of legislation. Challenges to customary practices have been particularly difficult, especially because customary practices have become enshrined in formal legal systems and have lost their earlier fluidity that had been embedded in daily practice (Chanock 1980).

Legislation pertaining to equality and addressing discrimination has been relatively uncontroversial in Africa when it comes to institutions tied to the state and market. At independence, there was no debate over women's right to vote or run for office. Early on, national machineries were adopted with little if any resistance, and later they were replaced with ministries of gender in many cases. Compared with other laws, gender-related legislation regarding labor practices, citizenship, and quotas has also not been as controversial. See Table 5.2 for examples of these types of policies regarding political rights (quotas); labor provisions (maternity leave); social policy regarding universal primary education (progress in eliminating gender differentials in primary enrollments): and economic rights (the existence of a gender budgeting initiative). These are all institutions created and regulated by the state rather than by familial institutions and therefore may be perceived as outside the domain of more localized institutions.

TABLE 5.2. *Measures of Political, Economic, Labor, and Social Policies Affecting Women*

| Country | Legislative Quota | Gender Budget Initiative | Weeks of Maternity Leave | Primary Enrollment: Ratio of Female to Male Students (2005) |
|---|---|---|---|---|
| Angola | Compulsory quotas | In progress | 13 | N/A |
| Benin | None | None | 14 | 0.8 |
| Botswana | Party quotas | In progress | 12 | 0.98 |
| Burkina Faso | Party quotas | None | 14 | 0.8 |
| Burundi | Reserved seats | None | 12 | 0.86 |
| Cameroon | Party quotas | None | 14 | 0.85 |
| Cape Verde | None | None | N/A | 0.95 |
| Central African Republic | None | None | 14 | 0.66 |
| Chad | None | None | 14 | 0.67 |
| Comoros | None | In progress | 14 | 0.88 |
| Congo-Brazzaville | None | None | 15 | 0.92 |
| Côte d'Ivoire | Party quotas | None | 14 | 0.79 |
| Democratic Republic of Congo | None | None | 14 | 0.78 |
| Djibouti | Compulsory quotas | None | 14 | N/A |
| Equatorial Guinea | Party quotas | None | 12 | 0.95 |
| Eritrea | Reserved seats | None | 9 | 0.81 |
| Ethiopia | Party quotas | None | 13 | 0.86 |
| Gabon | None | None | 14 | 0.99 |
| Gambia | None | None | 12 | 1.06 |
| Ghana | None | In progress | 12 | 0.96 |
| Guinea | None | None | 14 | 0.84 |
| Guinea-Bissau | None | None | 9 | 0.67 |
| Kenya | None | In progress | 8 | 0.96 |
| Lesotho | None | None | 12 | 1.0 |
| Liberia | Compulsory quotas | None | N/A | 0.73 |
| Madagascar | None | In progress | 14 | 0.96 |
| Malawi | Party quotas | In progress | N/A | 1.02 |
| Mali | Party quotas | None | 14 | 0.8 |
| Mauritania | Reserved seats | None | 14 | 1.01 |
| Mauritius | None | In progress | 12 | 1 |
| Mozambique | Party quotas | In progress | 9 | 0.85 |

| Namibia | Party quotas | In progress | 12 | 1.01 |
|---|---|---|---|---|
| Niger | Party quotas Compulsory quotas | None | 14 | 0.73 |
| Nigeria | N/A | In progress | 12 | 0.86 |
| Rwanda | Reserved seats | In progress | 12 | 1.02 |
| São Tomé and Principe | N/A | None | 10 | 0.98 |
| Senegal | Party quotas | In progress | 14 | 0.97 |
| Seychelles | N/A | In progress | 14 | 1.01 |
| Sierra Leone | Party quotas | None | None | 0.71 |
| Somalia | Reserved seats | None | None | N/A |
| South Africa | Party quotas | In progress | 14 | 0.96 |
| Sudan | Reserved seats | None | 12 | N/A |
| Swaziland | N/A | None | 8 | 0.93 |
| Tanzania | Women's list | In progress | 12 | 0.96 |
| Togo | N/A | None | 12 | 0.85 |
| Uganda | Reserved seats | In progress | 14 | 1.00 |
| Zambia | N/A | In progress | 8 | 0.95 |
| Zimbabwe | Party quotas | In progress | 12 | 0.98 |

Hence, because there are stronger feelings of ownership of family and clan institutions, it has been much harder to pass legislation affecting these institutions, such as ensuring women's rights to property through land and inheritance legislation. It has also been more difficult to pass laws that challenge the notion of women and children as property, such as bride wealth, child custody, and wife inheritance and property grabbing upon the death of a husband (i.e., levirate, or claims on the widow and/or her property and children by the eldest brother of the deceased husband and in-laws). Table 5.3 details the effects of family law upon women.

Interestingly, women's movements have accounted for changes both in policies tied to state institutions and those influencing family law. However, the postconflict impact has been felt more in the area of family law, whereas democratization correlates more strongly with state initiatives around education policy regarding girls and gender budgeting, while gross domestic product (GDP) and levels of foreign aid correlate with education (see Tables 5.1 and 5.2).

Only nine African countries have banned polygamy,[1] although increasingly the new family codes are discouraging the practice[2]; seven countries

---

[1] These include Angola, Burundi, Cape Verde, Eritrea, Ethiopia, Guinea, Madagascar, Mauritius, and Rwanda.
[2] Such codes are in effect in Benin, Mozambique, and Morocco.

TABLE 5.3. *Family Law Impacts on Women*

| Country | Marriage Age for Females and Males[a] | Polygamy | Head of Household | Women's Consent to Marriage[b] | Divorce[c] | Wife Inheritance[d] | Bride Price[e] |
|---|---|---|---|---|---|---|---|
| Angola | 18/18 | Prohibited | Husband | Required | Equal | | Permitted |
| Benin | 15/18 | Discouraged | Husband | Required | Equal | Permitted | Permitted |
| Botswana | 18/18 | Permitted | Shared | Required | Equal | Prohibited | |
| Burkina Faso | 17/20 | Permitted | Shared | Required | Equal | Prohibited | Prohibited |
| Burundi | 18/21 | Prohibited | Shared | Required | Equal | | Prohibited |
| Cameroon | 15/18 | Permitted | Husband | Required | Equal | Prohibited | Permitted |
| Cape Verde | 18/18 | Prohibited | Shared | Required | Equal | | |
| Central African Republic | | Permitted | Husband | | Equal | | Permitted |
| Chad | | Permitted | | | Equal | | Permitted |
| Congo-Brazzaville | 18/21 | Permitted | Husband | Required | Equal | Prohibited | Permitted |
| Congo-Kinshasa | 15/18 | Permitted | Husband | Not required | | Permitted | Permitted |
| Equatorial Guinea | None | Permitted | | | | | Prohibited |
| Eritrea | 18/18 | Prohibited | | Required | Equal | | |
| Ethiopia | 15/18 | Prohibited | | Required | | | |
| Gabon | 15/18 | Permitted | Husband | Required | Not equal | Permitted | |
| Gambia | None | Permitted | | Required | Not equal | | |
| Ghana | 18/18 | Permitted | | Required | | Discouraged | |
| Guinea | 17/18 | Prohibited | | Required | Not equal | | |
| Guinea-Bissau[f] | 14/16[b] | Permitted | | | | | |
| Kenya | 16/16 | Permitted | | Required | Equal | | |
| Liberia[g] | 18/21[c] | | | | | Prohibited | Permitted |
| Madagascar | 14/17 | Prohibited | | Required | Equal | | Permitted |
| Malawi | 15/15 | Permitted | | | | | |
| Mali | 15/18 | Permitted | | Required | | | |
| Mauritania | 18/18 | | | Required | | | |

116

| Country | | | | | | | |
|---|---|---|---|---|---|---|---|
| Mauritius | 18/18 | Prohibited | | Required | Equal | | |
| Mozambique | 18/18 | Discouraged | Shared | Required | Equal | | |
| Namibia | 15/18 | Permitted | | Required | Equal | | Permitted |
| Niger | 15/? | | Husband | Required | | | |
| Nigeria | None | Permitted | | | | | |
| Rwanda | 21/21 | Prohibited | | | | | |
| Senegal | 16/20 | Permitted | | Required | | | |
| Sierra Leone | 18/18 | Permitted | | Required | | | |
| Somalia | 16/18 | Permitted | | | | | |
| South Africa | 15/18 | Permitted | | | Equal | Permitted | |
| Sudan | At puberty | Permitted | | Required | Not equal | | |
| Tanzania | 15/18 | Permitted | | Required | | | |
| Togo | 17/20 | Permitted | | Required | Equal | | |
| Uganda | 18/18 | Permitted | | | Equal | | Permitted |
| Zambia | 16/16 | Permitted | | Not required | | | Permitted |
| Zimbabwe | 16/18 | Permitted | | Required | | | Permitted |

*Source:* CEDAW reports; Womanstats Project, http://www.womanstats.org/, accessed 27 May 2008.

Notes:

a Blank indicates no age specified or found in legislation.

b Blank indicates no mention of requirement of women's consent to marriage in legislation.

c Blank indicates no requirement for equal marriage.

d Blank indicates no legal prohibition of wife inheritance or levirate.

e Blank indicates no legal prohibition of use of bride price.

f The Civil Code sets the minimum age for marriage at fourteen for girls and sixteen for boys but is contracted by the Civil Procedure Code, which sets eighteen as the legal age for marriage.

g The Revised Administrative Law Governing the Hinterland sets the age limit at fifteen years only.

prohibit levirate or wife inheritance,[3] and only three countries prohibit bride price. Thirteen countries have set a minimum age of marriage at eighteen,[4] whereas thirty-six countries require women's consent to marriage (see Table 5.3). Laws pertaining to women's reproductive rights, which are also indirectly related to claims on offspring and women's reproductive capacities to produce children, are also potentially problematic. Much of the active and organized resistance to improving women's legal status has come from religious leaders, chiefs, elders, clan leaders, and individuals who are wedded to older norms and cultural practices and who stand to benefit politically and even economically from older practices and beliefs.

But state capacity and historical experiences require further refinements in this distinction. For example, there is considerable difference between legislation passed in a postconflict context and legislation passed outside of that context. Thus, legislation pertaining to violence against women, land legislation, and legislation regarding family codes has been easier to pass in postconflict contexts than non-postconflict countries because of the heightened concern around these issues and the high incidence of rape and domestic violence during and after civil conflict.

The different levels of ease with which various types of legislation are passed are often tied to the meaning that is ascribed to the practices they seek to limit or reconfigure. This makes comparability across countries and nations challenging; however, Africa is not alone in this regard. For example, abortion laws have very different meanings in different societies given the political and economic contexts. Hipsher and Darcy (2000: 119) argue that the "right to an abortion" in countries such as China, India, and Singapore that have adopted strict population policies is less of a right and more of a "threat or obligation." Abortion is seen in these countries as a way of stemming overpopulation, promoting economic development, and improving living standards. This is hardly the same notion of reproductive freedom that American feminists advocate in pressing for pro-choice legislation. Such differences make crossnational comparisons of legal change challenging because what may seem like a positive reform for women in one society may be a violation of women's rights in another. In addition, what constitutes a woman-friendly policy may also be contested. One feminist camp may view prostitution as legitimate labor in which sex workers' rights need to be protected whereas another group sees prostitution itself as a violation of women's human rights. Moreover, some legislation that

---

[3] These include Côte d'Ivoire and Swaziland, which are not included in Table 5.3.
[4] These are Angola, Botswana, Burundi, Cape Verde, Congo-Brazzaville, Eritrea, Guinea, Mauritania, Mauritius, and Uganda.

is passed to assist women may create another set of problems. In Uganda, one of the first laws regarding women enacted after the cessation of civil conflict in 1986 addressed rape and the defilement of children. The death penalty that the crime carries has not only been challenged by human rights organizations but has resulted in few convictions. These are only a few of the many issues that make the task of developing a useful framework of crossnational comparison challenging.

Legislation is never passed in a vacuum. It is always tempered and shaped by possibilities afforded by the regime type and the pressures from those supporting legislation and those opposed to it (be they religious, ethnic, or clan leaders, ideologically conservative forces, or traditional authorities). Passage of legislation may also depend on state openness to gender-related reform; the history of gender-related policies, such as colonial legal legacies; international norms, conventions, and treaties; and the specific interests of those in power to ally themselves with or challenge opponents of gender-related reforms.

Moreover, whether the policy is successful or has a positive impact on women needs to be evaluated in terms of what "success" means, which women are affected positively, and who benefits most from the policies (O'Connor, Orloff, and Shaver 1999: 22). It is also determined by what unintended consequences might result from policy outcomes. Carol Lee Bacchi (1999) suggests that we need to look at what assumptions are made in the particular representation of the issues in a policy debate or policy proposal. What are the competing ways in which the policy is being framed and what is the impact of those representations? These considerations will differ from society to society and do not necessarily fall along the lines of roles versus rights, strategic versus practical interests, or role-equality versus role-changing legislation. The weakness of African legislatures until recently has not encouraged scholarship into legislative processes generally or with respect to women's concerns.

Finally, there is the framing of legislation. One of the main reasons that some legislation is so difficult to pass is that it is framed as omnibus legislation (e.g., Domestic Relations Bill in Uganda, family codes in the Sahel, or the Child Rights Act in Nigeria) with multiple controversial provisions within one piece of legislation. Experiences in Latin America and elsewhere have shown that it is easier to pass legislation around narrower issues than to try to find common ground on multiple controversial issues at one time that virtually everyone will find objectionable for one reason or another (Htun 2003: 181).

In Chad, for example, the proposed Family Law that was to replace the 1958 civil code provisions had something in it for everyone to object to, resulting in opposition from a group of prominent Muslim lawyers, businesspeople, and media executives, the Union of Muslim Cadres in Chad, and southern Christians. For example, it banned wife beating, raised the minimum age of marriage for girls from fourteen to sixteen, established new divorce rules, and gave children born outside of wedlock the same inheritance rights as others – all of which rankled Muslim leaders. It also legalized polygamy, which upset the Christians leaders. Each one of these issues is controversial, but when separated out might have been easier to pass in a piecemeal fashion, starting with the least controversial provisions.

## Constitutional Reform

In spite of the challenges that women activists face with respect to legal reform, women are making important gains in this area, often for the first time since independence. Interestingly, women had been involved in constitution-making efforts in several African countries such as Ghana, Mali, Nigeria, and Sierra Leone at the time of independence (Turrittin 1993: 63). In fact, when women were excluded from the Sierra Leonean process, they were outraged and the Sierra Leone Women's Movement petitioned to be included, arguing that the government had deliberately ignored half the population and that the constitution needed to protect women's rights (Denzer 1987: 450). Two women were eventually included and ended up playing a pivotal reconciliatory role between the delegates.

As with these earlier constitution-making efforts, women sought to influence new constitution-making processes after the 1990s. Since 1990, thirty-eight African constitutions have been rewritten and six have had major revisions. Some of these new constitutions were adopted in the aftermath of major conflict, while others took place in the context of shifts toward multipartyism and political opening. After the 1990s, we witnessed in countries such as Malawi, Mozambique, Namibia, Sierra Leone, South Africa, and Uganda the emergence of new constitutions that stipulated that in the event of a conflict, nondiscrimination or equality provisions were to override customary law. This provision was included primarily in constitutions of postconflict countries such as Mozambique, Namibia, Sierra Leone, South Africa, and Uganda, whereas the only non-postconflict country that adopted such a provision as of 2007 was Malawi. These constitutions can be contrasted with constitutions passed prior to 1990, in which customary law generally has not been subject to any restrictions and where the gender provisions have not generally changed from the way that the colonial powers drafted the constitutions at the time of independence in countries such as Botswana and Zimbabwe. The South African constitution is somewhat ambiguous in that it also energizes traditional authorities in a way that has had the consequence of creating tensions between them and women's rights activists on issues such as land rights.

In Mozambique, a Legal Reform Commission was put in place after 1998 to ensure that the laws did not contravene the constitution or international conventions. One of the main women's umbrella organizations, Fórum Mulher (Women's Forum) – as well as the Mozambican Women Lawyers Association; Women, Law and Development in Mozambique (MULEIDE); and Women and Law in Southern Africa–Mozambique – were working with the Commission to ensure that the country's laws would be consistent with the constitution with respect to women's rights.

In Uganda, it was widely acknowledged that no other societal group was as organized and cohesive as women's organizations when it came to making a concerted effort to influence the constitution-writing process. Women's organizations wrote more memoranda submitted to the Constitutional Commission than any other sector of society (Bainomugisha 1999: 93). Women's groups spearheaded a countrywide effort to educate women about the constitution and to gather their views. Female members of the Constituent Assembly formed a nonpartisan Women's Caucus, which worked with women's organizations to make sure that their concerns were addressed in the Constituent Assembly. An umbrella body, the National Association of Women Organisations, supported the Caucus with a secretariat. The Link Programme of the women's organization Action for Development publicized the Caucus's views in weekly radio and TV programs as well as in a bi-weekly news bulletin on the Constituent Assembly debates. In addition, the Women's Caucus initiated a coalition with representatives of "marginalized" groups – people with disabilities, the youth, workers, and the armed forces – thus widening its support.

The Women's Parliamentary Caucus played an important role in getting key provisions passed within the Constituent Assembly (CA). It lobbied the CA; worked with sympathetic male CA members; held seminars and other functions to improve the lobbying, campaigning, and presentation skills of its members; collaborated with women's NGOs; and ran a CA Gender Information Center that provided support to women delegates in debating the constitution. It published educational materials, monitored debates, offered legal consultancy services to women delegates, and provided facilities for meetings (Tripp 2000).

The fruits of these efforts were seen in the final draft of the constitution, which included a provision requiring that gender equity be written into all laws passed by parliament; a prohibition of laws, customs, and traditions that undermine the position of women; and a call for expanding the number of women in parliament.

The constitutional provisions regarding women have made a significant difference in giving women's concerns legal legitimacy. In 2007, a constitutional court struck down key provisions of the Succession Act regarding women's right to inherit property. The law was found to be discriminatory and unconstitutional because it did not allow women to inherit property of a deceased person, including her husband. In a related ruling, the court also decriminalized adultery because the law, as it stood, discriminated against women. It penalized a married woman for having sex with any man but did not penalize a married man for having sex with an unmarried woman.

The Ugandan constitution has had additional impact in drawing attention to the issue of gender balance. Gender balance seems to be a regular concern, from political appointments to the allocation of government scholarships to secondary school students. Today, unlike in the past, the media and the general public take note when there have been shortcomings in gender balance. Media commentators, for example, pointed out that the 2006 cabinet had fewer women than the previous cabinet. Similarly, after people commented in the public media that the team negotiating peace between the Ugandan government and the Lord's Resistance Army had no women, the gender composition of the team changed in 2007. These observations were made not only by women, but also by men, both at the community and national levels.

In South Africa, the Women's National Coalition (WNC) was very active in influencing the constitution-writing process. The constitution guarantees women equality, freedom and security of the person, freedom from violence, the right to make decisions concerning reproduction, and the right over one's own body. No other group united as broad a spectrum of individuals during the transition from apartheid to democracy as the WNC, which was formed in 1991. It brought together eighty-one organizational affiliates and thirteen regional alliances of women's organizations, including organizations affiliated with the African National Congress, the Azanian Peoples Organization, the Democratic Party, the Inkatha Freedom Party, the National Party, and the Pan Africanist Congress. WNC also combined interests as diverse as the Rural Women's Movement, the South African Domestic Workers Union, and the Union of Jewish Women. Over three million women participated in focus groups organized by the WNC to voice their opinions on women's concerns. Regional and national conferences were held and a Woman's Charter was drafted and endorsed by the national parliament and all nine regional parliaments in 1994.

The Charter addressed a broad range of concerns, including equality, legal rights, economic issues, education, health, politics, and violence against women (Kemp, Moodley, and Salo 1995: 151). The Charter was used as a basis for reforming government policy regarding gender concerns. Although the Charter was presented to the Constitutional Assembly in August 1994, it was too late to be incorporated into the bill of rights. Nevertheless, it helped put pressure behind the adoption of gender equality and affirmative action ideas within the constitution.

The major achievement of the WNC was its ability to incorporate vast differences between women, as it put rural women into the limelight regarding key issues. For example, women delegates to the Multi-Party Negotiation Process such as Stella Sigcau of the Cape Traditional Leaders Organisation supported the WNC motion to subordinate customary law to the bill of rights, thus undercutting a key demand of the traditional leaders. Surprisingly, she took this stance without the support of women delegates of the political parties, which were seeking to appease the traditional authorities (Geisler 2004: 84).

In Zambia, the National Women's Lobby Group and six other NGOs succeeded in getting the Constitutional Commission to incorporate into the draft constitution a section on women's rights, focusing on discrimination, affirmative action, violence against women, and the implementation of the UN Convention on the Elimination of All Forms of Discrimination against Women. Despite fierce opposition from some female parliamentarians, leaders of the Movement for Multiparty Democracy, and officers of civic organizations, women's groups successfully pressed for the inclusion in the constitution of reproductive rights and equal opportunities for women and men in education (Chilaizya 1995). Under prior law, women needed spousal consent to use contraception, whereas men were under no such obligation. Similarly, many families chose to educate their sons but not their daughters in the belief that a son, unlike a daughter, was obliged to care for the family when the parents died. It was because of such discriminatory customs that many women's organizations fought to give women's rights explicit protection in the 1991 constitution.

Similar developments took place in Malawi, where women's organizations involved in the constitutional process had to be constantly on the alert to ensure that women's concerns were not downgraded or dropped from the agenda. A 1994 conference, held to prepare for Malawi's multiparty elections, agreed under pressure from women delegates to endorse specific women's concerns and incorporate many of them into the constitution. These included education for girls, equal rights and equal access for women in politics and business, and the development of HIV/AIDS prevention programs for both men and women. The National Commission on Women in Development (NCWID) recommended that women's concerns be included in the bill of rights and that the senate include equal representation of men and women. These provisions were incorporated into the constitution and then withdrawn four times prior to ratification in May 1994. A group of women in the NCWID lobbied the National Consultative Council against each successive attempt to remove the recommendations and was partially successful in the end.

The Swaziland branch of Women and Law in Southern Africa Research and Educational Trust (WLSA) and other such women's organizations succeeded in getting constitutional provisions approved that made men and women equal in a country that had been a holdout for decades when it came to women's rights. The 2006 constitution included provisions allowing women to own property, take out loans, sign contracts, and engage in financial transactions in their own names. An entire chapter (29) was devoted to women's rights. The practice of levirate was abolished and adult women were no longer considered minors ("Lack of Legal Status..." 2005). Although it permitted polygamy, the constitution banned forced marriage. Abortion laws were relaxed slightly to allow termination of pregnancy in the event that it would threaten a woman's physical or mental health ("For Women, Constitution..." 2005).

With the new constitution, women now hold one-third parliamentary seats (in the senate) by executive appointment. The constitution no longer gives only Swazi men the privilege that their children can claim Swazi citizenship: Women with children born to foreigners can now claim Swazi citizenship. The new constitution has a bill of rights providing for the right to life, liberty, and equality before the law; freedom of conscience and religion; and equal treatment for women.

## Ongoing Constitutional Challenges

In countries where constitutional reforms have not occurred since the 1990s or where they have occurred but have been limited with respect to women's rights, women's organizations have sought changes around a common set of concerns. They have sought gender-equality provisions (Kenya and Nigeria), an end to child marriages (Kenya and Nigeria), the conferring of citizenship rights to husbands and children of women married to foreigners (Kenya and Nigeria), an end to the practice of levirate and property grabbing by the widow's in-laws (Kenya), political representation of women (Kenya,

Nigeria, Sierra Leone, and Sudan), challenges to customary and religious laws that violate women's rights (Kenya, Nigeria, Sierra Leone, and Zimbabwe), provisions regarding violence against women (Sudan), and greater reproductive rights (Kenya) (Babalola 2004; "Women's Unequal..." 2006; "Zim's Marriage Laws..." 2006).

Kenya has had one of the most active women's movements in regard to constitution making. In 1997, women's organizations, with the help of parliamentarians such as the Honorable Martha Karua were able to get significant constitutional amendments that banned discrimination based on gender. The word "sex" was incorporated into Section 70 of the bill of rights. Up until then, women were prohibited from receiving certain tax exemptions, opening bank accounts in their own name, and obtaining bank loans without the approval of a husband or father. They could not be employed in certain jobs, obtain club membership, or enter hotels unaccompanied, and were paid less than men for the same kind of work.

Women were also very active in the process at all levels during the constitutional review process. The head of the Constitution of Kenya Review Commission, Yash Ghai (2005), referred to Kenyan women as the most active civil society group within the constitution-making process. In fact, at one point in 1998, it was the Kenya Women's Political Caucus that took the initiative to break the stalemate in the constitution review process.

In 2006, the debate over the constitution in Kenya became intertwined with a debate over the Mwai Kibaki presidency and his attempt to expand the powers of the executive. The Kenyan Constitutional Commission had drawn up an earlier draft of the constitution that was endorsed by the National Constitutional Conference, a body representing a cross section of interests, which held discussions at a cultural center near Nairobi referred to as the "Bomas of Kenya." This "Boma" draft was to be replaced by Attorney General Amos Wako's draft (known as the "Wako" draft), which was defeated in the 21 November 2006 referendum.

In both drafts, women sought the right to inherit and use property equally. This was aimed at putting an end to the practice whereby in-laws grabbed the property from the widow. It meant that parents would be able to bequeath property to any of their children. It also provided for one-third representation for women in the legislature and allowed women citizenship rights equal to those of men. They sought to remove the provision in the Kenyan constitution that prohibited women from transferring their citizenship to their spouses or children. They also wanted the right to apply for passports and identification cards without permission from their spouses or fathers.

However, the Wako constitution allowed for Christian, Muslim, and Hindu courts to rule on matters of marriage, divorce, burial, inheritance, succession, and other concerns of family law, thus reversing the Boma constitution's provision that civil law superceded customary law if it violated women's rights. Unlike the Boma constitution, which provided specific rules for increasing women's political representation, the Wako constitution provided only for the passage of legislation to increase women's political representation to one-third of all decision-making posts, which women feared would push the issue to the side, given the general disposition of the parliament against women's rights. The lack of progress for women was tied to the difficulties in overall constitutional reform, which as of 2008 had stalled.

Women in Zimbabwe were also actively engaged in the constitution reform process, forming in 1999 a Women's Coalition on the Constitution made up of academics, activists, and representatives of thirty women's organizations. As in Kenya, two constitution reform processes emerged early on, one representing the government and the other representing civil society. The Women's Coalition had members from both camps. However, it was not long before the coalition had to take a stand. Thoko Matshe, the head of the civil society–led coalition the National Constitutional Assembly (NCA), was a feminist. As one coalition member pointed out: "To a large extent during the latter 1990s, the whole civic process was in the hands of the women's movement, through the Coalition and our presence in the NCA. The media would call us the group of thirteen because we were the thirteen biggest women's organizations" (Essof 2005: 34).

Women were not only promoting their own concerns but were actively involved in a fight for democracy itself. The government's draft constitution did not guarantee women's rights in key areas and in the end was not supported by the Women's Coalition, which mobilized across party lines against it. The Coalition played a key role in the outcome of the referendum, which rejected the constitution. Women's organizations were shocked by the state-sponsored violence that ensued, targeting both women who supported the Zimbabwe African National Union–Patriotic Front (ZANU-PF) and those supporting the opposition party (Essof 2005: 37).

The processes in Kenya and Zimbabwe illustrate the central leadership role that women's organizations played in the constitution-making efforts to democratize both countries.

## Legislative Changes

In the 1990s, women's movements helped push through a new generation of legislation that was a break from past legislative reforms affecting women.

The new laws, for example, pertained to women's bodily integrity, addressing violence against women and female genital cutting. They actively chipped away at harmful and discriminatory customary laws through changes in family law/codes, land laws, and other such laws. These laws were distinct from the earlier legislative efforts of the 1960s and 1970s that focused on maternity leave, employment practices, and the taxation of women as well as on marriage and inheritance. In Tanzania, to take one example, pressure from women's groups in the 1990s led to a series of new legislation, including the Sexual Offenses Act, revisions of the Marriage Act, repeal of a law banning pregnant girls from school, and changes in land laws.

As the following discussion of areas of legislation demonstrates, several forces have helped ensure the passage of pro-women legislation. Women's movements have been especially important in providing the necessary pressure and strategic mobilization to see that legislation is drafted, introduced, and adopted. Legislative commissions, supportive parliamentarians, a sympathetic media, donor support, and the endorsement of key societal coalitions or civil society organizations have all facilitated legislative change. Conversely, organized resistance from societal organizations such as religious groups and traditional authorities has slowed down or constrained processes of change, depending on the issue.

The implementation of legislative commissions was essential in ensuring that constitutional reforms were translated into law. In South Africa, a Commission on Gender Equality was established to ensure that the country's laws would be fully implemented. Women fought to be included in the budget process so that state expenditures would better reflect women's interests and to see to it that the Labour Relations Act recognized maternity rights and women's rights against sexual harassment in the workplace. They also lobbied for an Employment Equity Act requiring employers to hire without discrimination based on race, gender, or disability.

Similarly in Mozambique, the Legal Reform Commission, created in 1997, played an important role in introducing and removing laws pertaining to equal rights. Several key women's groups worked with them on drafting laws relating to the family, domestic violence, and succession and on revising the civil and penal codes.

Women's parliamentary caucuses were another crucial institution for mobilization. They could be found throughout Africa from Mozambique, Seychelles, South Africa, Tanzania, and Uganda to Sierra Leone. It took over twelve years to create the Woman's Parliamentary Forum (WPF) in Mozambique after the 1994 multiparty elections. Women from different parties came together and tried to organize themselves around this forum. But party politics sometimes divided the women. During the discussions in parliament about the Family Law, even women MPs from the ruling Frente de Libertação de Moçambique (FRELIMO) party did not always adopt positions to defend women's rights, following instead what the party directed them to do. Women from the WPF, however, participated actively during a civil society meeting in 2006 to adopt the Draft Law about violence against women. Their meeting and public statement after the Coordination and Articulation Workshop between the WPF and women from the civil society was crucial. They decided to continue coordinating efforts to pass legislation regarding domestic violence, labor concerns, the penal code, and the succession law; to monitor and ensure the ratification of international instruments; to incorporate women's and reproductive rights into work in fighting HIV/AIDS; and to write legislation to introduce more gender quotas in a variety of areas. They also sought to incorporate gender perspectives into their joint work.

Representatives of the AIDS National Commission, the Ministry of Parliamentary Issues, the Ministry of Woman and Social Action, the WFP, and twenty-two women's organizations, including Associação Moçambicana para Desenvolvimento da Família [Mozambican Association for Family Development], Fórum Mulher, the Islamic Association of Maputo, the Rural Women's Association, WLSA-Mozambique, the Woman Lawyers and Jurists Association, and others, signed the Final Declaration. This is just one example of what could be accomplished through such collaborative efforts by parliamentary caucuses, gender ministries, and civil society.

Similar initiatives have been adopted by the Uganda Women's Parliamentary Association, which belongs to and works with the key women's networks in Uganda. Its aim is to advance common goals cutting across party lines within the parliament, to establish common legislative priorities, and to promote activities to enhance women's political participation, such as carrying out training to develop public speaking and debating skills.

Cameroon has had a less favorable experience with its parliamentary Women's Caucus, which functioned between 1992 and 1997 in a parliament where there were only 10 women out of 180. The caucus eventually fell apart under pressure from male parliamentarians who felt threatened by the existence of the caucus (Adams 2004b).

The following sections document some of the areas where the efforts toward legislative change have been most challenging.

FAMILY LAW

One area in which women's movements have sought changes and have met resistance has been in the reform of family codes and family laws to give women stronger inheritance rights, property rights, and child custody settlements in the event of divorce. Religious authorities, local customs, and localized power structures can at times pose serious obstacles to realizing these goals. Some countries such as Mozambique and South Africa have been more successful than others in negotiating changes within family law.

Dozens of women in the gallery of Mozambique's parliament burst into song when the new Family Law was passed on 9 December 2003 (going into force in 2005), overturning key provisions of the 1967 Portuguese Civil Code. It was a major hard-won victory after two decades of efforts to pass the law. The Family Law defends monogamy and does not encourage polygamy. In a country where one-fifth of the population was Muslim, this was an issue of concern, but Justice Minister Jose Abudo, a practicing Muslim, diffused the tension, arguing against polygamy and calling it an "attack upon the dignity of women."[5]

The Family Law grants women the same rights as men in acquiring, administering, and controlling land and assets from inheritance or divorce. It is path-breaking in this regard. The new law provides for equal rights in inheritance between men and women. This means that either surviving spouse has rights to his or her own property, half the joint property, and any willed property (Silva et al. 2005: 65–7).

The 2003 Family Law recognizes rights previously denied to women: It goes a long way in reconciling common and customary legal systems, protects women from discrimination, and lays the basis for future legal reforms. It provides women and children greater protection within polygamous and customary marriages, allowing them to seek alimony, maintenance, or custody in the event of divorce or separation if the parents have been cohabiting for at least three years. It abolishes the earlier distinction between legitimate and illegitimate children, giving both equal rights. The law increases the age of marriage to eighteen for both women and men (up from fourteen for women and sixteen for men) – one of the more controversial provisions in the law.

The law also recognizes civil, religious, and customary marriages. By recognizing customary unions, the law allows women married under customary law to claim property and custody rights and allows women who have lived with their husbands in common law marriages over a year to inherit their property. Women have new property rights, and jointly owned property can be inherited by women or transferred to them.

---

5 Mozambique News Agency, No. 267, 5 January 2004.

The Association of Women Lawyers, MULEIDE, Women's Forum, and WLSA played key roles in drafting legislation and researching popular attitudes toward the family and the Family Law. Women's organizations carried out hundreds of workshops, conducted extensive interviews, and held focus groups regarding the need for legal reform. They published their findings, aired them over the radio and TV, and used them to help draft the Family Law.

The Family Law reform process also benefited from the donor-supported reform of the judiciary in Mozambique. The Danish International Development Agency (DANIDA) funded the Legal Sector Program, which together with the attorney general, the Ministry of Justice, and the Supreme Court sought to improve the functioning of the legal system by training, building, and rebuilding the courts at the national, provincial, and district levels. They built houses for judges; wrote new laws/codes, and formed special commissions linked to the Ministry of Justice to revise the civil and penal codes. Thus, a Sub-Commission for the Reform of the Family Law began working in 1998. Also in 1998, the Judicial and Juridical Training Centre (Centro de Formação Jurídica e Judiciária) was formed to train judicial personnel at all levels, provide one-year specialized training to those who finished law school, and undertake research on the various forms of conflict resolution (Santos and Trindade 2003).

The timing of the legislation in 2003 after two decades of failed attempts at passage is also indicative of the possibilities that emerged with the end of conflict and the creation of a new foundation for the political order. The legislation had languished for twenty years. Its final passage was delayed from 2001 to 2003. When finally one thousand women marched on the parliament and demanded the passage of the Family Law, one month later it was passed (Disney 2005: 17). The passage of the Family Law in many ways typified the catalyzing role of independent women's movements in Africa, the need for autonomy as they engage the state, the need for allies within the state sector, and the importance of donor support.

On the other side of the continent, in West Africa, one of the most surprising changes was the unanimous adoption of the Personal and Family Code of Law by the Beninois parliament in 2004. The bill had been passed in 2002 but had been declared unconstitutional by the Constitutional Court. The parliament argued that the Court had exceeded its authority and voted once again in favor of this law, which recognizes only monogamous marriages certified by a civil status registrar. It discourages polygamy by providing legal protections and benefits, especially inheritance rights, only to monogamous unions, that is, to one registered wife in a polygamous marriage ("Polygamy Somewhat Out..." 2004).

## LAND RIGHTS

Laws that challenge customary authority and resources in the area of land rights have been particularly contentious in Africa. The bases of customary ownership have eroded since the time of colonialism, making women's access to land significantly more precarious as the protections traditionally ensured by the clan system have been peeled away. With increased commercialization of land and problems of land scarcity, local leaders have felt mounting pressures to protect the clan system, and in so doing have placed even greater constraints on women's access to land (Gray and Kevane 1999). However, the clan system that they are seeking to preserve is no longer one that affords women the supports that it was once said to have guaranteed. For this reason, women, both rural and urban, have responded to the renewed interest by elders to protect customary laws and practices that exclude women by involving themselves in movements to ensure women's access to and ownership of land.

Land is of critical importance to women because they depend on it for agricultural production and therefore their livelihoods. Unequal access to land is one of the most important forms of economic inequality between men and women and has consequences for women as social and political actors. Women provide a large percentage of all agricultural labor and especially labor involving food production, yet they own only a fraction of the land in most African countries. Women are often responsible for providing for the household, and thus their access to land for food production is critical to the welfare of the entire household. Even women who want to get into business need land as collateral to obtain bank loans. Because women are almost completely dependent on men to access land in patrilineal societies, women who are childless, single, widowed, separated, or divorced or who have only female children often have little or no recourse because they may have no access to land through a male relative.

In patrilineal societies, women generally do not inherit land from either their fathers or their husbands. Their fathers may not bequeath land to their daughters because daughters marry outside the clan and will therefore take the land with them to another clan. Husbands often do not bequeath land to their wives for the same reason.

In this context, women's movements in Africa have increasingly been adopting rights-based approaches that challenge customary land tenure arrangements. Feminist lawyers working with these movements have argued that customary law in the present day has been used to preserve practices selectively that subordinate women. Women's attempts to assert their rights in ways that challenge customary land tenure systems are often perceived as efforts to disrupt gender relations and society more generally. This explains why so much is at stake in battles over women's rights to land, and why women's gains in this area have been so slow.

Women have been active in a variety of land alliances and coalitions throughout Africa, many of which have arisen in response to legislative and constitutional changes in tenure laws. New land laws were enacted in Eritrea, Mozambique, Namibia, South Africa, Tanzania, Uganda, Zambia, and Zanzibar in the 1990s. Lesotho, Malawi, Rwanda, Swaziland, and Zimbabwe also adopted new land policies. Women and women's organizations have been at the forefront of coalitions such as the Kenya Land Alliance, the Namibian NGO Federation, the National Land Committee in South Africa, the National Land Forum in Tanzania, the Rwanda Land Alliance, the Uganda Land Alliance, and the Zambia National Land Alliance – all of which have fought for the land rights of women, pastoralists, the landless, and other marginalized people. Regional networks such as Landnet in East Africa were also formed to network between countries. At the regional level in eastern and southern Africa, Women in Law and Development in Africa (WILDAF) has been active since the early 1990s on land and other issues, as has WLSA in seven southern African countries. These movements have been especially pronounced in the former British colonies of eastern and southern Africa, although one is increasingly seeing similar movement pressures for land rights in Nigeria and Francophone countries such as Madagascar, Mali, and Senegal, where women have formed their own organizations to ensure that any changes in land laws incorporate women's concerns.

The new movements have been galvanized by mounting pressures in some countries that are placing undue constraints on women, who do not have sufficient access to and control over land. Although the focus of the women's movements has been on customary land practices, they have also been concerned with the negative effects of the privatization of land and land grabbing as governments have increasingly sought foreign investment through tourism, mining, and other businesses. Women have joined forces with pastoralists, who have often found themselves shut out of vast grazing lands in many parts of East Africa, Botswana, and Namibia as a result of large land sales (Palmer 1998).

In this next section, we examine the difficulties these alliances and organizations have had in gaining access to land for women because of the intractability of older forms of governance that persist within clan systems. It contrasts the legislative difficulties that women faced in Uganda with the relative successes of women in Mozambique with respect to land rights while recognizing that women in Mozambique still face difficulties of translating laws into positive realities on the ground.

## THE STRUGGLE OVER LAND RIGHTS IN UGANDA

In Uganda, a major struggle erupted over the 1998 Land Act. The debate centered on an amendment to the act regarding women's coownership (common property) of land with their spouse.[6] The coownership amendments were, in fact, passed by the parliament, but political maneuvering on the grounds of technicalities left women without the clause. Member of Parliament and Ethics Minister Miria Matembe was about to read the amendments into the microphone for the Hansard (legislative record) when someone interrupted her in midsentence and announced that amendments were finished and that she did not need to read them. Later she was told that because she had not read the clauses into the microphone, they could not be included in the Hansard and hence into the amendments to the Land Act. As she explained in her book:

I want to make one thing clear. If this had not been an amendment to give women their due rights, if this had had to do with things that the male MPs consider important, Parliament would have found a way to bring the matter back for more review. They would have said, this is just a technicality, and the provisions would have found their way into that law. (Matembe 2002: 251)

When the minister of state for lands brought the amendments to the Land Act before the cabinet, it was the president, by his own omission, who decided to pull out the coownership clause.

Those who rejected the clause wanted to preserve clan cohesion and power. Key parliamentarians, ministers, and the president rallied against the coownership clause in the Land Act in defense of "tradition" and "custom" in the face of challenges from some women parliamentarians, the women's movement, and the Uganda Land Alliance (ULA),[7] all of whom believed

---

[6] Actually there were four clauses that were being contested. These included the following: (1) An individual bringing land into the marriage can continue to own that land after marriage; (2) in monogamous marriages, home and land used for sustenance by the couple are to be co-owned; (3) in a polygamous marriage where each wife has a separate home, each woman would co-own with her husband her home and the piece of land that sustains her and her children; and (4) wives living in the same house with their husband would co-own the single home and land together with the women.

[7] The Uganda Land Alliance was a consortium of thirty-five NGOs, funded by the British charity, Oxfam International. It included the Legal Aid Project, the NGO Forum, and the Uganda Law Society, in addition to women's organizations such as Action for Development

that customs pertaining to land ownership needed changing. A coordinator of the ULA, Rose Mwebaza, said during a 17 December 1998 press conference that with the dropping of the coownership clause, "Women lost one major revolutionary clause that was to be the basis to challenge the very foundations of a patriarchal system... its effects would be a tool for social change, a provision for protection and security for women on land." (Mucunguzi 1998). The land clauses were moved into the Domestic Relations Bill (DRB), which was eventually shelved in 2006 with little hope of being revived. Many women's activists saw the move to put the land clauses into the Domestic Relations Bill as a way to kill them once and for all. The DRB had many controversial provisions – especially on inheritance, marriage, and divorce – that met with considerable resistance from religious groups.

It should be pointed out that there were some positive provisions in the Land Act that have led to increasing numbers of women taking their disputed claims to magistrate's courts, especially in areas where land pressures are great, such as Kigezi. Men need the consent of their wives to sell land, and lawyers are adamant about observing this.

There has been progress on other fronts as well. As mentioned earlier, as a result of activities of Law and Advocacy for Women in Uganda, the Constitutional Court threw out key provisions in the Succession Act in 1997 on grounds that it was discriminatory, thus laying the basis for new legislation pertaining to land and other property inheritance.

## MOZAMBIQUE'S LAND LAWS AND WOMEN

The Mozambican women's movement had success in reforming Mozambique's Land Act, in part because of more coordinated mobilization. One of the most active civil society campaigns in Mozambique emerged in response to proposed land legislation in 1997. Under the auspices of the Land Forum (Forum Terra), roughly two hundred national and local organizations of all kinds participated in the discussion and dissemination of the law approved by the parliament in 1997. They organized meetings in all parts of Mozambique to introduce, discuss, and collect proposals for parliament to consider. There was simultaneously a project to train paralegal specialists through the Juridical and Judiciary Training Center to adjudicate land disputes.

(ACFODE), Akina Mama wa Afrika, the Association of Women Lawyers in Uganda (FIDA-U), the Uganda Media Women's Association (UMWA), and the Uganda Women's Network (UWONET).

The activities of the Land Forum were premised on a new development paradigm, which according to the coordinator of the Land Forum, José Negrão, was guided by seven main factors: (1) equitably distributed development, (2) gender balance, (3) regionally sensitivity, (4) development that takes the individual as the starting point, (5) cultural decentralization, and development that is (6) participatory and (7) sustainable (Negrão 1998: 10–11).

Women's and peasant associations, in particular, played an important role in the discussion around land. At least 85 percent of the Mozambican population lives in the rural areas, and women are the most active among the population involved in cultivation of the land. The new Land Act emphasizes that the land belongs to the state, and that the state gives it to those who work on it. The Land Act also ensures that land tenure rights are acquired by occupation of individuals and local communities according to customary norms and practices. These norms sometimes disqualify women who are not seen as heads of households or decision makers in patrilineal families. But this is not the case in most matrilineal societies that still exist in Mozambique, mainly north of the Zambezi River. The law brings comparative advantages to the family sector, particularly women, who as citizens are given control over land as a resource and the right to ownership of land titles.

The new law protects women, especially those who are widows, divorced, and single mothers, who need access to land to survive. It protects small-scale farmers, who make up over 90 percent of all agricultural producers and form the base of the economy. The law recognizes customary tenure systems and unwritten customary law, which many see as a breakthrough, together with the provision that customary laws, practices, and tenure systems cannot violate the constitution, nor can they violate the rights of women. Moreover, the law guarantees women the right to own land, which together with the constitutional provisions grants women greater protections and access to and control over land. Some fear that by recognizing customary law and land tenure systems, the law creates a certain ambiguity that leaves open the door to conservative interpretations of the law that can be taken advantage of to deny women land rights. They see this as a potential reversal of the gains that have been made in women's rights. Moreover, there are still large gaps in knowledge of the laws and their implementation. Women similarly need to be empowered to exercise their rights (Silva et al. 2005).

More generally, thus far neither men nor women are fully benefiting from advantages afforded by the law, partly due to lack of knowledge about their rights, and partly because the administrative and judicial practices have yet to incorporate the norms and dynamics that the Land Act seeks to encourage (Pitamber and Hanoomanjee 2004; SARDC 2004). Moreover, in spite of the fact that land is state-owned, there exists an "informal" trade of land, involving some traditional leaders and other decision makers. Because of poverty, owners of small plots are selling them and thus losing the only resource that they have. The International Monetary Fund and World Bank, together with some voices in the Mozambican private sector, are encouraging the privatization of land in Mozambique.

In general, women's movements across the continent have come to the recognition that women need to have control over land for long-term security and for development. They need to reap economic gains from the land, as they are key contributors. Even where laws have been passed and where gains have been made, women's movements in Africa believe they have many hurdles ahead, especially in passing and implementing land legislation. There is now continentwide recognition that lack of land is a problem and a development barrier. The fact that in some countries men can no longer sell land without the consent of their spouses is important. The fact that women can acquire land through purchase is an important step toward social acceptance of full rights to land for women.

### DOMESTIC VIOLENCE

Violence against women has been an area in which there has been considerable international mobilization, especially after the Fourth World Conference on Women, held in Beijing in 1995, that placed it in the Platform of Action. NGO presentations at the Beijing +10 Conference reinforced the importance of this issue (UNDP 2005). It has been recognized that until society is made aware of the negative effects of domestic violence on women and the family, there will be little progress in other areas identified as key to the advancement of women. Only a handful of countries such as Madagascar, Mauritius, South Africa, and Zimbabwe have passed legislation regarding domestic violence.

In 2000, the Women's Forum in Mozambique organized a group of representatives of various organizations to work on a Law against Domestic Violence.[8] In 2004, national seminars were organized in most parts of Mozambique and Maputo city to discuss and modify a draft of the legislation. The same coalition had been working together on Family Law

---

[8] The organizations included All Against Violence (TCV), the Association of Mozambican Women Law Professionals (AMMCJ), the Center of African Studies, the Ministry of Women and Coordination of Social Action (MMCAS), MULEIDE, and WLSA.

legislation and on questions of unemployment and poverty together with a foreign antidebt NGO, the unions, and the Ministry of Planning and Finance.

The coalition reasoned that legal change is often most effective when combined with other educational and community action programs. For example, one of the coalition members, All Against Violence Group (Programa Todos Contra a Violência [TCV]), was initiated in 1996 as a direct outcome of the 1995 UN Beijing conference as a collective initiative to revise and change all legislation that discriminates against women. However, it also provides medical, counseling, and legal services to women who have suffered violence. The organization carries out civic education, disseminates information about women's rights, and carries out educational campaigns within schools, neighborhoods, workplaces, NGOs, and other locales.

Similarly, the Mozambican Association Woman and Education (Associação Moçambicana Mulher e Educação), formed in 1997 and based in Maputo, has a program on "Violence against the female teacher and the girl student in the community." MULEIDE and the Organization of Mozambican Woman (Organização da Mulher Moçambicana [OMM]) provide counseling and legal aid services, disseminate information about women's rights, and organize activities for women victims of violence. The Association of Mozambican Women Law Professionals (Associação Moçambicana das Mulheres de Carreira Jurídica [AMMCJ]) does much the same but also works on revising laws. Woman's Forum organizes networking activities, including a monthly newsletter on TVC activities. KULAYA is a shelter for battered women, located at Maputo Central Hospital, that provides counseling services to women, while Centro de Estudos Africanos (Center of African Studies) at Eduardo Mondlane University carries out participatory action research on legal issues.

Given the difficulties of passing legislation affecting issues that directly challenge male dominance and authority in the household, women's organizations have mobilized on multiple fronts, working for legislative change while addressing the legal, financial, psychological, health, relief, and social dimensions of the issues.

CONCLUSIONS

Since the 1990s, new constitutions throughout Africa have increasingly included nondiscrimination or equality provisions while prohibiting customary practices if they undermined the dignity, welfare, or status of women. These were new developments in African constitution making and can be contrasted with constitutions passed prior to 1990, in which customary law generally was not subject to any gender-related restrictions. Women's movements played an important role in ensuring that these clauses were included.

Rather than examining all the areas where legislative advances have been made with respect to women's rights, this chapter has looked at the areas of greatest resistance. The fact that women's movements in the 1990s started tackling some of the most intransigent and difficult societal issues is an indication of how much has changed. Some of the issues being taken up could not even be mentioned in public and were considered taboo well into the 1990s (e.g., domestic violence and female genital cutting).

The very fact that there is resistance to many efforts at legislative reform regarding women's rights suggests that laws matter and that laws are not merely passed to satisfy changing international norms, only to be filed away and ignored. The capacity to enforce many of the laws remains problematic and corruption is rampant in many African judicial systems, but the passage of these laws is a mark of changing societal norms, expectations, and sensibilities regarding women's and girl's rights.

It is evident from efforts to pass legislation in many African countries that the most resistance is elicited by efforts to challenge customs that affect family relations and male–female relations within the family, clan, and community. It is interesting to note that legal provisions that promote equality and nondiscrimination in state and market-related institutions are much less problematic than laws that directly challenge customary and family law. This lack of congruence is evident from such constitutions as the 1999 Nigerian constitution, which does not permit discrimination on the grounds of sex yet fails to place clear constraints on discrimination when it comes to marriage, inheritance, divorce, and family law (Toyo 2006: 1300). Many of the difficulties in reforming customary law derive from colonial times, because the colonial authorities had solidified or reified this sphere of law by creating a plural system of law that included coexisting legal systems of formal written law and customary and religious laws.

We make a final note about our cases. Cameroon has been absent from this discussion, largely because efforts to pass legislation regarding these issues are still in process. Women's organizations such as Association Camerounaise des Femmes Juristes, the Association de lutte contre les violences faites aux femmes, International Federation of Women Lawyers (FIDA)– Cameroon, the League for the Education of Women and Children, and the National Association of Professional Media Women have advocated the adoption of laws such as a family code, a law on violence against women, and a law on gender quotas. Once again, as in the aforementioned cases of constitutional reform in Kenya and Zimbabwe, the issue is not so much one of a lack of progress in these countries – all of which have active women's movements. Rather, it is the fact that those countries that have made the most progress have had other conditions that have allowed change, including fundamental shifts in gender relations as a result of upheaval and war. These disruptions have permitted women's movements to intervene while dampening and demobilizing voices of opposition to women's rights. These ruptures have also made the countries more susceptible to new international influences and pressures from regional associations such as the Southern Africa Development Community (SADC) that are seeking to enhance gender equity.

# 6

## In Pursuit of Equal Political Representation

One of the most remarkable changes since the mid-1990s in Africa has been the rise of women political leaders. Rwanda claimed the world's highest ratio of women in parliament in 2003, with close to 49 percent of its seats held by women. Mozambique has 35 percent of its legislative seats held by women, and in many other African countries today, women hold over one-third of the parliamentary seats. There have been six female prime ministers since the mid-1990s and women Speakers of the House in Ethiopia, Lesotho, Gambia, Nigeria, and South Africa.

Liberia's Ellen Johnson-Sirleaf became the first elected woman president in Africa in 2005 and there have been two unelected female heads of state since 1995.[1] Until the 1990s, it was virtually unheard of for women to run for the presidency in Africa. In the 1990s, women ran for the top executive office in the Central African Republic, Kenya, and Liberia. Since 2000, increasing numbers of women have run for office in about half the presidential elections held in Africa.

Six women have held the position of vice/deputy president. Uganda's Wandera Specioza Kazibwe became the first female vice president in Africa in 1993 and served for close to ten years. Women are also visible at the cabinet level; they are heading up key ministries and are no longer relegated only to the ministries of women, education, health, youth, and community development as they were in the past. Today they are taking up ministerial portfolios in foreign affairs, defense, finance and planning, trade and industries, and other such ministries. For example, Mozambique not only has a female prime minister but also ministers of foreign affairs, justice, labor, energy,

---

[1] Ruth Perry served as chair of the on the six-member collective presidency of Liberia (1996–7), and Carmen Pereira was briefly acting head of state in Guinea-Bissau.

parliamentary issues, and women and social action. Cape Verde, Guinea-Bissau, Malawi, Senegal, Uganda, and Zimbabwe have all had female ministers of defense since 2000.[2] Similarly, Burkina Faso, Burundi, the Gambia, Liberia, Mozambique, Nigeria, Namibia, São Tomé e Príncipe, and Tanzania have had ministers of finance and/or planning since 2000[3] and Benin, Burundi, Guinea, Malawi, Nigeria, and Tanzania had female ministers of foreign affairs in 2006.

In countries such as Nigeria, where women have been slow to gain access to power, Dame Virginia Etiaba was sworn in as the first woman governor in the country in 2005. Even at the local level, women make up 58 percent of local government positions in Lesotho and Seychelles ("Women Legislators..." 2007), 43 percent of the members of local councils or municipal assemblies in Namibia, and over one-third of local government seats in Mauritania, Mozambique, Tanzania, and Uganda (Morna 2003: 3).

Women are also forming and heading up political parties on an unprecedented scale (see Table 6.1). In southern Africa, women have often outnumbered men as voters. Women frequently make up the majority of grassroots party activists, workers, and volunteers. They are often more visible than men in attending rallies and demonstrating in countries such as Zambia (Osei-Hwedie 1998: 85; Zaffiro 2000: 4, 15). There are no legal restrictions or impediments to women running for office. Yet it has only been since the 1990s that women have begun to make their presence felt in the political leadership of post-independence states. Women's movements have played an important role in bringing about these changes.

As a result of pressure from women activists, these changes have even affected regional fora. The Pan-African Parliament of the African Union

---

[2] These include Minister of Defense Cristina Fontes Lima, Cape Verde (2006–); Minister of Home Affairs and Internal Security Anna Kachikho, Malawi (2005–); Minister of Security Betty Akech, Uganda (2005–6); Minister of Defense Filomena Mascarenhas Tipote, Guinea Bissau (2003–4); Minister of Defense Mame Madior Boye, Sénégal (2002); and Acting Minister of Defense Joyce Mujuru, Zimbabwe (2001).

[3] These cabinet members include Minister of Finance Zakia Hamdan Meghji, Tanzania (2006–); Minister of Economy Cristina Maria Fernandes Dias, São Tomé e Príncipe (2006–); Minister of Finance Antoinette Sayeh, Liberia (2006–); Minister of Finance and Planning Maria do Carmo Silveira, São Tomé e Príncipe (2005–6); Minister of Finance Dr. Ngozi Okonjo-Iweala, Nigeria (2003–6); Minister of Development Planning and National Reconstruction Marie Goretti Nduwimana, Burundi (2005–); Secretary of State of Economy and Finance Margaret Keita, the Gambia (2005); Minister of Planning, Development, and Reconstruction Seraphine Wakane (2003–5), Burundi; Minister of Finance Saara Kuugongelwa-Amadhila, Namibia (2003–); Minister of Planning and Finance Maria dos Santos Lima da Costa Tebús Torres, São Tomé e Príncipe (2002–3 and 2006–); and Minister of Planning and Finance Luísa Días Diogo, Mozambique (2000–5).

TABLE 6.1. *Women Party Leaders and Founders, 1944–Present*

| Leader | Country | Years | Position | Party |
|---|---|---|---|---|
| Amália de Victoria Pereira | Angola | 1992– | Chairperson | Partido Liberal Democratico and President of the Parliamentary Group |
| Rosine Vieyra Soglo | Benin | 1992–4 | President | Parti de Rennaissanince du Benin |
| Karimou Rafiatou | Benin | 1999–2003 | President | Parliament Group of Parti de Nation et Developpement |
| Limakatso Ntakatsane | Lesotho | 1992– ? | Founder | Kopanang Basotho |
| Marléne Zéban | Burkina Faso | 1990– | Secretary general | Parti de Convergence por Les Libertés et l'Integration |
| Joséphine Tamboura (née Sama) | Burkina Faso | Ca. 2002– | Secretary general | Alliance pour le Progrès et la Liberté |
| Sylvie Kinigi | Burundi | 1994?– | Co-leader | Progrés National Unifie |
| Nicole Okala | Cameroon | 1991–7 | Founding president | Union Sociale Camerounais |
| Lydia Effimba | Cameroon | 1996 | Chairperson | Liberal Democratic Alliance |
| Ruth Rolland-Jeanne-Marie | Central African Republic | 1992–6 | President | Parti Républicain Centroafrican |
| Judith Renazou | Central African Republic | 2004 | Chairperson | Carrefour Démocratique Centrafricain pour le Développement |
| Marie Claire Mbolidi Damada | Central African Republic | 2004 | Chairperson | Union Nationale Démocratique du Peuple Centrafricain |

| Name | Country | Years | Position | Party |
| --- | --- | --- | --- | --- |
| Angèle Gnonsoa | Côte d'Ivoire | N/A | Party Secretary (also deputy president and spokesperson in 1990–) | Parti Ivoirien des Travailleurs |
| Henriette Dagri Diabaté | Côte d'Ivoire | 1999 | Acting leader, previously vice president, secretary general 1999–, and deputy leader (1994–9) | Rassemblement des Républicains |
| Simone Ehivet | Côte d'Ivoire | 1999– | President | Parliamentary Group of Front Populaire Ivoirien |
| Antonieta Rosa Gomes | Guinea-Bissau | 1994– | Leader | Foro Civic da Guiné |
| Charity Kaluki Ngilu | Kenya | 1992–7 | Leader | Parliamentary Group of the Social Democratic Party |
| Dr. Julia Ojiambo | Kenya | Ca. 2002– | Chairperson | Labour Party of Kenya |
| Dr. Wangari Maathai | Kenya | Ca. 2002 | Founder | Mazingira Green Party of Kenya |
| Limakatso Ntakatsane | Lesotho | Ca. 1994– | Founding chairperson | Kopanang Basotho Party |
| Ellen Johnson-Sirleaf | Liberia | 1997– | Leader | Unity Party |
| Ayesha Keita Conneh | Liberia | 2004 | Co-founder and leader | Liberians United for the Reconciliation and Demokracy (LURD) |
| Giselle Rabesahala | Madagascar | 1975–90 1995– | Secretary general Co-leader | Parti Communiste Parti du Congres de l'Independence du Madagascar |

(continued)

TABLE 6.1 *(continued)*

| Leader | Country | Years | Position | Party |
|---|---|---|---|---|
| France Vallet | Mauritius | 1972–ca. 1987 | Leader | Parti du Centre Republicain |
| Sheilabai Bappo | Mauritius | 1973–1996– | President | Partie Mouvement Militant Mauricien Mouvement Socialiste Mauricien |
| | | | Secretary general | |
| France Félicité | Mauritius | 1983–ca. 2000 | Co-leader | l'Organisation du Peuple de Rodrigues |
| Nora Schimming-Chasee | Namibia | Ca. 1999–2004 | National president | Congress of Democrats |
| Carola Engelbrecht | Namibia | 2003– | Secretary general | Republican Party |
| Alivera Mukabaramba | Rwanda | Ca. 2003– | Leader | Party for Progress and Concord |
| Dr. Hilda Stevenson-Delhomme | Seychelles | 1964– | Leader | N/A |
| Annette M.S. George | Seychelles | 1992–5 | Leader | United Opposition Party (today named Seychelles National Party) |
| Kathleen Pillay | Seychelles | 1992– | Leader | National Party |
| Jeredine Williams | Sierra Leone | 1995–7 | Leader | Coalition for Progress Party |
| Dr. Sylvia O. Blyden | Sierra Leone | 2002 | Leader | Young People's Party |
| V. Margaret Ballinger | South Africa | 1953–4 | President | South African Liberal Party |
| J. McPherson | South Africa | Ca. 1961 | Chairperson | Labour Party |

| | | | | |
|---|---|---|---|---|
| Helen Suzman | South Africa | 1970–89 | Parliamentary Leader | Progressive Party |
| Albertine Sisuli | South Africa | 1988–92 | President<br>Chairperson | United Democratic Front<br>African National Congress Parliamentary caucus |
| Zanele Magwaza | South Africa | 2005– | | Inkatha Freedom Party |
| Fatma Maghimbi | Tanzania/Zanzibar | 1999– | Leader of party and opposition in parliament | Civic United Front |
| Stella Nambuya | Uganda | 2004– | Leader | Republican Women and Youth Party |
| Miria Kalule Obote | Uganda | 2005– | President | Uganda People's Congress |
| Chamba Gwendoline G. Konie | Zambia | 2001– | Founding chairperson | Social Democratic Party |
| Dr Inonge Mbikusita Lewanika | Zambia | 1991–2001– | Founder President | National Party Agenda for Zambia |
| Edith Zewelani Nawakwi | Zambia | N/A | Secretary general Vice President | Forum for Democracy and Development |
| Margaret Dongo | Zimbabwe | 1999–1999 | Chairperson<br>Founder and co-leader | Movement for Independent Candidates<br>Zimbabwe Union of Democrats |

*Source*: Worldwide Guide to Women in Leadership, http://www.guide2womenleaders.com/, accessed 5 September 2008.

now has a woman president, Gertrude Mongella – a first in the history of such a pan-African body. Mongella became internationally known for her role as chair of the Fourth United Nations World Conference on Women in Beijing in 1995. The African Union has also elected another woman, Loum N. Ne'loumsei Elise from Chad, as one of its four vice presidents. Moreover, half the members of the ten-person African Union Commission are women. By comparison, only one-third of the members (nominees) of the European Union Commission are women (eight out of twenty-four). Women on the African Union Commission head up key portfolios, including political affairs, trade and industry, human and peoples' rights, human resources, science and technology, and rural economy and agriculture.

Women's new presence in political leadership in Africa is being felt in other arenas as well, reaching onto the global stage. For example, Tanzania's Mongella was selected secretary-general of the UN Fourth World Conference on Women in 1995; another Tanzanian, Dr. Asha-Rose Migiro, became deputy secretary-general of the United Nations in 2007; the World Bank's managing director is Ngozi Okonjo-Iweala, the former finance minister of Nigeria; Kenyan environmentalist Wangari Maathai won the Nobel Peace Prize in 2004; Justice Sebutinde is chairing the UN-backed Special Court for Sierra Leone in the trial of former Liberian president Charles Taylor at the Hague; the deputy chief justice of Uganda, Laeticia Mukasa Kikonyogo, was elected president of the International Association of Women Judges (IAWJ) in 2001, and the World Association of Women Entrepreneurs elected Françoise Foning of Cameroon as the president of the organization in 2005. These are just a few examples of the ways in which African women have leapt into new global arenas, especially after 2000.

Returning to the national leaders within Africa, the bigger question, and one for future investigation, relates to the impact of these new women leaders. This chapter focuses on the issue of equal representation because it has been a central goal of the women's movements. Women's movements have sought to address the lack of women in political decision-making positions and have sought to increase the numbers of women running for and being elected to office. They have also sought to address the constraints that work against women being elected to office.

## CONSTRAINTS ON WOMEN'S POLITICAL REPRESENTATION

In spite of dramatic changes in women's representation in many countries, important constraints have encumbered women's entry into the political sphere. The dominance of men in the public realm is reinforced by their dominance in the private realm. Men are seen as heads or powerholders in the family as they are in the public realm. Thus, cultural beliefs keep women subservient to men in the household, which has implications for political leadership in the public sphere. As in much of the world, cultural and religious practices and beliefs may reinforce a view that makes it difficult for women to run for office (Osei-Hwedie 1998: 91).

Sometimes male-dominated selection committees are not prone to selecting female candidates or placing them high on the party list. Political parties intent on winning elections in a new multiparty system often indicate that they don't want to "waste" their chances on a woman who is perceived of as unlikely to win.

Although some constraints on women's political leadership are imposed, women themselves also may be reticent to run for office for a variety of reasons. Partly the reluctance may stem from cultural prohibitions on women speaking in public in front of men and campaigning in public places. Campaigning often involves travel, spending nights away from home, and meeting potential voters in public places, all of which puts women politicians at risk of being thought of as "loose women" or "unfit mothers." As one former Zimbabwean politician, Sarah Kachingwe, explained about running for office:

One also needs to do a lot of socialising, staying out late and meeting potential voters. Then there are the cultural inhibitions: while men can go out and drink, without their wives, our African socialisation says that women cannot do it. They are barred by restrictions which are based on their individual conscience. (quoted in Mumba 1997: 4)

Not only may women find themselves and their families under attack or the subject of malicious gossip, but husbands will sometimes forbid their wives from engaging in politics. Some husbands are threatened by the possibility that their wives will interact with other men. Others fear the social stigma directed against their wives, or they worry that their wife's political preoccupations will divert her attention away from the home. Anne Ferguson and Beatrice Katundu found in Zambia that most women who were active in politics claimed that they experienced marital problems as a result of their involvement (1994: 18). Women who do run for office are often single or divorced.

Many of the stereotypes of women politicians are reflected in comments made by men and women in Tanzania's Sukumaland in a rural area near Mwanza. Although one cannot generalize from these perceptions for all of Tanzania, let alone Africa, these types of comments are often heard in other parts of Africa, giving some indication of the cultural constraints that women face in entering into politics, especially at the local level:

When I was elected as a village secretary some people told me that I would become a loose woman, a prostitute. I told them that I could never do such a thing and second, I asked them whether they had any proof of the misbehavior of other women leaders to which they referred? Their answer was "No, this is just what we have heard." (Young woman CCM leader)

There are women who are capable of being leaders, and good leaders too. But it is not easy. Men very often do not trust their wives and think that if they go for seminars, they will betray their husbands; and that a woman is like a child as far as the brain is concerned; she can easily be convinced by another man to give way for sex. (Young male CCM leader)

Normally husbands are the main causes for their wives not to be leaders.... Many of the women are very eager to be leaders. But your husband can ban you and then that is the end. We ask husbands to allow their wives to contest, but many of them dislike it.... Here there are many women who are able to work, to lead, and who can build our nation. After all, some are properly educated, but because the husband is in a panic, his wife remains a housewife (Woman CCM official) (Andersen 1992: 161, 260, 263).

Women (and sometimes men) also tend to associate politics with being "dirty" or even "dangerous" and, as such, something that only men engage in. As Kenyan women's rights activist Dr. Maria Nzomo put it:

Women are still afraid of power... we need to realize that politics does not make itself dirty, people make it dirty and that we can't continue to say it is dirty and sit on the sidelines. We need to jump in and change politics. We have to deal with it. (Nzomo 1995)

But there are also practical considerations that constrain women from being office holders. Such considerations are related to gender inequalities in the division of labor. Women tend to bear heavier household and community responsibilities that give them less time for running for office or for keeping the long hours required for holding office. Women leaders in Uganda frequently complain that men tend to schedule meetings in the evenings and arrive too late for them, making it difficult for women who have to cook dinner and put children to sleep (Tripp 2000).

There may be enormous personal and social costs to becoming active in politics, from financial constraints to a lack of logistical support. Some find it an isolating life. It can place excessive strains on marriages and on husbands who demand the full attention of their wives (Ferguson and Katundu 1994: 17–18). Moreover, women are more often than men limited by the lack of financial resources. Under the single-party system in Zambia, the ruling party assisted all candidates running for office. With multipartyism, parties are not a major source of financial support and each candidate is responsible for mobilizing his or her funds from friends, family, supporters, and his or her own resources. This puts women at a significant disadvantage in Zambia. One consequence of this is a disproportionately high number of divorced and single women in office who don't have to negotiate with reluctant husbands on how to use household funds (Ferguson et al. 1995: 9).

In spite of these constraints, women who do run may find that they have better chances of getting elected than men. In Zambia, for example, in the six elections between 1968 and 1991, the percentage of successful females averaged 44 percent whereas successful men averaged 26 percent. Moreover, the rate of success almost tripled for women after the 1988 election (Osei-Hwedie 1998: 85).

In spite of all the aforementioned limitations on women's involvement in political leadership, women are not reluctant to participate in other aspects of politics. Women often vote in numbers very similar to those of men if not greater numbers than men, as seen in electoral turnout figures of elections in Mozambique and Zambia in the 1990s (Jacobson 1995; Longwe and Clarke 1991). As one Zambian former member of parliament put it: "Women do all the campaigning and organize rallies for men. But now we have to switch to do the same for ourselves. Women are still in the mold of campaigning for men, not for women. Women are waiting to be invited to participate but no one will invite them" (Mbikusita-Lewanika 1995).

WOMEN'S REPRESENTATION IN LEGISLATURES

Increasing numbers of African countries have among the highest rates of female legislative representation in the world, with women claiming in 2007 as much as or more than 30 percent of the parliamentary seats in Burundi, Mozambique, South Africa, Tanzania, and Uganda, with 49 percent in Rwanda (see Table 6.2).[4] After consistently being below the world average for decades, women in Africa today hold on the average 17 percent of the legislative seats (in the single or lower house), which is roughly the same as the world average. Moreover, the percentage of women in Africa's parliaments doubled between 1990 and 2005 (see Table 6.3).

---

[4] Women in Seychelles held 46 percent of parliamentary seats in 1993.

TABLE 6.2. *Women's Political Rights and Representation in Africa*

| | Right to Vote | Right to Stand for Election | Year Woman Elected (E = elected, A = Appointed) | Women Ministers % of Total, 2005 | Lower or Single House % of Total, 2005 | Lower or Single House % of Total, 1990 | Lower or Single House % of Total, 2008 | Upper House or Senate % of Total, 2008 |
|---|---|---|---|---|---|---|---|---|
| Angola | 1975 | 1975 | 1980 E | 0.1 | 15 | | 9 | – |
| Benin | 1956 | 1956 | 1979 E | 0.2 | 3 | | 8.4 | – |
| Botswana | 1965 | 1965 | 1979 E | 0.3 | 5 | | 11.1 | – |
| Burkina Faso | 1958 | 1958 | 1978 E | 0.1 | – | | 15.3 | – |
| Burundi | 1961 | 1961 | 1982 E | 0.1 | – | | 30.5 | 34.7 |
| Cameroon | 1946 | 1946 | 1960 E | 0.1 | 14 | | 14.1 | – |
| Cape Verde | 1975 | 1975 | 1975 E | 0.2 | 12 | | 15.3 | – |
| Central African Republic | 1986 | 1986 | 1987 E | 0.1 | 4 | | 10.5 | – |
| Chad | 1958 | 1958 | 1962 E | 0.1 | – | | 6.5 | – |
| Comoros | 1956 | 1956 | 1993 E | – | 0 | | 3 | – |
| Congo | 1961 | 1961 | 1963 E | 0.1 | 14 | | 7.3 | 13.3 |
| Congo, Dem. Rep. of the | 1967 | 1970 | 1970 E | 0.1 | 5 | | 8.4 | 4.6 |
| Côte d'Ivoire | 1952 | 1952 | 1965 E | 0.2 | 6 | | 8.5 | – |
| Equatorial Guinea | 1963 | 1963 | 1968 E | – | 13 | | 18 | – |
| Eritrea | 1955 | 1955 | 1994 E | 0.2 | – | | 22 | – |
| Ethiopia | 1955 | 1955 | 1957 E | 0.1 | – | | 22 | 18.8 |
| Gabon | 1956 | 1956 | 1961 E | 0.1 | 13 | | 12.5 | 15.4 |
| Gambia | 1960 | 1960 | 1982 E | 0.2 | 8 | | 9.4 | – |
| Ghana | 1954 | 1954 | 1960 | 0.1 | – | | 10.9 | – |
| Guinea | 1958 | 1958 | 1963 E | 0.2 | – | | 19.3 | – |
| Guinea-Bissau | 1977 | 1977 | 1972 A | 0.4 | 20 | | 14.0 | – |
| Kenya | 1919, 1963 | 1919, 1963 | 1969 E+A | 0.1 | 1 | | 7 | – |

| | 1965 | 1965 | 1965 A | | | | |
|---|---|---|---|---|---|---|---|
| Lesotho | 1965 | 1965 | 1965 A | 0.3 | – | 25 | 30.3 |
| Liberia | – | – | – | 0.1 | – | 5.3 | – |
| Madagascar | 1959 | 1959 | 1965 E | 0.1 | 7 | 7.87 | 11.1 |
| Malawi | 1961 | 1961 | 1964 E | 0.1 | 10 | 14.44 | – |
| Mali | 1956 | 1956 | 1959 E | 0.2 | – | 10.2 | – |
| Mauritania | 1961 | 1961 | 1975 E | 0.1 | – | 17.9 | 17.9 |
| Mauritius | 1956 | 1956 | 1976 E | 0.1 | 7 | 5.7 | – |
| Mozambique | 1975 | 1975 | 1977 E | 0.1 | 16 | 35.6 | – |
| Namibia | 1989 | 1989 | 1989 E | 0.2 | 7 | 27 | 27 |
| Niger | 1948 | 1948 | 1989 E | 0.2 | 5 | 12.4 | – |
| Nigeria | 1958 | 1958 | – | 0.1 | – | 7.0 | 8.3 |
| Rwanda | 1961 | 1961 | 1981 | 0.4 | 17 | 48.8 | 34.6 |
| São Tomé and Príncipe | 1975 | 1975 | 1975 E | 0.1 | 12 | 1.8 | – |
| Senegal | 1945 | 1945 | 1963 E | 0.2 | 13 | 22.0 | 40.0 |
| Seychelles | 1948 | 1948 | 1976 E+A | 0.1 | 16 | 23.5 | – |
| Sierra Leone | 1961 | 1961 | – | 0.1 | – | 12.9 | – |
| South Africa | 1930, 1994 | 1930, 1994 | 1933 E | 0.4 | 3 | 32.8 | 33.3 |
| Swaziland | 1968 | 1968 | 1972 E+A | 0.1 | 4 | 15 | 30 |
| Tanzania, U. Rep. of | 1959 | 1959 | – | 0.2 | – | 31.6 | – |
| Togo | 1945 | 1945 | 1961 E | 0.2 | 5 | 8.6 | – |
| Uganda | 1962 | 1962 | 1962 A | 0.2 | 12 | 30.7 | – |
| Zambia | 1962 | 1962 | 1964 E+A | 0.3 | 7 | 14.6 | – |
| Zimbabwe | 1919, 1957, 1978 | 1919, 1978 | 1980 E+A | 0.1 | 11 | 14.3 | 33.33 |

*Source*: Human Development Report, United Nations Development Programme (UNDP), http://hdr.undp.org/statistics/data/, accessed 22 May 2008; EISA, http://www.eisa. org.za.index.html, accessed 1 August 2008.

TABLE 6.3. *Change in Representation of Women in Legislatures (Single House or Lower House), Percent, 1960–2007*

|                     | 1960 | 1970 | 1980 | 1990 | 2000 | 2007 |
|---------------------|------|------|------|------|------|------|
| Sub-Saharan Africa  | 0.6  | 1.6  | 5    | 6    | 10   | 17.8 |
| World               | 4    | 5    | 9    | 9    | 12   | 17.7 |

*Source:* Data compiled from Inter-Parliamentary Union, Women in Parliaments, 1945–1995: A World Statistical Survey, Series "Reports and Documents," No. 23, Geneva, 1995; http://www.ipu.org/wmn-e/world.htm ("Women in National Parliaments: Situation as of 25 September 2000").

These changes are linked to (1) the influences of domestic and international women's movements, which, as this chapter shows, are related to three other factors: (2) the introduction of electoral quotas for women, (3) opportunities emerging in the process of ending major armed conflicts after 1986 in some countries, and (4) pressures from regional bodies such as the Southern African Development Community (SADC) as well as pan-African organizations (Tripp 2008; Tripp and Kang 2008). Perhaps surprisingly, the increase in women's representation is not linked directly to the democratizing trends that swept the continent in the 1990s. This is because many undemocratic countries such as Rwanda and Sudan have adopted quotas and have been in this way able to increase their rates of female representation.

## Women's Movements and Legislative Representation of Women

Today, women's movements demanding 50 percent representation in Africa have emerged in countries such as Kenya, Malawi, Namibia, Senegal, Sierra Leone, South Africa, Tanzania, Uganda, and Zambia. In fact, the majority of these 50–50 campaigns in the world are found in Africa. Only a handful of these 50–50 movements can be found in Europe (e.g., Bulgaria and Slovenia).[5] In Sierra Leone, the goal of the 50/50 Group was to have equal representation at every level of decision making. It has sought to recruit, train, and teach women how to raise funds in order to reach that goal (Steady 2006: 56).

These domestic-level pressures are influenced by changing international norms. The 1985 UN Conference on Women in Nairobi, in particular, served as a catalyst for women's mobilization throughout the continent. Over fifteen thousand women from 140 countries attended the Nairobi conference. National women's organization leaders in Uganda, for example, point to the Nairobi conference as a turning point in the history of Ugandan

[5] http://www.wedo.org/, accessed 21 May 21 2008.

TABLE 6.4 *Quota Type: Reserved Seats/Women-Only Lists*

| Country | Women in Legislature % | Constitutional Provision for Quota for Women | Quota % | Year Quota Introduced |
|---|---|---|---|---|
| Burundi | 30.5 | Reserved seats for women | 30 | 2005 |
| Rwanda | 48.8 | Reserved seats for women in upper and lower house | 30 | 2003 |
| Tanzania | 30.4 | Reserved seats | 30 | 2000 |
| Uganda | 29.8 | Reserved seat | 23 | 1989 |
| Country | Women in Legislature % | Legal Provision for Quota for Women | Quota % | Year Quota Introduced |
| Eritrea | 22.0 | Reserved seats for women | 30 | 1994 |
| Mauritania | 17.9 | Reserved seats for women | 20 | 2006 |
| Somalia Transitional National Government | 8.0 | Women-only lists | 12 | 2004 |
| Sudan | 18.1 | Reserved seats | 9.7 | 2000 |

*Sources:* Inter-Parliamentary Union Data, http://www.ipu.org/wmn-e/classif.htm. Global Database of Quotas for Women. A joint project of International IDEA and Stockholm University, http://www.quotaproject.org/.

women's associations but also for women's political empowerment. They returned from the conference and not only started creating independent women's organizations but also began to make demands on the government for political representation.

## Introduction of Quotas

One of the main strategies of women activists was to advocate the adoption of quotas and other mechanisms to advance female representatives. The adoption of quotas accounts for many of the increases in female representation in African legislatures. Today, about twenty-eight countries on the continent have some form of quotas. In sub-Saharan Africa, countries with quotas have an average of 19 percent female-held seats compared with 11 percent female-held seats in countries without quotas.

There are four main types of quotas in Africa: (1) reserved seats, which from the outset determine the number of seats that are to be won by women in an election (see Table 6.4); (2) measures determined through national

TABLE 6.5. *Quota Type: Compulsory Quotas*

| Country | Women in Legislature % | Legal Provision for Quota for All Parties | Quota % | Year Quota Introduced |
|---|---|---|---|---|
| Angola | 9.0 | 30% of all party seats allocated for women | 30 | 2005 |
| Djibouti | 10.8 | 10% of all party seats allocated for women | 10 | 2002 |
| Liberia[a] | 12.5 | Each accredited electoral coalition or alliance is required to nominate women as 30% of the candidates | 30 | 2005 |
| Niger | 12.4 | 10% of all party seats allocated for women; 25% of all nominative posts for women | 10 | 2002 |

*Note:*
[a] Quota not enforced.

*Sources:* Inter-Parliamentary Union Data, http://www.ipu.org/wmn-e/classif.htm. Global Database of Quotas for Women. A joint project of International IDEA and Stockholm University, http://www.quotaproject.org/; EISA, http://www.eisa.org.za./index.html, accessed 1 August 2008.

legislation or constitutional mandates requiring all parties to nominate a certain percentage of women as electoral candidates (see Table 6.5); (3) measures adopted voluntarily by political parties aimed at influencing the number of women candidates (see Table 6.6); and (4) executive appointments to legislative seats (see Table 6.7). The fourth type of quota has rarely been adopted.

Although democratic and nondemocratic countries alike have adopted quotas, the more democratic-leaning countries in Africa (Botswana, Mali, Mozambique, Namibia, Senegal and South Africa) have tended to prefer quotas or targets set by parties themselves rather than adopting reserved seats or compulsory quotas. Conversely, no democracies in Africa have adopted reserved seats. Of the proportional representation electoral systems, nine out of fourteen have some form of quota. Of the majoritarian/plurality systems, twelve out of twenty-eight have a quota and one out of four of the semiproportional systems have quotas. Thus, there are no clear patterns of quota adoption based on electoral system.

Quotas, which are to be a temporary measure to create greater gender balance, are not uniformly considered a welcome strategy in Africa nor are

TABLE 6.6. *Quota Type: Party-Mandated Quotas for Women*

| Country | Women in Legislature[a] % | Party Mandate of Quota for Women | Quota % | Number of Seats Held by Party | Year Quota Introduced |
|---|---|---|---|---|---|
| Botswana | 11.1 | Botswana Congress Party | 30 | 21 | 1999 |
| | | Botswana National Front | 30 | 2 | 1999 |
| Burkina Faso | 15.3 | Alliance pour la Démocratie et la Federation | 25 | 13 | 2002 |
| | | Congrès pour la Démocratie et le Progrès | 25 | 50 | 2002 |
| Cameroon | 14.1 | Cameroon People's Democratic Movement | 30 | 83 | 1996 |
| | | Social Democratic Front | 25 | 12 | 1999 |
| Côte d'Ivoire | 8.5 | Front Populaire de Côte d'Ivoire | 30 | 43 | N/A |
| Democratic Republic of Congo | 8.4 | People's Party for Reconstruction and Democracy | 30 | 111 | 2006 |
| | | Movement for the Liberation of Congo | 30 | 64 | 2006 |
| | | Congolese Rally for Democracy | 30 | 15 | 2006 |
| Equatorial Guinea | 18.0 | Convergencia para la Democracia Social | | 5.8 | N/A |
| Ethiopia | 21.9 | Ethiopian People's Revolutionary Democratic Front | 30 | 85 | 2004 |
| Mali | 10.2 | Alliance for Democracy | 30 | 40 | N/A |
| Mozambique | 36.6 | Frente de Libertação de Moçambique (FRELIMO) | 30 | 49 | 1994 |
| Namibia | 27.0 | South West Africa People's Organisation of Namibia | 50 | 55 | 1997 |
| | | Congress of Democrats | 50 | 5 | 1999 |
| | | National Unity Democratic Organisation | 50 | 3 | 2003 |
| Niger | 12.4 | National Movement for a Society in Development | 12 | 42 | N/A |
| Senegal[b] | 22.0 | Senegalese Liberal Party | 33 | 74 | 2001 |
| | | Parti Socialiste | 25 | 8 | 1982 |
| Sierra Leone | 12.9 | At least five parties have made a commitment to have 30% women on their lists of candidates, and two made a commitment to have 50% | – | – | – |
| South Africa | 32.8 | African National Congress | 33 | 70 | 1994 |
| Zimbabwe[c] | 14.3 | ZANU-PF | 30 | 65 | 2005 |

*Notes:*

[a] Figures refer to lower house or single house in case of unicameral legislature.

[b] In 1982, Parti Socialiste reserved 25 percent of all posts in the party for women. In 2001, fourteen political parties in Senegal urged political parties to reserve at least 30 percent of the places on their candidate lists for women.

[c] Seats set aside for women in thirty-six districts equaling 30 percent.

*Sources:* Inter-Parliamentary Union Data, http://www.ipu.org/wmn?e/classif.htm. Global Database of Quotas for Women. A joint project of International IDEA and Stockholm University, http://www.quotaproject.org/.

TABLE 6.7. *Quota Type: Appointed*

| Country | Women in Legislature | Type of Quota: Appointment | Quota | Year Quota Introduced |
|---|---|---|---|---|
| Kenya | 7.3 | Executive appointment | 3 seats | 1997 |
| Swaziland | 10.8 | Upper house: executive appointment | 28% | 2003 |

*Sources:* Inter-Parliamentary Union Data, http://www.ipu.org/wmn-e/classif.htm. Global Database of Quotas for Women. A joint project of International IDEA and Stockholm University, http://www.quotaproject.org/.

all forms of quotas considered equally useful. Quotas have been promoted by women's movements for a variety of reasons, ranging from questions of justice, equity, democratization, development, and the need to reverse the historic preferential treatment of men. Others point out that women's representation will not increase of its own accord. Moreover, qualified women do not win because of cultural beliefs, societal practices, and lack of economic and institutional supports. Often quotas are initially aimed at creating a critical mass in representation (30 to 35 percent), which is seen as a sufficient level of female representation to provide the momentum for advocacy for full gender parity. For some, they are a form of affirmative action, whereas for others, the goals are broader.

"It is an issue of democracy, it is an issue of human rights and equality. It is about social justice, about the fact that we both go to school and have achievements and knowledge hence, we deserve to be treated equally," University of Botswana lecturer Elsie Alexander told a *Mmegi* journalist. In Botswana, Emang Basadi is an NGO that has been advocating for 50 percent representation for women in Botswana's legislature. The two leading parties, Botswana Congress Party and the Botswana National Front, both introduced a 30 percent quota for women on electoral lists in 1999, but neither party has met the target (Konopo 2005).

Much of the lobbying for quotas came from Botswanan women's organizations such as Emang Basadi, which have been at the forefront of efforts to implement quotas. However, pressures from transnational women's movements and regional organizations have also played a role in influencing these changes, most of which began in earnest after the mid-1990s.

In sub-Saharan Africa in the decades leading up to 1995, only six countries had adopted quotas. Ghana's Convention People's Party had a provision for the election of ten women to parliament already in 1959 when women held 10 percent of the seats in parliament, and by 1965 there were 19 women in a legislature of 104 members. This lasted until the 1966 takeover by General

Joseph Ankrah, when female representation declined (Fallon 2003: 166–7). In 1975, Tanzania reserved fifteen legislative seats for women. Senegal's Parti Socialiste announced in 1982 that it would reserve one-quarter of its seats for women. Uganda adopted reserved seats for one woman in each district in 1989.

The big change, however, occurred between 1995 and 2005, when twenty-three countries adopted quotas, bringing the ratio of countries implementing quotas to twenty-four out of a total of forty-eight sub-Saharan African countries. The 1995 UN Conference on Women held in Beijing adopted a Platform of Action in which governmental delegations sought to ensure women's equal participation in all forms of "power structures and decision-making." This conference played a key role in helping foster these changes not only in Africa, but globally as well.

## Impact of the End of Conflict

The timing of the implementation of quotas is linked to the 1995 UN Conference on Women in Beijing. But in many countries it is also linked to the end of conflict. A large number of countries introduced quotas or adopted other measures to increase women's legislative representation after emerging from longstanding wars after the late 1980s (Burundi, Eritrea, Mozambique, Rwanda, Somalia's Transitional National Government, and Uganda) or wars of liberation (South Africa). With the exception of Tanzania, all the countries where women hold as many as or more than one-third of seats in parliament came out of conflicts after 1986, including Burundi, Mozambique, Rwanda, South Africa, and Uganda. Liberia placed large numbers of women within top government positions in a country that was headed by a woman.

There are several reasons that the end of conflict provided propitious opportunities for women activists to demand greater representation. Conflicts disrupted traditional gender roles, thus opening up opportunities for women and men to reenvision new roles for women, including political ones. Often women's movements were able to demand increased representation in peace negotiations or constitution-making exercises that generally occurred with the end of conflict. Countries coming out of conflict also tended to be more permeable with respect to international influences, such as new norms relating to women's political representation advocated within the UN system (e.g., UN Security Council Resolution 1325), but also by regional organizations such as SADC. Conflict may have diminished the power of potential opposition forces. In some cases, conflicts also disrupted potential opponents

of gender-based reform and weakened their base. Conflict leveled the playing field for new aspirants to power. Postconflict countries may increase
women's representation because women are often perceived as outsiders to
politics and therefore untainted by corruption, patronage, and the factors
that may have led to conflict. This gives them greater credibility in the newly
reconstituted political order (Tripp 2001a, 2008).

There has been a steady increase in the numbers of major conflicts coming to an end in Africa since 1985 and especially after 2000. Three major
conflicts ended between 1990 and 1999 and twelve ended in the next five
years between 2000 and 2005. This increased possibilities for women to
press for representation in these countries as opportunity structures shifted
in the postconflict context.

The timing of the end of conflict was critical. Such increases in female
representation did not occur after the end of wars of independence prior
to 1985 (e.g., Guinea-Bissau in 1974, Mozambique in 1974, Cape Verde
in 1974, Angola in 1974, and Rhodesia/Zimbabwe in 1979) (Tripp 2008).
Even though women sought greater representation at the end of these earlier
conflicts, having played important roles in many of the wars of liberation,
they were told to put their demands on the back burner and wait until development reached levels that could accommodate women's political emancipation (Staunton 1990; Sylvester 1989). This lesson was not lost on women
in countries such as Namibia and South Africa, which became independent
in the early 1990s.

In Zimbabwe, women had made up one-third of the fighters in the guerrilla movement that led to the end of colonialism. Women had also aided
the fighters in innumerable ways. Zimbabwean President Robert Mugabe
acknowledged that that the war would not have been won without the help
of women (Mugabe 1984). Nevertheless, Zimbabwean women activists were
extremely bitter about the fact that they were told to wait for an indefinite
time until they could assert their demands (Jirira 1995; Lueker 1998).

This was not the case in postconflict situations after the mid-1980s. From
Uganda to Namibia, South Africa, Mozambique, Rwanda, Burundi, Somalia, the Democratic Republic of Congo, and Liberia, after the end of major
conflicts, women's organizations vigorously pressed for increased representation, often in the form of quotas. They demanded a seat at the peace talks
and on constitutional commissions that drafted new constitutions. They
pushed for increased representation through legislative processes in other
instances. Unlike during the pre-1985 postconflict situations, they now were
able to realize their demands in most, but not all, cases.

This change in the mid-1990s and especially after 2000 in adopting quotas
occurred as a result of changing international norms and a greater openness

to strategies to advance women's status. By 1985, eighteen African countries had ratified the Convention on the Elimination of Discrimination against Women (CEDAW) and were obligated to report on progress on a regular basis. The UN Conference on Women held in Nairobi in 1985 served as a catalyst in putting women's rights on the agenda in many African countries. A decade later, the 1995 Beijing Conference on Women energized both women's movements and governments in Africa to take women's political representation more seriously.

## International Pressures

States have faced both regional and subregional pressures to give women greater political representation.

### Pressures from the Southern African Development Community

International pressures to increase female political representation were mediated through subregional organizations such as the SADC, with fourteen member states; the Economic Community of West African States (ECOWAS), with sixteen member states; and, more recently, by the Economic Community of Central African States (ECCAS). ECOWAS set targets to improve gender representation and pressured countries that were lagging and in 2004 ECCAS adopted a Declaration on Gender Equality (Déclaration sur l'Égalité Entre les Hommes et les Femmes),[6] which proposed steps to mitigate discrimination against women in its member states.

SADC, which has achieved relatively greater success than other regional bodies in promoting gender balance in governing institutions, has been especially aggressive in this regard, setting deadlines for increasing female representation. A SADC Regional Women's Parliamentary Caucus was formed in April 2002 in Luanda, Angola, to advocate and lobby for the increased representation of women in SADC parliaments. As a result, SADC set a goal in which female-held legislative seats of its member countries would reach 30 percent by 2005 and in 2005 a goal of 50 percent was set for 2015. This body also helped form women's parliamentary caucuses in Lesotho, Zambia, and Zimbabwe (Morna 2004: 111). The caucuses are nonpartisan and are aimed at bringing women parliamentarians together across party lines to address issues of common concern.

As a result of this type of regional lobbying, of the ten countries with the highest rates of legislative represention of women in the lower house

---

[6] See the document at http://www.ceeac-eccas.org/docs/hos/brazzaville03/declegalite.pdf.

in Africa, six are SADC countries. Additionally, Zimbabwe, Lesotho and Swaziland, which have lower rates of female representation in the lower house, have respectively 35 percent, 29 percent, and 37 percent seats held by women in the upper house or senate.

### Trans-African Pressures

Lobbying efforts have been evident at the regional level as well. For example, NGOs and networks have been pressing for changes within the African Union, which in turn has had implications for national movements pressing to advance women's status at the national level. Much of this lobbying began with the African Union predecessor, the Organization of African Unity, whose 1981 Charter on Human and Peoples' Rights included the goal of advancing gender equality and opposing gender discrimination. Although the African Charter on Human and Peoples' Rights embodied a commitment to eliminate discrimination against women and had an equal protection clause, it was not until 1995 that it decided to proceed with a protocol specifically on the rights of women. This decision was a result of a high degree of mobilization and strategic activism by African women's networks and organizations, working in full cooperation with governments and expert organizations.

The Organisation of African Unity and the Economic Commission for Africa established the African Women's Committee on Peace and Development (AWCPD) in 1998. The AWCPD itself included government representatives, prominent African women leaders, and representatives of leading NGOs in various countries.[7] The AWCPD and a network of women's organizations from throughout Africa were instrumental in getting gender issues placed on the table during the formation of the African Union. These networks were the driving force behind the "50–50" requirement stipulating that half of the African Union Commission be women. They had lobbied for this provision at the African Union summit in Durban in 2002 and brought it to fruition at the Maputo conference in 2003. At the latter conference, women's organizations campaigned successfully to have Gertrude Mongella elected to the presidency of the African Union parliament. These organizations have also lobbied vigorously for women to be included in peace processes around the continent.

---

[7] These included Ethiopian Women's Lawyers Association (Ethiopia), the Federation of African Women's Peace Networks (Zambia), Femmes Africa Solidarité (Senegal), Pro-Femmes (Rwanda), and Save Somali Women and Children (Somalia).

African women's networks[8] throughout the continent, particularly the Solidarity for African Women's Rights network, successfully pushed for the Protocol to the African Charter on Human and Peoples' Rights on the Rights of Women in Africa. After years of lobbying and meeting,[9] the Assembly of the African Union's second summit in Maputo, Mozambique, adopted the protocol on 11 July 2003, which went into effect 25 November 2005 (Adams and Kang 2007). This protocol calls for equal representation for women in political office and a broad range of economic and social rights for women.[10] For the first time in international law, the protocol specifically calls for the reproductive right of women to medical abortion in cases where pregnancy is the result of rape or incest or when the continuation of the pregnancy threatens the mother's life. Also for the first time, the protocol endorses the legal prohibition of female genital cutting.

## PRESIDENTIAL ELECTIONS

In the 1990s, women started seeking party nominations to run for the presidency and ran for the presidency in Angola, the Central African Republic, Kenya, and Liberia. Ruth Rolland-Jeanne-Marie from the Central African Republic had been Africa's first female presidential candidate in 1993. Since 2000, increasing numbers of women have run for the presidency in Africa.[11] In 2006, for example, out of nine presidential elections, women ran in at least four of them. Women's movements took advantage of situations at the end of conflict to push for women's representation. The most dramatic example of this was the election of Ellen Johnson-Sirleaf to the presidency

---

[8] These include Foundation for Community Development (FDC) in collaboration with UNIFEM (Southern Africa Regional Office), Femmes Africa Solidarité (FAS), African Centre for Constructive Resolution of Disputes (ACCORD), Centre for Human Rights (University of Pretoria), Southern African Development Community (SADC) Gender Unit, Forum Mulher (Mozambique), Women and Law in Southern Africa (WLSA) Mozambique, and the African Women's Development and Communication Network (FEMNET).

[9] The new protocol builds on the Dakar Strategy on Mainstreaming Gender and Women's Effective Participation in the African Union (26 April 2003) and the Durban Declaration on Gender and Mainstreaming and the Effective Participation of Women in the African Union (30 June 2003).

[10] http://www.hrea.org/erc/Library/display.php?doc_id=806&category_id=31&category_type=3, accessed 22 May 2008.

[11] Women candidates, for example, ran in presidential elections in Congo-Kinshasa (2006), Ghana (2007, 2008), Guinea Bissau (2005), Liberia (2005), Madagascar (2006), Malawi (2004), Mali (2002, 2007), Mauritania (2003), Mauritius (2000), Nigeria (2003), Rwanda (2003), Sierra Leone (1995, 2002), Somalia (2003), Tanzania (2005), Uganda (2006), and Zambia (2001, 2006).

in Liberia in 2005, where women rallied in large numbers to support and campaign for her. Up until that time, only three women had been head of modern states in Africa, none elected. Ruth Perry was appointed chair of the Liberian Council of State in September 1996 after the overthrow of dictator Samuel Doe. Sylvie Kinigi acted as president in Burundi following the murder of President Melchior Ndadaye in October 1993, and Carmen Pereira acted as head of state in Guinea-Bissau for two days in May 1984.

Uganda had the first woman vice president in Africa, Dr. Wandira Kazibwe, who served 1994 to 2003. Since the mid-2000s, Burundi, Gambia, South Africa, and Zimbabwe have had women vice presidents.[12] Rwanda and Burundi had women prime ministers in the mid-1990s, and Mozambique, São Tomé e Príncipe, and Senegal, had female prime ministers after 2001.[13]

Vabah Gayflor, Liberian minister of gender, explained at a conference of women politicians in 2005 immediately following Johnson-Sirleaf's election that her victory in the polls was a direct consequence of the mobilization of women:

Women realized that people's continued silence and marginalization was perpetuating a culture of violence. Liberia experienced an upsurge in advocacy of women especially after 2003. Women's advocacy had taken deep roots among women. In the past women's voices were hardly recognized by international mediators and Liberian politicians. Every resolution only talked about men and the warlords as stakeholders. Women were grossly marginalized in National Transitional Assembly, where there were 4 women for 19 men. Women saw this as indicative of discrimination, as men were presumed to be main actors. Women's advocacy was ignored and undervalued. This left women with little option but to seek political equality and that is why they backed Ellen Johnson-Sirleaf so forcefully. (Gayflor 2005)

### CASES OF UGANDA, MOZAMBIQUE, AND CAMEROON

These general trends regarding women's representation are reflected with our three cases. Both Mozambique's leading political parties have shown commitment to women's representation. In 2004, 40 percent of FRELIMO's seats were held by women whereas 22 percent of RENAMO's seats were claimed by women. This has resulted in almost 35 percent of all legislative

---

[12] These include Vice President Marina Barampama (Burundi, 2006–), Deputy President Phumzile Mlambo-Ngcuka (South Africa, 2005–), Vice President Joyce Mujuru (Zimbabwe, 2004–), Vice President Alice Nzomukunda (Burundi, 2005–6), and Vice President Isatou Njie Saidy (Gambia 2006–).

[13] These include Mame Madior Boye (Senegal, 2001–2), Maria do Carmo Silveira (São Tomé e Príncipe, 2004–6), Luisa Dias Diogo (Mozambique, 2004–), Sylvie Kinigi, (Burundi 1993–4), Maria das Neves (São Tomé e Príncipe, 2002–4), and Agathe Uwilingiyimana (Rwanda, 1993–4).

seats being claimed by women. In 2008, Mozambique has a female prime minister, six female ministers, four deputy ministers, and six permanent secretaries. This is a major improvement from 1997, when Mozambique had only one minister and three deputy ministers. Moreover, there are female provincial governors, six provincial secretary generals, and thirty-three provincial directors (compared to only twelve provincial directors in 1997) (SIDA 2007).

Although party commitment has been an important factor in explaining these changes, all key factors that we have identified in explaining the increase in female representation were present: Women's movement advocates for female representation within and outside of the state have exerted pressure to promote women leaders; Mozambique is a postconflict country; and it is a member of SADC.

Although Uganda was one of the first countries to adopt legislative quotas in 1989 and to promote women in key ministerial positions and into the position of vice president, today it is no longer leading in this regard. However, women still hold close to 30 percent of all legislative seats and one-third of all local government positions. Uganda's outcomes can similarly be explained by the pressures from the women's movement, especially in the late 1980s and early 1990 and its postconflict status after 1986. However, unlike Mozambique, Uganda is not a member of SADC and has not had to commit as rigorously to the various targets set by the organization to increase female representation.

Unlike Mozambique and Uganda, Cameroon has not experienced the disruptions of civil conflict and the pressures for increased female representation that have arisen in postconflict countries. Cameroon belongs to the regional body ECCAS, which unlike SADC has only recently begun to pay attention to gender equity. Moreover, the women's movement has faced greater challenges in pressing for legislative quotas and other mechanisms to promote women's leadership.

Thus, women held 14 percent of all legislative seats in Cameroon after the 2007 election, which is an increase from 9 percent in 2006. Although women actively participated in the struggles for the restoration of multiparty politics in Cameroon in the 1980s, they did not make gains in terms of access to leadership and decision making in the more than seventy parties that were created. Only one woman, Lydia Effimba, rose to the position of party chairperson within the male-dominated structures of the Liberal Democratic Alliance (LDA) in 1996, when a nine-member committee of which she was the only woman voted her to office in the absence of the incumbent. Another woman, Nicole Okala, created a party, the Union Sociale Camerounaise, in 1991, making her the first woman to create and head a political party in independent Cameroon. She later dissolved her party to join another party in 1997.

Women are also underrepresented in the leadership of all major parties represented in parliament, including the Union des Populations du Cameroun (UPC) and the National Union for Progress and Democracy (NUDP), both of which maintain separate wings for women. Currently, the main opposition Social Democratic Front (SDF) party upholds formal gender equality. In the aftermath of the 1997 legislative elections, which saw only one woman out of forty members of parliament elected on its ticket, the party adopted a 25 percent quota for women in all leadership positions within the party. The party elected Madame Marie-Louise Wandji to the post of second vice chair in 1994 and included nine women in its national governing body, the National Executive Council.

CONCLUSIONS

Women started to make their mark in politics in the 1990s to a degree not seen before in post-independence history. In spite of their efforts, women had yet to see enormous payoffs in terms of elected officials and political appointments. Women often lacked the resources, political experience, education, and political connections to run for office. Popular perceptions often suggested that women's "proper" place is still in the home rather than in politics. Prohibitive cultural attitudes against women's involvement persisted among both men and women. These were reflected in voting patterns, in media coverage of female politicians, and even in blatant attempts to suppress women's assertion of their political rights and views. But women themselves were also reticent to run for office (both national and local government positions) for many reasons. Even in parliamentary bodies, women have had difficulty being taken seriously or listened to and were frequently subjected to humiliating stereotypes and derogatory remarks. One study of women in parliamentary politics in Uganda found sexual harassment rampant, even in a parliament where women had been active and visible for over a decade (Tamale 1999). Over half of the women who had been elected in 1994 in South Africa, according to one study, did not plan to return to parliament when their terms expired because they believed there was no room for them to be heard and felt they could contribute more through community work (Britton 2005). This sentiment changed in subsequent elections as more women were elected into parliament and gained experience. Many African National Congress (ANC) women parliamentarians in South Africa, in fact, improved their position on the ANC list between the 1994 and 1999 elections. This is evidence that after getting elected to parliament, women have won credibility and acceptance (Mtintso 1999). In Uganda, with each subsequent election, significantly larger numbers of women were running for office and the numbers of women running for open seats (i.e., nonreserved seats) had increased with the introduction of affirmative action measures (Tripp 2000).

Women in Africa after 1990 were setting their political sights higher than ever before in postcolonial history. An increasing number of women aspired to be presidential candidates; they formed and led political parties and claimed leadership positions as ministers. Women's organizations made concerted efforts to increase female representation in parliaments. Even though the results of many of these efforts were often disappointing, new trends were being set. Women's movements were important to these early successes, forming nonpartisan organizations to train leaders, support women candidates, and lobby for quotas.

As we have seen throughout Africa and in our cases of Mozambique, Uganda, and Cameroon, the main factors that explain the increase in women's legislative presence in Africa have to do with the influences of domestic and international women's movements, which pressed for the adoption of legislative quotas, took advantage of opportunities that emerged with the end of major armed conflicts between 1986–2006, and pressured regional bodies such as SADC as well as pan-African organizations to promote women's political representation.

The influence of the African Union, ECOWAS, and SADC on African states suggests that the most important locus of transnational diffusion occurs at the regional and subregional level in diffusing transnational norms, practices, and strategies. Thus, pressures from such regional bodies mediated international pressures, such as those emerging from the United Nations conferences on women in Nairobi (1985) and Beijing (1995). Women activists in their home countries often encounter resistance to their efforts to advance women politically, economically, socially, and in multiple other arenas. Thus, their influence on the African Union and the subregional organizations has put pressures on governments to advance women's rights, creating greater openness to change on the part of governments. It has also removed the foil of transnational feminism from the picture, thereby helping eliminate the dubious charge that the advancement of women's rights must be equated with Western influences alien to one's society. The regional pressures are emanating from Africa and are eliciting new and important African responses.

# 7

# Engendering the State Bureaucracy

In Africa, as in other parts of the world, women's movements have wrestled with how best to address women's concerns by working with the state. From independence through to the early 1990s, the presence of authoritarian one-party regimes and/or military regimes posed enormous constraints on what was feasible and the extent to which women's movements were able to influence policy. Nevertheless, various governments initiated policy changes to improve the status of women, especially in the area of social policy and in some of the legislation adopted regarding women's employment, maternity leave, and, to some extent, family law.

African governments were generally responsive to United Nations efforts to create national machineries to advance women and to international treaties such as the Convention on the Elimination of All Forms of Discrimination against Women (CEDAW). However, the readiness and capacity to commit resources toward realizing the goals of these institutions were often illusive. This has been the biggest challenge in incorporating women's concerns into the state and policy apparatus, although, as this chapter shows, it is by no means the only one.

It was not until the 1990s that coalitions of international women's movements and UN agencies began to exert pressure on governments to deliver on their promises and to adopt policies to advance women's interests through a process of "gender mainstreaming" (True and Mintrom 2001). This created both tensions and opportunities for domestic women's movements with respect to the national machineries, which were the main governmental units charged with developing and implementing gender policy.

This chapter looks at the creation of national machineries and the eventual formation of ministries of gender/women; it examines various women in development (WID) and gender and development (GAD) approaches that guided their work, including the notion of gender mainstreaming. The chapter takes a critical look at the successes and problems with gender mainstreaming, both in its conceptualization and its application in various African contexts – in particular, the Cameroonian, Mozambican, and Ugandan cases. Finally, the chapter looks at gender budgeting policies as an example of gender mainstreaming. The chapter confirms the overall claim of the book regarding the difference between Mozambique and Uganda on the one hand and Cameroon on the other hand.

## FORMATION OF NATIONAL MACHINERIES

Under colonialism, women's affairs were often lodged within departments of community development, as in the countries administered by Britain's Colonial Office between the 1920s and 1960s. Much of the actual work was carried out within women's clubs or community development clubs, where the focus was on women's handicrafts and income generation; education in hygiene, nutrition, and childcare; cultural activities; civic education; organizational skills, including public speaking and handling of club finances; and discussions of issues of the day (Smyth 2004; Tripp 2002, 2004). These initiatives were continued in the early post-independence period under the rubric of the departments and ministries of community development.

Similar initiatives called *foyer sociaux* (social homes) were formed in Belgian colonies in Africa in the 1920s by the Union des Femmes Coloniales, a consortium of private voluntary agencies and the Catholic missions. Nuns, social workers, and African women in urban communities ran them. After World War II, the Belgian colonial authorities sent their own social workers to help run *foyer sociaux*, which were institutions that tended to impose Western notions of gender, domesticity, morality, and household divisions of labor on African women (Hunt 1990).

In the post-independence period, the emphasis shifted to enhancing women's status and rights in most sub-Saharan governments, and with only a few exceptions (e.g., the Central African Republic, Chad, and Liberia), most countries made an effort to create a governmental body to address these new concerns. The majority of women's national machineries were formed in response to the calls for the establishment of institutional mechanisms to promote women's advancement made at the first United Nations World Conference on Women, held in Mexico City in 1975. These objectives were incorporated into the UN International Decade for Woman (1976–85), so that by 1980 at least forty-one African nations had a women's national machinery (Parpart and Staudt 1989: 9). By 1985, 127 countries around the world had created some type of national machinery.

In response to the UN resolution, some countries set up ministries early on (e.g., Togo in 1975 and Côte d'Ivoire in 1976), while others established women's bureaus, departments, or divisions within a ministry. In other countries, government commissions, committees, or councils were established, such as the National Council on Women and Development formed by the ruling National Redemption Council in Ghana and the National Council of Women in Uganda formed by Idi Amin, who situated the council inside the prime minister's office. In creating the Council, Amin simultaneously banned all other independent women's organizations.

After the 1970s, the national machineries sought to promote a women in development (WID) approach. Women were to be integrated into existing institutions; they were seen as recipients of aid, which would help them become more productive. Through increased educational and employment opportunities and greater access to health and other social services, women were to gain equality and social justice. Gradually, women's roles were to expand and stereotypes that limited women would break down.

By 1991, almost all African countries had set up a national machinery of some sort. Starting in the 1990s, many countries upgraded the machineries to ministries so that by 2006, the majority of countries (thirty-six) in sub-Saharan Africa had gender ministries (see Table 7.1).

Most African countries today have national gender policies to guide the implementation of a gender equality agenda. Many are implementing programs and projects that address gender issues, including mainstreaming gender in macroeconomic policy frameworks and in sector policies. Some are reviewing constitutions and laws, enacting new gender equity–related laws, organizing training and capacity-building programs, and collecting gender-disaggregated data. A few countries have gender budgeting initiatives and are engaged in national-planning initiatives (Warioba 2004: 13).

GENDER MAINSTREAMING APPROACHES

The UN Fourth World Conference on Women in Beijing in 1995 marked a watershed in terms of government initiatives regarding women beyond the national machineries for women. The Platform of Action incorporated the terminology of "gender" and "gender mainstreaming" that became popular in the early 1990s in development circles. Women's movements started targeting government ministries and agencies as well as international organizations such as the United Nations and World Bank to incorporate gender

TABLE 7.1. *National Machineries in Africa*

| | Year National Machinery Formed | Year Ministry Formed | Current Designation of National Machinery |
|---|---|---|---|
| Angola | 1991 | 1997 | Ministry for Family Affairs and Women's Promotion |
| | | 2007 | Gender focal points (GFPs) in all ministries Ministry of Family, Development, and Gender Promotion |
| Benin | 1993 | 1997 | Ministry of Social Protection and Women Affairs GFPs in all ministries |
| Botswana | 1981 | N/A | Women's Affairs Department in the Ministry of Labour and Home Affairs GFPs in all line ministries |
| Burkina Faso | 1993 | 1997 | Ministry for the Advancement of Women |
| Burundi | 1967 | 1983 | Ministry of Social Action and Advancement of Women Focal points in 50 departments |
| Cameroon | 1975 | 2004 | Ministry of Women's Empowerment and the Family (Ministere de la Promotion de la Femme et de la Famille) |
| Cape Verde | 1994 | N/A | Institute for Gender Equality and Equity Effort to include gender perspective into development plans and programmes |
| Central African Republic | Year of formation is unknown | Year of formation is unknown | Ministry for the Promotion of Women |
| Chad | 1982 | 1988 | Ministry for the Promotion of Women and Social Affairs (Ministère de la promotion Féminine et des Affairs Sociales) Committee for the Integration of Women in Development (Comité d'Intégration de la Femme au Développement) |
| Comoros | Year of formation is unknown | N/A | National Ministry of Social Affairs addresses gender issues General Planning Department is in charge of coordinating action plans |
| Congo-Brazzaville | 1990 | 1999 | Ministry for the Promotion of Women and Integration of Women in Development (Ministre de la Promotion de la Femme et de l'Intégration de la Femme au développement) |
| Congo-Kinshasa | Year of formation is unknown | 2003 | Ministry for Women's Affairs (Ministère de la Condition Féminine) |

*(continued)*

TABLE 7.1 *(continued)*

| | Year National Machinery Formed | Year Ministry Formed | Current Designation of National Machinery |
|---|---|---|---|
| Côte d'Ivoire | Year of formation is unknown | 1976 | Ministry of the Family and the Promotion of Women's Affairs (Ministere de la Famille et de la Promotion de la Femme) |
| Djibouti | 1999 | 1999 | Ministry of Women's, Family, and Social Affairs (Ministère Chargé de la Promotion de la Femme, des Affaires Sociales et du Bien Etre Familial) |
| Equatorial Guinea | 1980 | 1992 | Ministry of Women's Affairs |
| Eritrea | 1979 | N/A | National Gender Policy mainstreams gender issues in ministries |
| Ethiopia | 1992 | N/A | Women's Affairs Office within the Prime Minister's Office Women's Affairs Departments in line ministries Women's Affairs Bureaus in 10 regional governments |
| Gabon | 1983 | 2002 | Ministry for the Family, the Protection of Children, and the Promotion of Women |
| Gambia | 1980 | N/A | Women's Bureau in the Office of the Vice President and Department of State |
| Ghana | 1975 | 2001 | Ministry for Women and Children's Affairs |
| Guinea | 1991 | 1996 | Ministry of Social Affairs and the Promotion of Women and the Child |
| Guinea-Bissau | 1985 | 1991 | Ministry of Social Affairs and Women's Empowerment |
| Kenya | 1976 | 2003 | Ministry of Gender, Sports, Culture, and Social Services |
| Lesotho | 1976 | Year of formation is unknown | Ministry of Gender, Youth, Sports, and Recreation GFPs in ministries Gender Management Forum at central and district levels |
| Liberia | 1984 | 2003 | Ministry of Gender and Development |
| Madagascar | 1976 | 1996 | Ministry of Population and the Condition of Women and Children |
| Malawi | 1984 | 1992 | Ministry of Gender, Child Welfare and Community Services GFPs in all line ministries and stakeholder organizations Cabinet Committee on Gender Issues Technical Working Group of Principal Secretaries |

|  | Year National Machinery Formed | Year Ministry Formed | Current Designation of National Machinery |
|---|---|---|---|
|  |  |  | Gender Policy Advisory Committee |
|  |  |  | District Assembly at local level |
| Mali | 1975 | 1991 | Ministry for the Promotion of Women, the Child, and the Family |
| Mauritania | 1964 | 1992 | Secretary for the Promotion of Women |
| Mauritius | 1982 | 1985 | Ministry of Women's Rights, Child Development, and Family Welfare |
|  |  |  | Women's Unit and Family Welfare Unit operates through Family Support Bureaus |
|  |  |  | GFPs in all ministries |
| Mozambique | 1973 | 2000 | Ministry for Women and Social Action |
| Namibia | 1990 | 1995 | Ministry of Gender Equality and Child Welfare |
|  |  |  | GFPs in all ministries |
| Niger | 1975 | 1998 | Ministry of Social Development, Population, Promotion of Women, and Protection of the Child |
| Nigeria | 1974 | 1995 | Ministry of Women Affairs and Social Development |
| Rwanda | 1975 | 1996 | Ministry of Gender and Family Promotion |
|  |  |  | GFPs in line ministries |
| São Tomé & Principe | Year of formation is unknown | N/A | Director of Cabinet of Women and Family Affairs |
| Senegal | 1972 | 1978 | Ministry of the Family, Social Development, and National Solidarity |
| Seychelles | 1990 | N/A | National Gender Steering Committee |
|  |  |  | Ministry of Social Affairs and Employment |
|  |  |  | GFPs in ministries |
| Sierra Leone | 1975 | 1996 | Ministry of Social Welfare, Gender, and Children's Affairs |
| Somalia | 1969 | 2004 | N/A |
| South Africa | 1997 | 1997 | *Executive Branch:* |
|  |  |  | Office on Status of Women Gender Focal Points |
|  |  |  | *Legislature:* |
|  |  |  | Joint Monitoring Committee on the Quality of Life and Status of Women Parliamentary Women's Caucus |
|  |  |  | Women's Empowerment Unit |
|  |  |  | *Independent Statutory Advisory Research Body:* |
|  |  |  | Commission on Gender Equality |

(*continued*)

TABLE 7.1 *(continued)*

| | Year National Machinery Formed | Year Ministry Formed | Current Designation of National Machinery |
|---|---|---|---|
| Sudan | 1975 | N/A | Women in development units in several ministries |
| | | | Cabinet-level advisor on women's affairs |
| Swaziland | 1975 | N/A | Gender Coordination Unit in the Ministry of Home Affairs |
| | | | GFPs in each sector |
| | | | NGO Gender Consortium |
| Tanzania | 1985 | 1992 | Ministry of Community Development, Gender, and Children (Tanzania) |
| | | | Ministry of Youth, Employment, Women, and Children Development (Zanzibar) |
| | | | GFPs in all central ministries |
| Togo | 1977 | 1977 | Ministry for Social Affairs, the Advancement of Women, and the Protection of Women |
| Uganda | 1975 | 1988 | Ministry of Gender, Labour, and Social Development |
| Zambia | 1984 | 2006 | Ministry of Women's Affairs |
| | | | *National Level:* |
| | | | Gender in Development Division |
| | | | Parliamentary Committee on Good Governance, Gender, and Human Rights |
| | | | GFPs in all line ministries |
| | | | Gender Consultative Forum |
| | | | *Provincial Level:* |
| | | | GFPs |
| | | | Gender Committees of Provincial Coordinating Committees |
| | | | *District Level:* |
| | | | Coordinating Committees |
| Zimbabwe | 1980 | 1997 | Ministry of Women's Affairs, Gender, and Community Development |
| | | | Gender Management System |
| | | | GFPs in all ministries |
| | | | Provincial gender councils |
| | | | District gender councils |

concerns both leading up to the conference and after it through various initiatives that were referred to as "gender mainstreaming." Gender mainstreaming was seen as a key to the advancement of women. The definition of gender mainstreaming is a contested concept, as are the strategies by which it can be accomplished. Generally, the term refers to pragmatic efforts to eliminate gender-based discrimination and adopt measures to promote gender equality at all stages of policy making. The term has also referred to the process of evaluating the implications of any policy, program, or legislation to make women's concerns and experiences integral to their design, implementation, and evaluation, with the goal of achieving gender equality (Council of Europe 1998: 7–8). The idea behind gender mainstreaming is not especially new, but after the 1990s it came to characterize many of the activities of national machineries of women. There had been a keen interest in integrating women into development agencies since the UN Commission on the Status of Women declared 1975 to be International Women's Year, followed by the UN Decade of Women (1976–1985) that culminated in the Nairobi Conference in 1985. But it was not until after the 1995 UN Beijing Conference on Women that key international and regional organizations such as the Commonwealth Secretariat, the European Union, the Organization for Security and Cooperation in Europe, the United Nations and its related agencies (the International Labour Organization [ILO], United Nations Development Programme [UNDP], United Nations Educational, Science, and Cultural Organization [UNESCO], the World Health Organization [WHO], etc.), the World Bank, and others began to embrace the concept of gender mainstreaming seriously. Many nongovernmental organizations (NGOs), international nongovernmental organizations (INGOs), institutions of higher learning, and a variety of other institutions followed suit.

The earlier WID approaches were replaced in the 1990s by gender and development (GAD) approaches, which, combined with gender mainstreaming, sought to target gender inequalities from the outset rather than incorporating gender into policy considerations as an afterthought. GAD, in theory, was to address power imbalances in gender relations. This approach saw the transformation of institutions as critical to the empowerment of women, who themselves were agents of change. It would be necessary to introduce a gendered approach into all institutions and all aspects of women's lives, including their economic, social, and political dimensions.

Building on the GAD approach, Zambian scholar and activist Sarah Longwe developed an "empowerment framework" that has come to be widely adopted in African contexts and applied to many projects and programs for the advancement of women. She argued that unless interventions enabled women to go through specific stages of change successfully, no transformation would be achieved. The stages vary from awareness to control: the promotion of women's rights in general; women's need to gain access and control over land and agricultural technologies; microfinance programs and easier loan acquisition frameworks; provision of strategic information through training; documentation and the media; better family laws across the continent; and finally increased women's entry into decision-making, legislative, managerial, and other bodies.

The whole field of gender analysis (gender awareness, gender training, research focused on gender) has benefited from collective African experiences. For example, African practitioners have emphasized the need to use women and men gender trainers to better identify with the learners' experiences, demystify gender to eliminate fears, show the benefits of accounting for gender equity and equality, and demonstrate that good gender practices are not exclusive to women. African-based gender analysis and training manuals are increasingly filling gaps, drawing from African experiences and understandings at national and regional levels as well as in the academy.

The African Women's Communication and Development Network (FEMNET), the Department of Women and Gender Studies at Makerere University in Uganda, the Tanzania National Gender Network, and Women in Law and Development in Africa (WILDAF) have, for example, developed gender awareness training manuals relating to their own contexts.

Gaps are still evident at policy and management levels, where gender or women's concerns still turn up as appendages and afterthoughts rather than as integral parts of complete processes. Scrutiny of major sectoral government policy documents reveals such discrepancies in Uganda and elsewhere – Five-Year Education and Health Strategic Plans and the Five-Year Strategic Plans of General Education and Higher Education show such gaps. Some explanations point to lack of expertise at the various levels in state structures. In other cases, those concerned tend to hide their inefficiency with the assertion that there is no need to include women and gender into the planning process because they will be accommodated in the implementation process, given the general level of awareness in society about these important issues.

Thus far, one of the most vexing issues in the field of gender and development is how to reach out to the individual policy maker, implementer, development practitioner, activist, and academician, both male and female, to get them personally committed to the idea that both men and women need to be on the development train for African development.

Rather than relying solely on the national machineries for women to drive gender-related policy, some countries required various ministries to create focal points to ensure that mainstreaming was implemented. In some cases, as in Ghana, there was even resistance on the part of some women's organizations to the formation of the Ministry of Women and Children's Affairs, because it was felt that women's concerns should be addressed by all the ministries (Fallon forthcoming). In a few countries, some of the focal points succeeded in carrying out their goals. However, attempts to create focal points in the ministries were not always successful. Problems arose because these focal points were not part of the mainstream civil service arrangement, nor did the individuals working at those nodes have the clout to change things because they tended to be more junior representatives. Even in Mozambique, the focal points did not have their own funding and relied on the ministry in which they were housed. Because they were not regarded as important, they received the smallest allocation of resources (Silva et al. 2005).

Another concern in setting up the ministries of women/gender is that they ghettoized women's concerns. For this reason, the Ghanaian women's movement pressed for not only a constitutional guarantee of women's rights that would empower the national machinery, but also an independent statutory body that could work across ministries, because a ministry of gender often had little jurisdiction beyond its own activities. An independent civil society would serve as an additional source of pressure to make sure that a minister with little interest in broader changes regarding the women's agenda did not hijack the body or, as in the case of a Ghanaian minister of gender, was focused only on a narrow topic such as micro-credit (Mama 2005, 130–8).

A similar concern motivated the African National Congress (ANC)-led South African government to set up a national machinery that incorporated an independent statutory body as well as the women's movement/civil society as a component of the machinery. South Africa has a fairly unusual national machinery in that it has several structures within the state, legislature, and civil society as well as statutory bodies. The aim was to create greater accountability and build a sense of activism into the machinery to make government more responsive to interests of various groups of women. Within government, there is an Office on the Status of Women (OSW) in the president's office, with provincial-level offices that report to the OSW. There are Gender Focal Points in national departments and again within local government structures. Within the legislature, there is the Joint Monitoring Committee on the Quality of Life and Status of Women, a Women's Empowerment Unit of speakers from national and provincial legislatures, and a Parliamentary Women's Caucus (when it functions). There is an independent and advisory Commission on Gender Quality nominated by the public and appointed by the president to monitor and evaluate government policies and practices as well as those of the private sector. And finally, a fourth prong includes civil society, women's organizations, and religious organizations (Gouws 2006; Hassim 2006: 219; Warioba 2004: 4).

## CRITICAL PERSPECTIVES OF APPLICATIONS OF GENDER MAINSTREAMING

One of women activists' biggest criticisms of the way in which gender mainstreaming has been applied has involved the view, often adopted by the national machineries themselves and by various ministries, that all that is required is opening up greater opportunities for women in education, decision making, and other arenas and availing them of the resources that men have already enjoyed. This is referred to as an "integrationist" approach (Verloo 2005) that seeks to give women the same opportunities as men. With the integrationist approach, little attention is given to the need to transform the gendered nature of institutions themselves so that women are not marginalized in other ways through practices that create individual and group disadvantages (Rees 2000: 3). Women are seen as "the problem" rather than as agents of change involving both men and women.

This struggle over the integrationist view came to the fore in Mozambique, where an intersectoral coordination group was charged with supervising, promoting, and following up with the implementation of the policies and programs approved by the government regarding gender and women issues. The group drafted the 2002–6 National Plan for the Advancement of Women, in which there is no reference to equality but rather only to the advancement of women. Mozambican women activists saw this as an approach that did not question the dominant power relations that perpetuated inequality, but rather sought simply to integrate women into existing institutions (Arthur, Maman, and Pedro 2000: 12).

Along similar lines, some have argued that existing gender mainstreaming models have relied too much on technocratic solutions and focus excessively on procedures and checklists rather than goals (Arnfred 2001). They have felt that the machineries were not sufficiently responsive to women's movements and had been appropriated by bureaucrats, policy makers, and consultants.

Some commentators have observed that as a result of the creation of institutions charged with gender mainstreaming and promoting gender equality, one unintended consequence is the shifting of a women's rights agenda out of the political realm and into a more technical arena, which even with the best of intentions can get gender concerns wrapped up in institutional hierarchies and obstacles. Given that most of the machineries are underresourced in Africa, having a concern "taken up" by a ministry may mean that it gets swallowed in bureaucracy and can lose key dimensions such as attentiveness to the concerns of the poor. South Africa's gender budget all but died when the Ministry of Finance took it up and initially downgraded the project and then eliminated it. Although state-initiated policies regarding women are essential, they pose serious challenges for activists when they fail (Hassim 2005: 24).

Sometimes, in practice, the notion of "gender" in gender mainstreaming becomes watered down from a notion of power relations between men and women to the idea that men also have to be incorporated in development. Many have felt that although gender equality means the equal participation of both men and women, such a focus on men would end up pushing women out of the picture once again. In other contexts, gender has been taken to mean adopting a gender-disaggregated approach to research and data, treating gender simply as a variable (Baden and Goetz 1997; Razavi and Miller 1995).

The World Bank's adoption of an older WID-type instrumental approach to gender mainstreaming, portraying it in various documents as a means to greater economic growth and efficiency, is a frame that has been adopted by various government agencies in Africa trying to make gender mainstreaming more palatable. But as Sally Baden and Anne Marie Goetz (1997) point out, it is perilous ground on which to make claims for women's advancement should it be discovered that women's education does not directly lead to increased productivity or a drop in fertility. Does that mean then that women don't need to be educated or have access to birth control if these woman-friendly policies don't directly and immediately lead to greater production efficiencies and other economic benefits for society?

Thus, the notion of gender has in recent years come to mean for some women activists not subsuming women's interests into the national goals as it did in the past, but rather paying particular attention to the advancement of women's status within the context of uplifting the entire society. Improving women's status in the household means improving the welfare of the entire household. At the same time, women's welfare will not improve without addressing the political and economic constraints that impede development more generally. Women continue to struggle for recognition of their active citizenship and their contributions in the context of opening spaces for more political participation, protecting human rights, promoting greater governmental transparency, and institutionalizing pluralism and political democracy. Women have been making important contributions to all these processes, but their roles have not always been acknowledged, as seen in their peace initiatives in civil conflicts, because politicians see them as a threat to their power.

## NATIONAL MACHINERIES AS AGENTS OF CHANGE?

Some women's movements in Africa have supported the formation of national machineries as a mechanism to promote gender equality. Others, however, have seen them as sources of cooptation of women, especially where women's movements are weak. In some countries such as Ghana and Mozambique, some women's organizations even opposed the formation of the ministries, having seen how little they had done for women in other parts of Africa due to underresourcing. When there was talk of creating a national machinery in South Africa in 1994, there was concern that such an agency would entrench the worst tendencies of state-directed feminism that involved cooptation of the women's movement and protection of the interests of a small elite of women inside government without altering women's subordinate status in society. In addition, there was concern about the machinery's inability to defend women's interests in the face of competing interests, including dominant political interests, and an unwillingness to address power inequalities between men and women and among women themselves. In South Africa, these concerns led to an elaborate set of mechanisms and strategies to create accountability within the national machinery and multiple sites of activism (Hassim 2006: 214–16). These types of apprehensions have driven many of the debates surrounding national machineries globally, according to Shirin Rai (2003).

In general, national machineries have not been very effective in most African countries, largely because they have tended to be underresourced by central government (Mama 1995: 40; Rai 2003; Tsikata 1989: 81). When national machineries have been embedded in ministries, it has usually been within those related to social or welfare activities such as ministries of social work or community development rather than within the most important strategic units of government, such as the ministry of finance. Moreover, the machineries do not always coordinate properly with national planning and budgeting structures, especially in countries that do not have gender budgeting initiatives.

Sometimes the machineries lack the authority with which to influence various ministries. In South Africa, the Office on the Status of Women is situated in the Office of the President but has no direct access to the cabinet or interministerial committees. The gender focal points within the ministries similarly have little or no authority to integrate gender equity concerns into policy frameworks in their ministries. This is further hampered by the lack of a broad framework setting priorities and establishing policy goals that could be legitimated politically, thereby forming the basis for advocacy within the ministries (Hassim 2006: 225–7).

In Mozambique, prior to 1999, the older Ministry for Coordination of Social Action had been charged with supervising intersectoral activities, including those relating to gender. The ministry had little clout and even less money. There was no plan to approach gender concerns in a concerted and holistic fashion. Thus, most ministers did not pay attention to gender, which they relegated to the Ministry of Social Action. National machineries find themselves with weak central government commitments to mainstreaming and a lack of accountability in monitoring and evaluating its effects. Gender units, or focal points in ministries, are often accorded low status within organizations and are staffed by junior people, making it difficult for them to carry sufficient weight. Thus, many of the problems facing the national machineries flow from this indifference and relatively weak funding base.

National machineries often do not have clear mandates or their mandates are too broad for the resources allocated to them. In Mozambique, the committee coordinating intersectoral gender-related activities and the gender units within the various ministries do not have a clearly defined mandate or set of responsibilities. This hampers the committee's work, especially at the provincial and district levels.

Frequently, any gender issue that comes into the public eye is expected to be solved by the ministry or department of gender, which in turn gets blamed for not doing enough despite the lack of supportive mechanisms and resources. They may be called on by other ministries, by parliamentarians, by communities, and by a broad range of constituencies. They often work with poor data and information at their disposal. Machineries generally have poorly paid and trained staffs, with rapid turnover as a result. Many African countries have developed national gender policies. However, because the ministries have no means of enforcing adherence to these policies, with no carrots or sticks to offer, their plans remain largely on paper.

Some ministers of gender/women and heads of national machineries come from the women's movement and are fierce advocates for women's rights. But frequently they are political appointees with conflicting allegiances. How aggressively a national machinery pursues gender issues depends a great deal on the inclinations of the top leadership. Similarly, some national machinery employees are femocrats tied to women's movements, but others are simply government bureaucrats. The latter may not go out of their way to ensure gender equity and equality because they do not have adequate training, resources, and commitment to the broader goals of the national machinery.

## WOMEN'S MOVEMENTS AND NATIONAL MACHINERIES

One of the main debates and tensions in gender mainstreaming in Africa has revolved around the role of women's movements and ways in which they engage national machineries and gender mainstreaming strategies. Efforts to mainstream gender policy have frequently been contested and in some cases highly politicized. Women's movements have both collaborated and struggled with national machineries to shape the gender policy agenda: They have contested specific policies, goals, and strategies, and have questioned policies when they have neglected various key constituencies of women, especially rural women.

During the one-party era, the national machineries competed for power and resources with the women's wings and party mass women's organizations run by first ladies and relatives of top party leaders. Later, after the 1990s, their relations with independent women's organizations were strained as they vied for support from donors for legal awareness training, constitution-making programs, gender budgeting initiatives, and other such projects. Moreover, some women's rights activists have claimed that machineries have actively worked against women's associations. Not surprisingly, today, linkages and coordination with women's NGOs are often weak, resulting in duplication of efforts and competition for limited resources (Tsikata 2001; Warioba 2004: 14).

The authority of national machineries in developing gender policy has been a source of tension with women's organizations. This is because the machineries have the mandate and international recognition, but not always the commensurate capacity, whereas many NGOs are clearly in a better position to develop policy and articulate a coherent agenda regarding women's rights but do not have the institutional standing that they would need to negotiate with national machineries to advance their policy goals. In some countries, the women's NGOs or women's coalitions prepared the government policy statements for international conferences, such as the UN Beijing conference in 1995, and fruitful collaborations emerged between NGOs and the machineries, drawing on the respective strengths and capacities of both entities. In other countries, when national machineries reported to UN bodies, women's organizations did not always trust their data. Women's organizations were sometimes concerned that they were not being consulted by the national machineries. Some machineries would claim in advance that they had consulted women's NGOs in order to avoid such accusations, when in fact they had not, only raising further suspicions. In turn, the national machineries charged NGOs with lack of integrity and questioned their representativeness.

Mutual mistrust between the machineries and NGOs was exacerbated as the relations between the machineries and women's organizations were poorly defined (Tsikata 2001). Such was the case in the late 1980s in Uganda, when the machinery at the time, the National Council for Women, circulated a statement to all its branches around the country urging them not to welcome a new women's organization called Action for Development, which had suggested a restructuring of the Council to separate the official government component from the NGO unit.

In some countries, the ministries went out of their way to prevent the registration of women's NGOs or sought to deregister them. The Tanzania Gender Networking Programme (TGNP) had trouble registering because of fears in the Ministry of Community Affairs, Women and Children that it would eclipse the ministry's efforts and those of the ruling party's Women's Union (Umoja wa Wanawake wa Tanzania [UWT]) to coordinate women's mobilization. These tensions became especially apparent when TGNP began playing a leading role in mobilizing women's NGOs for the 1995 United Nations Women's Conference in Beijing. The Ministry of Community Development, Women's Affairs and Children also had a major hand in using the courts and the Ministry of Interior to try to destroy a semi-independent women's organization, the Tanzanian Women's Council (Baraza la Wanawake [BAWATA]), discussed in Chapter 3. In fact, the organization was the brainchild of the ministry, which had decided to form a nongovernmental umbrella organization that would include all women's groups in Tanzania, one that was ostensibly independent but still under the control of UWT. The ministry felt that because of the difficulties NGOs had working with the ministry, it might be easier to monitor and regulate them through a separate council. However, when BAWATA itself became more independent of UWT and the ministry than the ministry had intended, the ministry sought to ban it, claiming that the organization had become too "political." BAWATA took its case against the government to the High Court and won; however, in the process, the organization was destroyed as a result of intimidation and pressure on its leaders and their spouses. This suggests just how threatened the national machinery can become as a result of activities of independent NGOs.

The conflict between women's organizations and the national machinery in Zambia was especially acrimonious. In Zambia, historically the impetus for legislative change has not come from the national gender machinery, which was formed in 1984. No women's rights legislation had been enacted in the first decade after independence. The first steps in the mid-1980s to pass key gender-related legislation were taken by women's NGOs. The Non-Governmental Organization Coordinating Committee (NGOCC), the Zambia Association for Research and Development, and a group of new women's NGOs initiated a campaign to pass a bill that would entitle a widow and children to the family home and 75 percent of the estate. Polls showed that 96 percent of Zambians supported the bill but it was nevertheless initially rejected by the legislature in 1987. The bill finally passed in 1989 after concerted NGO lobbying of parliamentarians. Similarly, as indicated in Chapter 6, Zambian women activists from the National Women's Lobby Group and others were instrumental in changing discriminatory clauses in the 1991 constitution, although these activists succeeded with little support from the national machinery (Ferguson and Katundu 1994: 19; Osei-Hwedie 1998: 91; Schuster 1983: 24).

The depth of the chasm between the national machinery and the women's movement became evident when in 2006 Zambia's President Levy Patrick Mwanawasa created a Ministry of Women's Affairs and appointed a former leader of the opposition party as the minister. The NGOCC, Women for Change, and other women's organizations opposed the move, calling instead for a gender equality commission, as the women's movement had proposed in submissions to the Constitution Review Commission. They said they wanted a genuine mechanism that could enforce the implementation of international women's rights conventions and instruments in Zambia. The women activists argued that the position had been created as a carrot to reward the new minister for helping Mwanawasa's party gain a presence in the Eastern Province and it therefore was politically motivated as a means of obtaining votes rather than as a vehicle for genuine change (Phiri 2006). They felt that had the government been serious about women's rights, it would have done everything in its power to amend the constitution to give citizens full protection against discrimination and see that regional and international human rights treaties were realized in Zambian law.

The deep distrust of the machinery did not subside with its formation and many activists have felt it has not been effective in initiating, coordinating, and enforcing gender policy. The debates over the women's ministry in Zambia reflect some of the antipathy women's movements have had for national machineries and the ways in which these machineries have been used to signal concern for women's rights to international UN monitoring bodies without doing much substantively to advance women's status.

Women's movements in Zambia and elsewhere have increasingly become impatient with mere rhetoric and are demanding concrete change in women's status.

In Ghana, a similar rift between the ministry and women's NGOs emerged with the drafting of the Women's Manifesto, which had broad-based support and drew active involvement from women's organizations and districts throughout the country. The ministry refused to participate in the initiative and instead issued its own gender policy a day before the Manifesto was launched to preempt the activities of the NGO coalition (Mama 2005: 130–8). Earlier tensions had arisen when the Ministry of Women and Children had blocked a domestic violence bill being supported by a coalition of over forty local organizations and individuals. The activists accused the ministry of delaying the introduction of the bill in parliament by conducting a survey of views regarding the bill in all regions of Ghana. When the bill finally was enacted in 1995, it left out a key clause forbidding marital rape, which the minister and president had been instrumental in excluding despite fierce protests by women's rights activists (Fallon forthcoming).

One might argue that the gulfs between the movements and national machineries are ultimately counterproductive and will need to be bridged, because although the movements in general have greater capacity and knowledge, national machineries potentially have a critical role to play in developing policies and seeing that key legislation is enacted.

CONSEQUENCES OF UNDERFUNDING NATIONAL MACHINERIES:
THE CASE OF UGANDA

As mentioned earlier, the key constraint on national machineries has been a lack of resources. Sometimes ministries live or die depending on foreign donor support. Uganda's national machinery was a full ministry at its height in 1988, the Ministry of Women in Development. Already at that time it had gone through numerous permutations (see Table 7.2). It was then reduced to a department of Gender, Culture and Community Development in the Ministry of Gender, Labour, and Social Development in 1999, where it has been sidelined. Its various permutations have also put strain and uncertainty on the ministry and have been destabilizing to its functioning (Kwesiga 2003: 206). Its diminished status – with only two individuals in charge of the gender unit and a staff of eight, down from twenty-six in 1994 – have been accompanied by a shrinking budget (Gawaya-Tegulle and Kemigisha 2000: 1). As of 2003, the gender unit was receiving only 10 percent of the budget of the entire ministry with an annual allocation of USD 200,000 coming

TABLE 7.2. *Changes in Uganda's National Machinery Configurations, 1955–Present*

| Year | Bureau |
|------|--------|
| 1955 | Department of Welfare and Community Development |
| 1962 | Ministry of Community Development, Culture, and Sports; Department of Welfare and Community Development |
| 1978 | National Council of Women, Prime Minister's Office |
| 1988 | Ministry of Women in Development under a minister of state |
| 1992 | Ministry of Women in Development, Culture, and Youth |
| 1994 | Ministry of Gender and Community Development |
| 1998 | Ministry of Gender, Labour, and Social Development |
| 1999 | Department of Gender, Culture, and Community Development in the Ministry of Gender, Labour and Social Development |

*Source:* Kwesiga 2003.

from the Japanese Women in Development Trust Fund and the United Nations Capital Development Fund (Uganda 2003). Moreover, its responsibilities increased without commensurate authority and without political commitment from the top of the administration (Kwesiga 2003: 211).

At its height and prior to its downgrading to a small department, the ministry had succeeded in formulating a national gender policy. It had provided training in gender planning and analysis for permanent secretaries, heads of departments, magistrates, and state attorneys, which has helped move mainstreaming initiatives forward in the civil service. The ministry had also helped review sector policies for their gender outcomes and it had published gender-disaggregated data to be used by women's NGOs and other stakeholders. It strived to ensure that gender mainstreaming became part of the formulation and implementation of government policies such as the national Poverty Eradication Action Plan.

The ministry helped national- and district-level administrations in evaluating the extent to which both women and men benefited from various projects, including decentralization. It provided some legal education programs for women and collaborated with paralegal workers. Moreover, it had also been a mechanism through which awareness regarding gender concerns had been raised. The national machinery helped stimulate interest in gender inequality and legitimized gender concerns more broadly (Kwesiga 2003: 214–15).

The drop in support for the ministry is reflected in the decline in collaboration between the ministry and women's organizations, which had been strong between 1989 and 1996 at a time when the ministry benefited greatly from support from the Danish International Development Agency (DANIDA). During those years, the ministry and women's organizations collected memoranda for the Constitutional Commission from around the country in a countrywide exercise of constitutional consultations (1989–92). The NGO Law Reform Fund (1991–4) carried out countrywide consultations on the Domestic Relations Bill, which is now languishing. The Pilot Micro Credit and Legal Aid projects were conducted for women in Jinja, Kapchorwa, Mbale, and Mukono (1992–6). With the conclusion of ten years of DANIDA support, these programs effectively came to an end. DANIDA was unhappy with the fact that after all it had invested in the Ministry of Women, the national machinery was diminished and relegated to a small department within a larger entity. The end of Danish support, coupled with the reorganization of the ministry, the retrenchment of the civil service, and the subsequent drops in staff, dramatically limited the scope and possibilities for gender initiatives in the ministry (Mpagi 2002).[1]

Without a directorate of gender, many of the gains that had been made were lost, although those projects with continued funding – such as the gender budgeting initiative, described in the next section – continued and thrived. Uganda's experience with the downgrading, restructuring, and disruptions caused by the shifting of the locus of the national machinery from one ministerial configuration to another is similar to negative effects experienced in other countries as well and is indicative of the low status accorded national machineries (Rai 2003).

A COMMITMENT TO GENDER EQUALITY: THE CASE OF GENDER MAINSTREAMING IN MOZAMBIQUE

The Frente de Libertação de Moçambique (FRELIMO)–led government in Mozambique has a stated commitment to gender equality and has placed the goal of advancing the status of women at the center of its political, economic, and social policies.[2] The UN Beijing Conference on Women in 1995 reinforced this. Outside of government agencies, NGOs and civil society were seen as key to the success of gender mainstreaming, as were international

---

[1] Interview with Jane Mpagi conducted by Aili Tripp, January 2002.
[2] These policies include the Economic and Social Plan (PES), the Medium Term Fiscal Framework (MTFF), the Poverty Reduction Action Plan (PARPA), the Sector Integrated Programs (SIPs), and the national budget.

donors. In fact, Mozambique is unique in the extent to which NGOs and networks,[3] research institutions[4] and other women's rights entities serve on state bodies and government commissions. From the top level on down, there has been an expressed need to increase women's rights within Mozambican society, incorporate gender perspectives and analysis into national development plans, increase women's participation in decision making at all levels and in all arenas of society, review all legislation for gender bias, improve the working conditions for mothers, increase female enrollment in schools and universities, and improve the livelihood of female heads of households.

Thus far, only the sectors of education, health, and social welfare have demonstrated progress, while other sectors have not shown comparable results. According to a study by Maimuna Ibraimo (2003), the reasons for these discrepancies have to do with a lack of consensus on who should define and fund the gender initiatives and a lack of technical capacity to do so. Accompanying this lack of commitment is a lack of awareness of the importance of integrating gender into policy making and efforts by various ministries to shift the responsibility (and costs) of gender mainstreaming onto the Ministry of Finance and Planning.

As a result of the Mozambican state's political will and commitment to promote gender equality between women and men, the government transformed the Ministry for Co-ordination of Social Action (MICAS), created in 1995, into the Ministry of Women and Co-ordination of Social Action (MMCAS) by presidential decree in 2000. This transformation occurred in response to the Southern African Development Community (SADC) Declaration on Gender and Development in 1997. The main tasks of this new ministry were to direct the coordination and implementation of policies that ensure women's empowerment at all levels and areas and to see that women's needs and concerns are an integral part of the development agenda. MMCAS has developed a number of mechanisms to carry out gender mainstreaming. It established a Gender Institutional Capacity Building Project, which is aimed at enhancing the institutional technical capacity of the ministry for implementation and coordination of programs that promote equality and equity in gender and the improvement of gender integration in all aspects of social and economic plans. MMCAS set up the National Directorate of Women (DNM) within the ministry.

---

[3] Such networks include Fórum Mulher (Woman's Fórum), Link, NGO Forum, and Women and Law in Southern Africa (Mozambique).

[4] An example of such an institute is Cruzeiro do Sul–Instituto de Investigação para o Desenvolvimento (Southern Cross–Research Institute for Development).

At the national level, the Conselho Nacional para o Avanço da Mulher (National Council for the Advancement of Woman), created by decree of the Council of Ministers in 2004, brings together members of the Council of Ministers with representatives of government institutions, independent organizations, and other public and private institutions. The Council has forty-two members at the national level and thirty to thirty-five members at the provincial level (Silva et al. 2005). In 2005, the government created the Ministry for Women and Social Action, and the National Council or directorate continues to exist within it.

The Council of Ministers that oversees the ministries has an Operative Group for the Advancement of Women (Grupo Operativo para o Avanço da Mulher [GOAM]), which was created after the 1995 Beijing conference by MMCAS as an intersectoral coordination body to coordinate the implementation of gender policy and monitor the government's plan of action. This plan of action became the 2002–6 National Plan for the Advancement of Women. The GOAM combined representatives from the fifteen ministries, from the Center of African Studies at Eduardo Mondlane University, and from women's associations, including Fórum Mulher, the Mozambican Association for Women Law Professionals (AMMCJ), and Wakhela (an association on education). GOAM created gender units and focal points in all government institutions in order to implement sectoral programs (Silva et al. 2005).

Gender mainstreaming initiatives were incorporated into the mandates of all the ministries. GOAM not only works with the ministries, it brings together all the relevant stakeholders in the various sectors of health, markets, and social protection, including NGOs, donors, and others. One goal was to increase the number of girls entering primary school from 43 percent in 2000 to 48 percent in 2005. To do this, the Ministry of Education worked with various ministries with the help of GOAM. Mozambique increased the number of female teachers at a rate of 2 percent a year through a scholarship program, exempted most poor households from a tax, improved the quality of school principals, and provided school materials to children from the poorest households. Budget changes were made to provide reallocations to the most impoverished areas of the country. Curricular reform incorporated human rights awareness, the impact of sexual harassment and abuse, and other such issues.

There are a number of other mechanisms that contribute to the promotion of gender equality and women's empowerment programs and policies. These include the Commission of Social, Gender, and Environmental Affairs (CASGA) and the Office of Women Parliamentarians (Silva et al.

2005). Other partners include the Gender Donor Group (GDG), formed in 1998, which included gender advisors from donor agencies together with representatives of Fórum Mulher and the National Directorate of Women. After 2005, it was renamed the Gender Coordinating Group. The United Nations agencies have a Gender Thematic Group (GTG) to coordinate activities related to gender issues. Fórum Mulher, as the main network regarding women and gender, is the key mechanism of coordination among women's organizations and also with other civil society organizations. It trained over half the GOAM members in policy analysis from a gender perspective.

In spite of the existence of these important bodies linking government, civil society, and international institutions, women activists feel more could be done in terms of implementation. Problems remain with coordination at national, provincial, and local levels, and in many cases there is duplication of activities (Silva et al. 2005: 80). Mozambique faces many of the same problems that other African countries face in gender mainstreaming: a lack of authority on the part of the National Council for the Advancement of Women, limited resources to implement policies, a lack of training in gender mainstreaming, and an absence of a coherent policy to institutionalize gender equality.

In spite of all the problems with the ministries, the incorporation of the gender approach within the state institutions and NGOs contributed to advancing women's rights, but at the same time it institutionalized gender technocracy (Arnfred 2001). Women were incorporated but not always with a gender and holistic perspective. For example, with the creation of the Ministry of Women and the Coordination of Social Action, women gained the status of minorities and of victims rather than of political and economic actors. The ministry has been important for lobbying and pushing for the government to sign international documents regarding women's rights. But women's movements are also cognizant of the fact that the states can be the prime violators of human and women rights. Nevertheless, legal change has been an important tool in advancing respect for human rights (Facio 1997: 5–7).

LIMITED GAINS: THE CASE OF CAMEROON

Cameroon responded to the UN push to create national machineries for women by forming in 1975 a women's unit within the Ministry of Social Affairs. Almost a decade later in 1984, Cameroon was one of the first African countries to create a separate Ministry for Women's Affairs (MINCOF), prior to the UN Nairobi Conference on Women in 1985. Lack of funding, ill-defined relations with other ministries, and poor training of MINCOF personnel plagued the ministry in its early years. It did not have an institutional mechanism or the authority to hold other ministries accountable in spite of its mandate to provide oversight on how the ministries addressed women's concerns (Adams 2004a: 12).

In 1988, the Ministry of Women merged with the Ministry for Social Affairs and became the Ministry for Social and Women's Affairs, popularly known by its French acronym, MINASCOF. A directorate directed the Advancement of Women Affairs. A decade later, a 1997 Presidential decree reorganizing the government again split MINASCOF into the Ministry for Women's Affairs (MINCOF) and the Ministry for Social Affairs. The ministry underwent yet another transformation in 2004 and was renamed the Ministry of Women's Empowerment and the Family (Ministere de la Promotion de la Femme et de la Famille [MINPROFF]). The Ministry of Women's goals included the reduction of the gender gap, the strengthening of women's capacities, and the mainstreaming of women's development initiatives. After 1997, the reconfigured ministry expanded its presence in the provinces among grassroots women. Although the ministry gave women's advancement a larger profile, it remained hampered by budgetary constraints. MINCOF's share of the national government budget diminished from 0.66 to 0.41 percent between 2000 and 2002 (Adams 2004a: 17).[5] Nevertheless, compared to the budgets of gender ministries in other parts of Africa, MINCOF's is relatively large. The ministry reported in 2004 that it had 708 personnel.

The external services of the ministry reflect the administrative setup of the country: They are comprised of provincial delegations and of divisional and district offices across the country. The ministry runs thirty-five Appropriate Technology Centers and Centres for the Advancement of Women in nine out of ten provinces, focusing on information and skills training in petty trading and dressmaking and on primary and health education for girls and women. It organizes scholarships, capacity-building workshops, and seminars for women and conducts studies. More importantly, it has been able to deliver credit, farm tools, small machinery, and other farming inputs to local grassroots organizations.

It developed a National Policy on Women in Development (1999), which addresses women's living conditions, legal status, role in development and

---

[5] CEDAW/C/CMR/1 9 May 1999, Consideration of Reports Submitted by States Parties under Article 18 of the Convention on the Elimination of All Forms of Discrimination against Women, Cameroon.

decision making, the girl child,[6] violence against women, and improvement of the institutional framework to address these concerns (Adams 2004a: 16). The ministry also formulated a Multi-Sectoral Plan for the Advancement of Women to address goals set in the 1995 UN Beijing Platform for Action, including the improvement of the legal status of women and the elimination of violence against women.[7]

The ministry promotes women's political empowerment through activities such as the convening of interparty consultative meetings and the production of advocacy and sensitization materials. More importantly, it has the means by which to intervene through a general secretariat, gender inspectorate, and technical directorates and local departments in the provinces. The ministry has also facilitated the review of the draft Family Code initiated by the Cameroon Association of Female Jurists and was involved in developing a bill on violence against women. It has developed a national action plan on the elimination of female genital cutting and plans have been adopted to improve the health and living conditions of women.

MINCOF participated actively in regional and international events and activities of the women's movement. In 1994, Cameroon ratified CEDAW. MINCOF organizes international women's day events and generates public discussions of topics such as practices and customs that discriminate against women. The ministry formed a committee of Women Ministers and Parliamentarians and has promoted the advancement of women in the civil service. It has established focal points in various ministerial departments and contributed to programs relating to women under the purview of other ministries, including the ministries of agriculture, public investments and territorial development, public health, and national education.

In sum, Cameroon has made some important advances in developing policy regarding women's concerns. After the Beijing conference, there were some modest reforms taken: Women and men workers, for example, can claim housing benefits on an equal basis, and girls who leave school due to pregnancy can be readmitted (Adams 2003).

Nevertheless, in spite of best efforts, outcomes in Cameroon with respect to women have been less than impressive, especially when one compares the

---

[6] The girl child is a reference to particular issues girls face in Africa and elsewhere, including early marriage, female genital mutilation, child labor, sexual and physical abuse, sexual exploitation and trafficking, son preference, and discrimination in education, health care, food intake, and other areas.

[7] Committee on the Elimination of Discrimination against Women Twenty-Third Session Summary Record of the 476th Meeting Held at Headquarters, New York, on Tuesday, 20 June, at 10 A.M., 2001. CEDAW/C/SR.476.

outcomes with the kinds of changes that we are witnessing in other parts of Africa. Most of the new legislation that is being developed is still pending, Cameroon has not launched a major gender budgeting program, and women are poorly represented in the legislature and within government. The government's response to demands for legal reforms has been slow. MINCOF basically lacks the funds and necessary trained personnel to achieve its goals and is operating within a state that is at best ambivalent about its support for women's rights.

## GENDER BUDGETING

One of the most important gender mainstreaming initiatives that has generated considerable momentum in Africa has been the adoption of "gender budgets," or attempts to make the gender implications of national spending priorities more explicit and ultimately fairer. After the 1995 Beijing UN Women's Conference, many countries adopted women's budgets patterned along the lines of Australia's 1984 budget initiatives and South Africa's 1994 budget exercise. By 2000, gender-sensitive budget initiatives were under way in eighteen countries in four regions and by 2006 there were over thirty such efforts. The most progress has been made to date in East Africa and South Asia.[8]

The Ministry of Finance generally coordinated gender-responsive budget initiatives, which involved collaboration among nongovernmental organizations and the legislature. The gender budgeting process involved analysis of existing budgets to determine how government spending impacted women and men (also girls and boys) differently. The ministry also made recommendations for future budgets to improve equity in the way in which funds were allocated (Budlender 2000).

Much of the impetus for gender budgeting initially came through the Commonwealth Secretariat, which in the late 1990s started its Engender Budgets program. Finance ministers were engaged in the process and had to report on progress periodically at their annual ministerial meetings. This accounts for why most of the countries initiating the gender budget reviews were formerly part of the British Empire, including Barbados, Botswana, Malawi, Namibia, Sri Lanka, Tanzania, Uganda, and Zimbabwe as well as Australia. SADC has also encouraged gender budgets as well as the United

---

[8] Commonwealth Secretariat, Commonwealth Secretariat Panel Presentation on Gender Budgeting Experiences in Commonwealth Countries, http://www.gender-budgets.org/, accessed 21 May 2008.

Nations Fund for Women (UNIFEM). The majority of these initiatives in Africa started with nongovernmental actors, which engaged government.

## Gender Budgeting in Uganda

Gender mainstreaming efforts in Uganda focused on a Gender Budget Initiative (GBI), which came out of a project of the Forum for Women in Democracy (FOWODE), an independent NGO. Pressure from FOWODE was also responsible for attempting to create greater transparency and accountability in legislative decision making regarding the national budget, and several gains were made on this front, including the creation of a budget office. The GBI is now being implemented by the Ministry of Finance in conjunction with the Ministry of Gender, Labour, and Social Development in twenty-four districts (2002–8), prioritizing agriculture, water, sanitation, health, education, and roads. One aim of the GBI is to create a gender-responsive Poverty Eradication Action Plan (PEAP).

Research by women's associations in Uganda revealed that national and local government budgets had not considered gender an important variable. In some cases, consideration of gender at the district level was limited to the provision of funds to annual International Women's Day celebrations on 8 March.

From the outset, the Ugandan GBI focused on local governments, which were not receiving their share of resources. They discovered that 60 percent of the country's health resources were being directed to the teaching hospital in Kampala with minimal resources being allocated to the districts. As a result of the GBI, more health resources were redirected to the rural areas. Similar reallocations of funding have taken place in spending on agriculture, which no longer goes simply to bureaucrats in the capital but increasingly to male and female producers in the countryside. Likewise, more funds have been redirected to help girls to complete their primary education (Fleshman 2002: 4).

Training in gender budgeting therefore became very important and a relatively large number of women's rights associations have taken up this task, trained leaders, and produced manuals for reference.[9] As a result, at least at the local government level, there is evidence that this requirement

---

[9] Such organizations include ActionAid, Action for Development (ACFODE), the Association of Professional Women in Agriculture and Environment (AUPWAE), the Coalition for Political Accountability of Women (COPAW), the Council for Economic Empowerment of

is being taken into account, although at the national level the budget leaves much to be desired from a gender equity point of view (ACFODE 2005).

The central government made funds available to the districts' Local Government Development Program if the program could show how its activities were promoting gender equity and equality. Successful districts such as Luwero offered funds to initiatives led by women councilors. Other successful districts sought to improve representation of women in local government leadership positions, the gender distribution of contract awards for technical services provision, and the procurement of goods and services for the National Agricultural Advisory Services.

## Gender Budgeting in Mozambique

Fórum Mulher has been working with the Tanzania Gender Networking Program on developing a gender budgeting program, training personnel from various ministries, including the ministries of planning and finance, health, education, and home affairs. One of the challenges of gender budgeting in Mozambique is that it comes at a time when the country is both trying to privatize its economy and at the same time implement an action plan for the Reduction of Absolute Poverty (PARPA) to offset the social costs of privatization. Mozambique is also trying to increase public revenue by expanding its tax base. Because most Mozambicans are involved in smallholder production and the informal economy, this is enormously challenging because minimum wage earners, small-scale producers, low-income individuals, and basic goods and services are not subject to tax. Moreover, fees cannot be charged for primary education and health care services. Nevertheless, this taxation system protects women, who are generally at the lowest pay scales and can be found primarily in agricultural production and informal sector activities. They are frequently the main person in the household responsible for feeding the family and for taking care of the sick and elderly and seeing that children are schooled. The reduction of taxes in all these areas has direct bearing on women's lives and lightens the heavy burdens that they already shoulder. Free schooling lifts some of the financial constraints that one finds in other countries that prevent girls from being educated. Free health care has implications not only for a better quality of

Women in Africa (CEEWA), the East African Women Support Initiative (EASSI), and the Uganda Debt Network (UDN).

life, but also for increased labor productivity, fertility rates, and ultimately for poverty reduction.

CONCLUSIONS

The interest in gender mainstreaming evolved in Africa as a result of a conjuncture of multiple pressures from women's movements, international bodies such as the United Nations, and foreign donors. Regional bodies such as SADC also promoted gender mainstreaming, creating additional regional incentives to comply. Governments adopted these measures in response to domestic pressures and the availability of donor funds, and at times to present to the international community the aura of progress in the area of gender equality in order to be seen as moving toward "modernity."

Nevertheless, many of these gender mainstreaming initiatives were fraught with difficulties, in part because of tensions and competition between women's organizations and national machineries, but also because governments rarely provided the women's machineries with the requisite financial resources and personnel. Moreover, the machineries or focal points generally lacked sufficient authority with which to provide leadership to other ministries and units in gender mainstreaming.

Although Mozambique faces many of the same problems as other countries with respect to its national machinery, it has been able to do more because it has taken advantage of the productive synergies that have been produced by combining the resources, skills, and input of women's organizations, academics, and government officials. Each sector can compensate for the limitations of the other, and each has important but different contributions to offer. Without an independent women's movement, the utility of these kinds of synergies is diminished because of the absence of differing and alternative points of view, experiences, and resources.

# 8

# Women's Movements Negotiating Peace

The steady end to a significant number of conflicts in Africa since the mid-1980s has been an important change in the African political landscape. Sometimes low-grade conflict continued in the aftermath of a negotiated peace agreement. Major settlements occurred after the end of national wars of liberation in Namibia and South Africa. Civil conflicts diminished or came to an end in countries such as Angola (2002), Burundi (2004), Chad, (2002), the Democratic Republic of Congo (2002), Liberia (2003), Mozambique (1992), Rwanda (1994), Sierra Leone (2002), southern Sudan (2005), and northern Uganda (2007).

With the winding down of almost all these major conflicts, women's organizations vigorously pressed for increased political representation and changes in policy and legislation regarding women's rights. Unlike the post-conflict situations prior to the 1990s, and especially after 2000, women now were beginning to see many of their aspirations for greater rights addressed through new constitutions and the passage of legislation. International norms were changing, as evident in governmental commitments made at the 1995 Beijing United Nations Conference on Women and in other international and regional treaties and conventions.

One of the clearest examples of this change is in the area of women's legislative representation. In African countries where conflicts ended after 1985, women hold, on average, 24 percent of legislative seats compared with countries that did not experience conflict, where women account for only 13 percent of the legislative seats. Rwanda has the highest rate of representation for women in the world, with 49 percent of its parliamentary seats held by women. Women in postconflict Burundi, Mozambique, South Africa, and Uganda claim over 30 percent of their countries' parliamentary seats in a continent where the average percentage of women-held seats is

17 percent. The higher rates are in large part due to the introduction of quotas aimed at increasing the representation of women. Women have also been running in presidential elections in increasing numbers throughout Africa, but noticeably in postconflict countries, such as the Democratic Republic of Congo (2006), Liberia (2005), Rwanda (2003), and Sierra Leone (2002). Liberia's Ellen Johnson-Sirleaf became the first elected woman president in Africa in 2005.

There are a number of reasons for this heightened interest by women in political representation and policy change in postconflict countries. First, the conflicts had a leveling effect as societies sought to re-create themselves through the writing of new constitutions and the implementation of new rules of governance. Women's organizations seized on this window of opportunity and demanded greater political representation. They did not have male incumbents to contend with or to oust from legislative seats (Tripp 2001a).

Second, women themselves had experiences mobilizing for peace during the conflict and during the peace talks. They came out of long periods of conflict determined to prevent a reversal of the peace process and to participate in the new political order to ensure that their rights were protected. They had the organizing skills, experience, and political muscle to assert themselves in the postconflict context. They had tried both successfully (e.g., Burundi) and unsuccessfully to influence peace negotiations and wanted a place at the table in the new political arrangement.

Third, foreign donors and international agencies of the United Nations were putting pressure on governments to address women's rights in a concerted manner. New international norms had embraced the need for women's empowerment in postconflict contexts through constitutional, legislative, and other means.

Finally, prolonged conflict also disrupted gender roles, thrusting women into new activities in the absence of men. In many cases, they ran businesses and sought new sources of livelihood, took over household finances and supported the household, learned how to drive, and played active roles in communities in new ways. These transformations continued in the postconflict period.

This chapter explores the role of women's movements in the context of peace building. It situates the Mozambican and Ugandan cases in the context of the broader trends, showing how conflict and peace and the emergence of peace and women's movements in these countries represented key moments and turning points in the history of women's activism. The end of Mozambique's war with its Portuguese colonizers (1964–74) produced some changes for women, but like other conflicts ending at this time, the changes were not as far reaching as those that followed the end of Mozambique's conflict between Frente de Libertação de Moçambique (FRELIMO) and Resistência Nacional Moçambicana (RENAMO) (1974–92). This chapter examines the reasons for this shift, which occurred throughout Africa in the mid-1980s, beginning with the end of conflict in Uganda (1980–6). The more recent decline of conflict in northern Uganda after 2006 belongs to a later trend of decline in some of the deadliest and longest-lasting conflicts in Africa after 2000: Angola, Burundi, Democratic Republic of Congo, Liberia, Sierra Leone, and southern Sudan.

## TURNING POINT IN WOMEN'S MOBILIZATION

Uganda was the first of this new generation of postconflict countries that introduced quotas and adopted measures to increase the political representation of women in the late 1980s and demanded gender-related policy changes. As mentioned earlier, increases in female representation did not occur after the end of wars of independence prior to 1985 (e.g., Angola [1974], Cape Verde [1974], Guinea-Bissau [1974], Mozambique [1974], and Rhodesia/Zimbabwe [1979]), even though women had sought greater representation at the time. What had changed in the intervening years was the holding of the UN conferences on women in Nairobi (1985) and Beijing (1995) and new pressures mounting from the international women's movement. The Ugandan example illustrates the way in which women were able to take advantage effectively of the window of opportunity afforded by the end of conflict.

Uganda had plunged into years of civil war, internal conflict, and institutionalized violence beginning with Idi Amin's takeover in 1971. Unrest in most of Uganda (the north excluded) lasted roughly until 1986 when the National Resistance Movement (NRM) came to power after waging a prolonged guerrilla war. Fifteen years of conflict left over eight hundred thousand people dead, two hundred thousand exiled, and millions displaced within the country (Watson 1988: 14). Out of these crises, new spaces for associational life emerged.

National women's organization leaders point to the 1985 Decade of Women conference in Nairobi as a watershed moment for Ugandan women's associations. Women activists in nongovernmental organizations – many of whom had attended the conference on their own, independent of the official delegation – returned from Nairobi with a new sense of urgency to begin revitalizing and creating autonomous women's associations. At the Nairobi conference of fifteen thousand women from 140 countries, the Ugandan participants got a sense of how far women in other countries had come. The Ugandan attendees felt that the women's movement in their country had been stalled by tyrannical regimes and was badly in need of a jumpstart. The women left Nairobi inspired and committed to changing the status of women. Upon their return, they immediately started to mobilize women and stepped up their efforts after the NRM takeover in January 1986 (Tripp 2000).

The new government led by President Yoweri Museveni did not have any particular program addressing women's concerns. Human rights activist Joan Kakwenzire recalls that one of Museveni's first speeches to women in 1986 was a "disheartening speech," in which he spoke of transforming women's status by bringing about changes in society more broadly and asked women to "pull up their socks" and not to make too many pleas for help."[1] But gradually, as a result of women's lobbying efforts, Museveni changed his position regarding women's organizations. He also began to see possibilities for tapping into women's organizational capacity in order to promote his own goals and build his own base of support among women.

Shortly after 1986, twenty leaders of Action for Development, the National Council of Women, and other women's organizations paid a courtesy call to the president, requesting that women be represented in government leadership. Many of their recommendations were adopted immediately, including the appointments of nine women ministers. In 1989, a quota system had been put in place, allowing women to run for a minimum of one seat per district. By 2007, women held 30 percent of all parliamentary seats in Uganda. A woman, Specioza Kazibwe, served as vice president from 1993 to 2004. Thus, under pressure from women's organizations, Museveni encouraged women's leadership at all levels of the government, from local government on up. New women's organizations vigorously pushed for a provision that would allow women to contest all positions on the local councils (Ankrah 1996: 21; Tripp 2000).

The Ugandan case thus illustrates how women were inspired by the emerging norms that came out of the 1985 UN Nairobi Conference on Women to demand political representation. At the same time, one sees the beginning of a new strategy on the part of the NRM to use women's representation in

---

[1] Interview with Aili Tripp, Maxine Ankrah, Kampala, 19 June 1992.

these seats as a quid pro quo for women's votes and support. At times, this arrangement has reached cynical proportions, as when in 2005 Museveni allegedly cut a deal with women parliamentarians by following through on a constitutional provision to set up an Equal Opportunities Commission in exchange for their support for an effort to abandon presidential term limits.

The difference between the Ugandan women's experience in 1986 and the earlier postconflict situations had in part to do with the emerging international norms that gave women new impetus to demand a political presence. Women had fought in the independence wars in Rhodesia and Mozambique, yet they were unable to capitalize at the time on their new roles to advance their status after the war and were proverbially told to "go back to the kitchen and stay there until further notice." The new international norms coming out of the UN Nairobi conference, combined with Museveni's own efforts to build a patronage system on a new footing and create new bases of support that drew heavily on women, resulted in a new political configuration. Thus, one has to look at a confluence of strategies of both internal and external women's movements as well as of the state or dominant parties. Although the Zimbabwean experience did not result in changes, it gave rise to an active women's movement that has persisted to this day.

WOMEN'S NEW PEACE ACTIVISM

The end of conflict in Mozambique marked another shift in women's activism, which began to incorporate peace mobilization, even at the national level. With most conflicts that ended in the 1990s and especially after 2000, women activists were involved in trying to bring an end to conflict through a variety of strategies. The fact that women activists had common goals around equal rights, opposition to violence against women, and increasing the number of women leaders brought them together as women and created a basis for unity often across so-called enemy lines. This common cause allowed women to engage in peacemaking activities at the national and local levels by building coalitions across ethnic and party differences in ways that were often distinct from men's peacemaking activities. Although rarely acknowledged by the press, academics, or policy makers, women and women's organizations in Africa have been actively engaged in peacemaking activities at both the national and local levels. Women activists have employed a wide variety of peacemaking tactics, organizing rallies and boycotts, promoting small arms confiscation, and negotiating with rebels to release abducted child soldiers. Women's rights advocates sought to become more active in formal peace initiatives especially after the 1990s.

In the period leading up to the 1994 elections, the Association of Mozambican Women for Peace (MWFP) actively saw to it that the elections were carried out peacefully. These were the first democratic elections held after a ceasefire was reached following seventeen years of conflict between the FRELIMO-led government and RENAMO. The women's peace group appealed to the competing parties to stop making threatening statements against each other. They organized a major peace rally in Maputo and negotiated with ex-combatant organizations that were threatening to disrupt the elections. They successfully convinced them to allow the elections to proceed without event. The meetings with the combatants were organized by the National Committee for Elections, including the MWFP and several Christian organizations (Snyder 2000).

Other remarkable efforts were mounted at this time. After 1992, demobilized combatants from the government army and RENAMO formed the Mozambican Association for the War Demobilized (Associação Moçambicana dos Desmobilizados de Guerra [AMODEG]). Women ex-combatants from both sides played a very important role in this organization in building bridges. Jacinta Jorge, a former soldier from the government side and one of the founding members of AMODEG, was also the head of Propaz (ProPeace), an organization of ex-combatants, including a group of disabled veterans. Propaz has worked in four provinces providing peace building and conflict-resolution/transformation services.[2] These types of initiatives led Carolyn Nordstrom (1997: 11) to observe in her book *A Different Kind of War Story*, "The citizens in Mozambique demonstrated the most sophisticated country-wide conflict resolution practices and ideologies I have observed in the world."

Women peace activists have had good reason to intervene. Even as many conflicts came to an end, some of the worst violence in Africa occurred during the period described in this section. Africa has been one of the most conflict-ridden parts of the world. The human cost of conflict has been staggering. Nowhere in the world have the death tolls related to civil war been as high as in Africa. It is estimated that 5.4 million have died in the Democratic Republic of Congo between 1998 and 2008 from war-related causes, according to the International Rescue Committee (Polgreen 2008); roughly 200,000 have been killed in Burundi since 1993; about 2 million have died

---

[2] Interviews conducted by Isabel Casimiro with Jacinta Jorge and Flora Ngoma, an ex-combatant from RENAMO, Maputo, 12 January 2005.

in the southern Sudan conflict since 1983 (Lacina and Gleditsch 2005); and over 1 million (mainly Tutsis) died in the 1994 Rwanda genocide and conflict according to the 2000 Rwandan census. Millions more have become refugees or displaced persons in their own countries. Large numbers of women were raped during the conflicts while men have also suffered untold sexual violence during and after these conflicts. Tens of thousands of children have been kidnapped and forcibly conscripted into conflicts in Angola, Burundi, Congo, Congo-Brazzaville, Liberia, Mozambique, Rwanda, Sierra Leone, Somalia, Sudan, and Uganda. They have made up over half of the fighting forces in these countries. These figures do not even begin to capture the consequences of these conflicts on the physical and psychological health of the affected populations, the disruptions to family life, the impact of war on the capacity to grow food, and other devastating consequences of warfare.

## WOMEN AND FORMAL PEACEMAKING PROCESSES

In spite of women's brave and persistent efforts at grassroots peace activism, they have been largely left out of formal peace negotiations, even after the passage of UN Resolution 1325. In 2000, the United Nations Security Council adopted Resolution 1325 to provide women with a greater role in conflict prevention and resolution. The resolution gives strong support "for States to include women in the negotiations and implementation of peace accords, constitutions and strategies for resettlement and rebuilding and to take measures to support local women's groups and indigenous processes for conflict resolution." Although this resolution provides a basis on which to bring greater numbers of women into peacemaking processes and has had visible impacts, many have been disappointed with the slowness of its implementation.

In Uganda, women peace activists from around the country organized a Women's Peace Caravan in November 2006 that crossed the country from Kampala, to Kitgum, and then on to Juba, Sudan, where peace talks were being held between the Lord's Resistance Army (LRA) and Ugandan government representatives to bring an end to a conflict that had been dragging on for nineteen years. At two different times in the history of the conflict, in 1993 and again in 2005, Betty Bigombe, the chief government negotiator with LRA head Joseph Kony, had been close to a settlement. On both occasions, she was unable to complete the task as fighting resumed. Her efforts, nevertheless, ultimately paved the way and were essential for the signing of a ceasefire in September 2006. However, women, who had suffered every bit as much as men from the conflict, were not represented in the final negotiations. For this reason, members of the Civil Society Women's Peace Coalition, the Uganda Women's Network, and the Uganda Women Parliamentary Association led a caravan to Juba to demand women's inclusion in the process. They carried women's Peace Torch. As news commentator Mary Karooro Okurut said of the torch and women's absence from the peace talks:

> First it is a symbol of solidarity; a statement of togetherness – that the women of this country and region are fully behind the peace process. . . . The Peace Torch is the voice of women in the peace process, holding all players accountable to the women of Uganda and the Great Lakes region who have suffered most in the conflict. Lasting peace without the active input of women is unimaginable, which is why women must speak out as they are doing now. (Okurut 2006)

Up until 2006, the peace movement in Uganda was relatively small, as was women's role in it. Nevertheless, the insistence that women be part of all negotiations represented a change in women's movements that had already been evident for some time in Burundi, the Democratic Republic of Congo, Liberia, Sierra Leone, and Somalia. Women did eventually gain entry into the negotiations in Burundi, the Democratic Republic of Congo, Liberia, and Somalia after protracted lobbying.

### INTERNATIONAL AND REGIONAL MOBILIZATION

Women's movements in Africa have mobilized around peace issues not only domestically but also through regional and subregional networks. Women are coordinating their activities across state boundaries on an unprecedented scale. Peacemaking has been a central concern of networks such as the African Women's Committee for Peace and Development (AWCPD) and the Federation of African Women's Peace Networks (FERFAP). FERFAP, formed in 1997, includes representatives from sixteen countries and has been involved in activities ranging from petitions and peace marches to local alliance building and national reconciliation conferences (Manuh 1998). Perhaps most significantly, the importance of women's participation in peace initiatives has gained recognition from African governments not previously evident in the post-independence era.

The formation of the African Union in 2001 was an important turning point in African women's regional mobilization around peace issues. However, the groundwork had been laid through a series of meetings and conferences. The Conference on Women and Peace that was held in

Kampala, Uganda, in 1993 under the auspices of the Organisation of African Unity (OAU), the UN Economic Commission on Africa (UNECA), and the government of Uganda resulted in the Kampala Action Plan on Women Peace, which was which was endorsed by the OAU heads of state and government in 1995. The principles were incorporated in the African Platform for Action and were later folded into the UN Platform for Action adopted at the 1995 Beijing Women's Conference. The Kampala Action Plan aimed to increase the participation of women in conflict resolution and decision making; protect women living in conflict situations or under foreign occupation; reduce excessive military expenditures; control weapons availability; promote nonviolent forms of conflict resolution; protect human rights; encourage women's contributions in fostering a culture of peace; and provide protection, assistance, and training to refugee women and other displaced women.

In November 1996, the OAU and UNECA organized a Women Leadership Forum on Peace in Johannesburg, South Africa, which among other things discussed the participation of women in the OAU Mechanisms for Conflict Prevention, Management, and Resolution. A major outcome from this meeting was a recommendation for the formation of the African Women's Committee for Peace and Development (AWCPD). However, the lack of a clear policy environment and human and financial resource constraints hampered the committee. It did not have the necessary legal and policy framework and institutional supports to realize its mandate fully. Nevertheless, the AWCPD maintained strong and close partnerships with women's civil society organizations. Subsequent conferences organized by the OAU and UNECA in Kigali, Rwanda, in 1997 and another in Zanzibar in 1999 by OAU, UNESCO, and the Tanzanian government highlighted prevalent concerns regarding peace and women.

The African Union (AU) was formed in 2001 out of the unification of the OAU and UNECA. Gender equality was one of the founding principles of the AU. AWCPD seized the opportunity provided by the transition from the OAU to the AU to move gender issues to the forefront. Indeed, at the Fifth Extraordinary Summit of the OAU in Sirte, Libya, in March 2000, the AWCPD lobbied and engaged key foreign ministers on the need to highlight the gender components of the Constitutive Act of the AU. The AWCPD worked with the gender desks of UNECA's African Centre for Gender and Development, the African Regional Economic Communities, and the African Women's Development Fund (AWDF), to lay the groundwork for the establishment in 2002 of a Gender Directorate to be located under the office of the chairperson of the African Union and a Specialized Technical

Committee on gender equality at the level of commissioners. These institutional arrangements ushered in a new era in gender mainstreaming within the AU, which would not have happened without years of mobilization on the part of women activists.

The AWCPD remained an active presence in addressing various conflict situations around the continent. Together with the AU, the AWCPD and associated organizations organized a Solidarity Mission to the Democratic Republic of Congo in December 2001. This mission, for example, supported Congolese women's preparations for effective participation in the Inter-Congolese dialogue hosted by South Africa early in 2002. The tribute marking the end of the OAU in July 2002 in Durban, South Africa, had particular meaning for the AWCPD, as the ceremony marked the transition to a new era of activism in the context of the AU.

Another concrete manifestation of women's heightened mobilization across the continent regarding peace issues was the passage of the UN Security Council Resolution 1325. Women's organizations met in May 2000 in Windhoek, Namibia, and helped draft a document that was to become the basis of the aforementioned UN Security Council Resolution 1325 detailing women's role in peacekeeping. On 21 July 2003, the African Union adopted the Protocol to the African Charter on Human and Peoples' Rights on the Rights of Women in Africa that recognizes "the right of women to participate in the promotion and maintenance of peace." This was preceded by a women's summit in Maputo, Mozambique, in June 2003, organized by the United Nations Development Fund for Women (UNIFEM) and Africa-wide women's associations.

One important West African network is the Mano River Union Women Peace Network (MARWOPNET) of women activists from Guinea, Sierra Leone, and Liberia. The network mediated an intense conflict between Guinea and Liberia in 2001 in spite of minimal resources and being excluded from the formal peace process. MARWOPNET was able to get the feuding heads of state to a regional peace summit. At one point, President Lansana Conté of Guinea had been adamant about not meeting with Charles Taylor of Liberia. Mary Brownell, a Liberian peace activist of the MARWOPNET delegation, told Mr. Conté: "You and President Taylor have to meet as men and iron out your differences, and we the women want to be present. We will lock you in this room until you come to your senses, and I will sit on the key." Conté relented and met with Taylor as a result of the sheer audacity of a woman telling him what to do, saying, "What man do you think would say that to me? Only a woman could do such a thing and get by with it" (Fleshman 2003). As a result of their actions, the women were given delegate status at the Twenty-Fourth ECOWAS summit in December 2001, where they were able to make an appeal for African leaders to support women's peacemaking initiatives. They were also given observer status in the 2003 Accra talks that led to a ceasefire agreement and the establishment of an interim government in Liberia.

SIERRA LEONE

In Sierra Leone, the Women's Forum emerged in 1994 to serve as an umbrella organization for women's groups. It was a powerful group that included women from all political, religious, ethnic, and other groups, such as the National Displaced Women's Organization, the National Organization for Women, the Women's Association for National Development, the Young Women's Christian Association, the women's wing of the Sierra Leone Labour Congress, as well as women traders associations and several Muslim and Christian women's associations. Most groups were affiliated with different political parties, but they nevertheless joined forces to push for a common peace agenda. Their first objective was to prepare for the UN Women's Conference in Beijing in 1995. Soon they joined forces with the newly formed Sierra Leone Women's Movement for Peace (SLWMP), which had launched a series of demonstrations, rallies, and prayer meetings with government officials and diplomats to pressure the government for a negotiated settlement.

The first demonstration that SLWMP organized in 1995 was a carnival-like event led by a pediatrician Fatmatta Boie-Kamara. It was the first public demonstration by women since the 1960s. Professional women danced through downtown Freetown and linked arms with female soldiers, small-scale businesswomen, and nurses, singing "Try peace to end this senseless war." Bystanders were captivated by the festivity and joined this parade of women. The demonstration gave new legitimacy to existing peace groups that had previously been suspected of fronting for various political parties. For the first time, a negotiated peace settlement became a real possibility and rebels and government began to disengage. Women thus took leadership of the peace process, as other civil society groups felt that the military was more tolerant of the women because they were women.

Women were vital to the transition phase from military to civilian rule and played central roles at high levels during peace negotiations with the warring groups both as mediators and as civil society representatives. Women leaders had proposed the key provisions at the Freetown National Consultative Conferences in 1995 and 1996 (called Bintumani I and II) that pushed for elections at a time when the military was threatening a postponement of elections. Bintumani II, which was chaired by Shirley Gbujama, eventually led to presidential and parliamentary elections in 1996. Women had succeeded in creating an independent voice that put forward a nonpartisan women's perspective on basic issues. The 1996 elections brought about a civilian government but not a sustainable peace, as the May 1997 coup put to an end to women's efforts to intervene independently in the peace process (Haffajee 1999; Kamau 1999).

Women activists helped get two-thirds of the electorate to the polls, even as the rebel Revolutionary United Front (RUF) was terrorizing potential voters by chopping off hands. Women's hard work in the peace process failed to earn them seats at the negotiating table at Abidjan, but they made up four of a team of nine in the 1999 Lomé talks, which lead to the Lomé Peace Agreement. Although the notorious warlord Foday Sankoh had been convicted of treason, his rebels wreaked havoc on Freetown, after which the United States forced the government to free Sankoh in order to negotiate the peace agreement. Sankoh was made vice president and put in charge of the diamonds that he had been looting to fund his militia fighters. To get the UN peacekeepers out, his forces attacked them in 2000. As he planned an RUF takeover of the government, the Women's Forum and MAROWPNET bravely marched on 6 May to appeal to him to allow the peace process to move forward. He refused and a civil society demonstration was held two days later. It was attacked and the disruptions led to continued protest and the eventual arrest of Sankoh, paving the way for the peace process to continue. The UN-sponsored special court charged Sankoh with war crimes but he died while in detention (Gberie 2003).

## LIBERIA

Most women's organizations in Liberia had mobilized around relief until 1994, when Mary Brownell started a women's pressure group, the Liberian Women's Initiative (LWI), to speak out against the 1989–96 war. The organization was open to women of all ethnic, social, religious, and political backgrounds. Ruth Perry, who came to lead the National State Council of Liberia as the interim head of state in 1996, was a founding member of the LWI. The LWI worked with all parties to bring them into the negotiations. Women's associations also acted as monitors to see that promises were kept. At one point, they opposed UN-sponsored peace agreements that basically rewarded leaders of the armed factions with positions in the transitional government while doing little to disarm them. They challenged former U.S.

president Jimmy Carter and UN special envoy Trevor Gordon-Somers when they pursued a strategy of encouraging warring factions to meet separately with one another. They opposed all initiatives that lent credibility and power to armed factions (Moran and Pitcher 2004).

One of the primary aims of the women peace activists was to collect and confiscate small arms. Women's associations acted as monitors to see that promises were kept. LWI mobilizers also attended regional peace talks and engaged in letter-writing campaigns with the Economic Community of West African States (ECOWAS), the OAU, and the United Nations. Liberian women continued to mobilize across differences to oppose the 1999–2003 war. Some groups such as the Coalition of Political Parties Women in Liberia (COPPWIL) were formed explicitly to find a common agenda around women's rights concerns. The activists served as a backbone of support behind the victory of Ellen Johnson-Sirleaf, who became Africa's first elected woman president in 2005.

However, even though women's organizations were essential to the peace that was brokered, they were never given a formal role in the peace talks. Vabah Gayflor, minister of gender in Liberia, explained that women

were not considered as peacemakers at any time. Yet Liberian women drew attention to the horrible political situation and how the war adversely affected women. They took it upon themselves to serve as go betweens. Women shuttled between international and national actors through their women's organizations. Women's organizations like the Liberian Women's Initiative, Federation of African Women's Peace Networks (FERFAP) and the Mano River Union Women Peace Network (MARWOPNET) were very active. (Gayflor 2005)

In spite of the engagement of women, they were relegated to serving as peace observers.

One of the more dramatic incidents that contributed to the peace settlement in Liberia involved a refugee women's organization, the Women in Peace Building Network, based in Ghana. In 2003, ECOWAS sponsored peace negotiations in Accra, Ghana. At the talks, the women's refugee network locked negotiators in their meeting room and said they would not allow them out until they signed a comprehensive peace agreement. Drawing on funereal symbolism that has deep roots in West African history of women's protest, the women wept to protest the ongoing violations of a ceasefire on all sides and threatened to strip naked if the meeting did not produce a positive outcome. The protestors accused ECOWAS of pampering the negotiators and said that the talks should have been held instead in the Budumbram refugee camp on the Accra-Winneba road to help the negotiators understand the urgency for peace. The women complained that the negotiators had been housed in luxurious accommodations and were wearing expensive clothes and eating good food ("Paper Hails Liberian Women..." 2003). Eventually the "hostages" were freed, but the women had made their point.

Women were not entirely absent from the talks. In fact, one of the most forceful negotiators was Ellen Johnson-Sirleaf, who was to become Liberia's president in 2006. Another participant, Ruth Perry, had been the head of the Liberia's Interim Presidential Council in 1996 and was representing the aforementioned women's organization MARWOPNET at the talks together with several other members. Because of the important mediation role that MARWOPNET had played between the various factions involved in the peace talks, the network was one of the signatories of a peace agreement as witness to the agreement signed on 18 August 2003 by the government of Liberia, Liberians United for Democracy (LURD), Movement for Democracy in Liberia (MODEL), and all the eighteen political parties.

SOMALIA

Women in Somalia similarly faced an uphill battle to be included in peace talks. Much like the Liberian women, they also influenced peace talks in Somalia through collective and united action. In Somalia, state collapse and clan warfare followed the demise of the Siad Barre regime in 1991. Barre effectively fanned the flames of clan rivalry in order to divert attention from the failure of his rule. Competing clans vied for the control of the state as the country fell into civil war and disarray. Women from hostile clans bravely began meeting in the early 1990s amid clan-based factional warfare. When the women were excluded from the March 1993 National Reconciliation Conference in Addis Ababa, a group of activist women fasted until an agreement was reached after the men had failed to achieve consensus. Twenty-four hours later, the men had a peace plan that outlined provisions for a transitional government, elections, disarmament, and a UN-supervised ceasefire.

Women lobbied for and got 10 percent of the seats in the National Assembly of the Somali Transitional National Government. The assembly seats were balanced between competing clans. Each of the four major clans was also represented by one of five women with five remaining women representing minor clans. Interestingly, the women formed a bloc ("rainbow coalition") to advocate for women's interests across clan lines through a network called the Sixth Clan. Asha Haji Elmi, a member of the transitional government and chairperson of the Sixth Clan, believes women politicians' interests diverged from those of male politicians because of the different way in which they were positioned with respect to clans. Women in Somalia marry into their husband's clan and leave their own clan behind. In referring to women in the transition government, Elmi stated: "We are not here for decoration. Ten years of war and no government, that is enough. The women of Somalia are tired and will work to pressure the men to change the situation." Due in large part to Elmi's efforts, twenty-two Somali women came to serve in the national parliament. In January 2004, Elmi was the only woman to co-chair the final phase of the Somali National Reconciliation Conference and the first woman to sign the peace accord (Hollier-Larousse 2000).

## BURUNDI

From the time of independence from Belgium in 1962 until the 1994 genocide in Rwanda, nowhere else in Africa had there been so much violence in such a small area in such a short period of time as in Burundi (Lemarchand 1994).[3] Thousands died in ethnically based conflict in 1965, between one hundred thousand and two hundred thousand perished in 1972, government troops killed approximately twenty thousand in 1988, and another three thousand were killed in 1991. In 1993, there was a brief respite from three decades of authoritarian and military rule as a democratically elected president and the first Hutu president, Melchior Ndadaye, came to power in a country predominantly Hutu but one that had been dominated politically and economically by a Tutsi minority since the time of colonialism. No sooner was Ndadaye elected than Tutsi paratroopers assassinated him. His successor, Cyprien Ntaryamira, also a Hutu, was killed in a plane crash along with the president of Rwanda. With these deaths, the country became mired for five years in large-scale massacres and a civil war in which civilians became targets. At least three hundred thousand died in the battles and another million were forced into internal and external exile.

Formal peace talks were initiated in 1999 in Arusha, Tanzania, to lay the basis for a new constitutional arrangement. Seventeen out of nineteen existing Burundian parties signed peace accords in Pretoria, South Africa, on 28 August 2000. By the time of the parliamentary elections on 4 July

---

[3] This section is a modified version of paper presented by Aili Mari Tripp, "Empowering Women in the Great Lakes Region: Violence, Peace and Women's Leadership," for a conference organized by Gender Equality and Development Section, Social and Human Sciences, UNESCO, Addis Ababa, Ethiopia, 13 May 2005.

2005, all parties were on board. Women had lobbied for and got a minimum of 30 percent (thirty-six) of all parliamentary seats reserved for them in the elections.

The most dramatic changes in women's participation took place in the context of the peace talks in 1998. Burundian women's peace efforts go back to 1993 when the organization Women for Peace was formed with the support of African Women in Crisis (AFWIC) and UNIFEM. The following year, the Collectif des Associations et ONGs Féminines du Burundi (CAFOB) was formed as an umbrella for seven organizations and quickly grew to fifteen organizations by 1996. The organizations focused on training women in leadership skills, on peace building, and on getting women into positions of decision making (Burke et al. 2001: 11). Peace talks aimed at bringing an end to civil conflict in Burundi were held in Arusha, Tanzania, in June 1998 and women's organizations were determined to be included. The parties involved had not even consulted their own party women with respect to these negotiations.[4] At these talks, seventeen political parties committed themselves to finding a solution to a conflict that had incurred untold suffering on the Burundian people, displacing over eight hundred thousand refugees to the Democratic Republic of Congo, Rwanda, and Tanzania and another eight hundred thousand internally. The majority of the refugees were women and children.

The women lobbied Tanzania's former president Julius Nyerere, who started as facilitator of the talks. After Nyerere's death in 1999, the former president of South Africa, Nelson Mandela, began guiding the peace process. Nyerere arranged for a women's group of three Hutu and three Tutsi women and one woman in exile in Kenya to meet with the heads of the party delegations. The head of the women's delegation was Catherine Mabobori, president of CAFOB and founding member of Women for Peace. Mabobori and the group argued that women in Burundi, who made up 52 percent of the population, had been at the forefront of efforts to find peace through local-level associations but had continued to remain marginalized at the national level. Their involvement in the talks could only broaden the channels for spreading efforts toward peace and reconciliation (Burke et al. 2001: 8). As a result of this meeting, seven women were allowed to come as a nonaccredited delegation to the 20–29 July 1998 meeting in Arusha but were told that they could not attend the following session.

---

[4] Email communication from Marie Nduwayo to women-armdconf@phoenix.edc.org on women peace-building actions in Burundi, 2 November 1999.

One of the participants in the Arusha conference, Alice Ntwarante, was struck by how unity was the starting point for the women delegates in contrast with the men at this meeting:

We [the women] were united in purpose, despite our ethnic split – three Hutus and three Tutsis. The various political parties to which we women belonged tried to split us up, but we resisted them. We said, no! We stand together with our sisters. We are here to represent women, not as members of such-and-such a political party. Our unity spoke for us. We said to all Burundian women: "Come and join us! There is a place for you!" This was the big success of Arusha for women – that we remained united.

She contrasted the stance of the women to that of the male party negotiators: "I told myself, here are the men, the key players, who are going to negotiate, but right at the start of the conference they can't communicate with one another. Each was turning his back on his adversary. Each had brought his ideas to the peace table. They were partisan, even extremist" (Burke et al. 2001: 14). Imelda Nzirorera made a similar observation from her experience in the Burundian peace negotiations: "What worries us most is that our Burundian brothers, who are members of political parties, are putting the division of the national pie first. In other words, they are thinking, at the end of the negotiations, what position and post will we get?" (Anderlini 2000: 33). This is not to say that the women did not have differing views or disagreements, but they started from the point of unity.

The focus of the women's efforts was to protest the sanctions that had been placed on Burundi by Kenya, Rwanda, Tanzania, and Uganda, and in January 1999 it is believed that their efforts had an impact on the lifting of the sanctions by neighboring countries. When their efforts to continue to join the peace talks were rebuffed at the July 1998 meeting, the women continued to press their case not only at Arusha but with international donors, international communities, the facilitation team, regional leaders, and African women's organizations (Anderlini 2000: 10).

By February 2000, with the help of the Mwalimu Nyerere Foundation, UNIFEM, and others, the women had gained permanent observer status at the talks. In July 2000, they succeeded in getting the nineteen negotiating parties to accept the need for women's involvement in the peace process. An All-Party Burundi Women's Conference was convened in 2000, where delegates insisted that women's concerns be taken up in all aspects of the peace process, given the particular effects of the conflict on women. Each party sent two delegates to the conference. The document that they drew up, *Women's Proposals to Engender the Draft Arusha Peace and Reconciliation*

Agreement, is an important one because it provided a road map for how women's concerns needed to be addressed in the peace-building process.

The group insisted that women be represented in all aspects of the peace process and that all issues raised needed to be looked at from a gender perspective. They also demanded a 30 percent quota for women in the legislature, the judiciary, and the executive branches of government, as well as in all bodies created by the peace accord. They argued that the final agreement include rights to property, land, and inheritance along with a recognition of the fact that Burundi girls and women suffer discrimination because of culture and policies that are not sensitive to women's particular needs. The declaration highlighted the need for equal access to education for girls and for an end to impunity when it comes to rape, sexual violence, prostitution, and domestic violence. It talked about the importance of paying attention to the needs of women refugees and in particular female- and child-headed families and many other crucial concerns (All-Party Burundi Women's Peace Conference 2000). Twenty-three of these recommendations were ultimately included in the final peace accord as a result of the group's lobbying efforts.

Women's efforts to be included in the peace process were part of a series of broader initiatives that emerged from the growing women's movement, which included a wide range of organizations. For example, the Burundi Women Refugee Network and AFRICARE Burundi had been involved with internally displaced women and refugees in promoting peace-related activities. When men negotiators at Arusha said there were insufficient numbers of qualified women to hold office, CAFOB compiled a list of women with the education and skills necessary to serve in the government. Since its formation in 1997, the Burundi Women's Journalists Association (BWJA) has been promoting women's rights and the freedom of the press. Dushirehamwe ("Let's Reconcile") serves as a network of women's peace-building organizations from ten provinces in Burundi. It has been initiating inter-ethnic dialogues and engaging in conflict resolution. Traditional birth attendants are being trained to help women survivors of rape. Many other organizations provide other important services and play advocacy roles in the current context in Burundi and are an important resource for changing the status of women in this country.

DEMOCRATIC REPUBLIC OF CONGO

In neighboring Congo, five years after the 2002 ceasefire and in spite of the 2006 elections, various peace efforts, and the presence of United Nations troops, the situation remained volatile, especially in the eastern part of the country.[5]

An Inter-Congolese Dialogue between the various Congolese rebel forces and the government was initiated in October 2001. At the final stage in the peace process in Sun City, South Africa, on 2 April 2003, the factions signed a peace agreement that provided for the establishment of a two-year transitional government and constitution that allowed the Democratic Republic of Congo its first democratic elections in forty years in 2006.

When the country plunged into civil war in 1998, women's groups, together with human rights activists, formed lobby groups, organized marches, wrote memoranda, and made trips abroad to bring attention to the conflict and seek a resolution to it. They sought to educate women at the grassroots about the peace process, electoral politics, and their rights as voters. They had two objectives: (1) to convince the contending male-led factions that dialogue was essential and (2) to convince them to include women in the negotiations.

The women produced a joint statement that called for an immediate ceasefire, provisions to include women and their demands throughout the peace process, and adoption of a 30 percent quota for women at all levels of government. The women held the men accountable in the negotiations and presented themselves as representatives of ordinary people back home whom they would report back to if the negotiators failed to come to an accord at the 2002 Sun City, South Africa, meeting (Fleshman 2003). When male negotiators were spending too much time enjoying themselves at the Las Vegas–style resort, women attendees representing all parties and factions convened the men to see a play that they had produced. It highlighted the impact of the war on women and how the suffering of one woman represented the suffering of all. They got the negotiators involved in the play, singing and acting. They gave each of the men a piece of paper in the shape of the part of Congo from which they came and had them bring the pieces together to form a whole country. The event had a profound impact on the negotiators and humbled them into returning to the negotiating table.[6]

---

[5] This section is a modified version of paper presented by Aili Mari Tripp, "Empowering Women in the Great Lakes Region: Violence, Peace and Women's Leadership," for a conference organized by Gender Equality and Development Section, Social and Human Sciences, UNESCO, Addis Ababa, Ethiopia, 13 May 2005.

[6] Discussion with member of negotiating team Claudine Tayaye Muyala Bibi, 29 August 2007.

Women adopted a variety of other strategies to influence the negotiations. Women representing opposing sides of the conflict held prayer vigils to pressure warring factions to honor the 2002 peace accords in Ituri (Kapinga 2003: 25–6). They held work stoppages, such as the one in Ituri on International Women's Day, 8 March 2002, to protest the civil war (Mwavita 2002). An October 2002 workshop in North Kivu Province called for integrating women into the decision-making process, increasing regional trade among the local populations, and opposing the recruitment of children by armies and militias.

In the capital of Kinshasa alone over 150 women's organizations had been formed to address women's rights concerns. Regional organizations were also created, such as the Réseau des Femmes pour la Défense des Droits et de la Paix (Women's Network for the Defense of Rights and Peace), which mobilized women in the Kivus in order to get female representation into the dialogue. In February 2002, over forty Congolese women from a wide range of groups convened in Nairobi, Kenya, to discuss issues to be included in the dialogue and to bring women's concerns to the table in the peace talks. They also demanded that the country's new constitution mention the Convention on the Elimination of All Forms of Discrimination against Women (CEDAW), which has been ratified by Congo. Women marched in Bukavu to protest Rwanda's involvement in the Congo, saying that "enough was enough." Their statement, which was read by Zita Kavungirwa, said that women were fed up with the eight years of atrocities and the number of victims, which has far exceeded the numbers of victims in the Rwandan genocide (DRCongo Radio 2004). The women targeted the international community, calling for a suspension of foreign aid to Rwanda.

In the peace negotiations, women were given 40 out of 340 seats. Having forged a common position before the negotiations, Inter-Congolese Dialogue in 1999 resulted in the Lusaka ceasefire agreement. "We knew that we had to be together for the men to hear what we had to say," said Aningina Bibiane, a Congolese peace activist of the Caucus of Congolese Women and Women as Partners for Peace in Africa (WOPPA-DRC). She continued:

At first, the men were hostile because there was this group of women entering "their" space. But we approached them in a way that made them feel secure. In African culture the woman is your mother. The woman is your wife and sister. If your mother or sister is talking to you, you have to listen. We didn't demonize the men or try to take their place. (Fleshman 2003)

CONCLUSIONS

Women have sought to influence peace processes and the postconflict peace in a variety of ways at both the national and local levels. The cases of Mozambique and Uganda exemplify some of the constraints and opportunities that women have encountered since the 1970s. After Mozambique's liberation from Portugal, women had few opportunities to advance themselves in significant ways, especially as the country plunged into renewed conflict. It was not until Uganda emerged from years of conflict in 1986 that women, energized by their experiences at the 1985 UN Nairobi conference, sought and gained greater political representation and expansion of their rights. Uganda was a turning point in postconflict experiences as women united to push for a common agenda. Mozambique's experiences after 1992 were also critical, because from that time on we began to see women in various conflicts throughout Africa engaged in peace activism and linking these efforts with a common agenda of advancing women's rights and political representation in the postconflict context. The activism most notably cut across party, ethnic, and other lines that had divided citizens during the conflicts.

After 2000, we witnessed many efforts by women to be represented in peace negotiations, some successful and others less so. The 2006 efforts by Ugandan women to be part of the northern Uganda peace settlement fall into this last phase of women's activism. Women, who had been totally shut out of formal peacemaking initiatives since independence in some cases, were now actively seeking a seat at the table after 2000, with moderate success in countries such as Burundi, the Democratic Republic of Congo, Liberia, Sierra Leone, and Uganda. Furthermore, they sought and often gained greater political representation in postconflict governments. Their initiatives were linked to the growth of the women's movements throughout Africa that sought greater political representation for women at all levels. They were also indicative of the changing international norms regarding women's representation and rights. Preparations for the Beijing conference were one of the priorities of the newly formed Women's Forum in Sierra Leone in 1994, illustrating the importance of these international influences and linkages on the evolution of the women's movement.

Women's marginalization from politics and their outsider status has, on the one hand, made them attractive contenders for power as the ends of conflicts open up new political spaces. Their shared exclusion has given them a common agenda and capacity for being remarkably broad-based regardless of partisanship, ethnicity, religion, or other factors, and many of women's strategies in peacemaking are indeed shaped by and arise from their marginalization in society. To what extent do these strategies simultaneously lock them into limited forms of peacemaking and keep them excluded from other roles? To what extent does their participation in these gendered structures perpetuate institutions that marginalize women rather than challenge them? These are some of the many questions women face as they rebuild their societies together with men.

# 9

## African Women's Movements and the World

This book is about a social transformation that is revolutionizing women's status in African societies in ways that it would have been hard to imagine even a couple decades ago. For those involved in the movements, it still seems like there is a long way to go and the hurdles ahead are daunting. However, if one takes a step back to examine the overall crossnational picture in Africa, the patterns of change are unmistakable and there is no question that there have already been significant changes in gender-related norms, government objectives, and, to a more modest extent, in the advancement of the status of women.

The cases of Cameroon, Mozambique, and Uganda in many ways typify some of the key trends that we see today in Africa, both in women's status as well as in the persistence of the status quo. Each case points to both possibilities as well as the limitations of these changes.

Women's movements were critical to the legislative and constitutional changes related to women's rights, facilitating gender mainstreaming in the state bureaucracy, carving out new roles for women in postconflict contexts, and promoting expanded political leadership roles for women at all levels. But women's movements were not alone in their efforts to bring about radical changes. They took advantage of opportunities that had converged at the international and regional levels as well as trends within Africa, such as the end of major civil conflicts. International women's movements pressured the United Nations agencies and other multilateral institutions to expand women's rights and roles. These institutions in turn held governments accountable through treaties, conventions, and platforms of action. African women's organizations pressured the Organisation of African Unity (OAU) and its successor, the African Union (AU), as well as subregional bodies such as the Economic Community of West African States (ECOWAS) and the Southern African Development Community (SADC), which also promoted accountability among their member states.

Furthermore, there was a convergence internationally of developmental and human rights–based approaches in the 1990s that helped put women's rights on the agenda, especially because they embodied both strands of these new rights–based approaches: the need for women to be seen as integral to development as well as the notion of women's rights as human rights. Countries with greater resources or access to donor resources more easily incorporated women's rights and the promotion of gender mainstreaming, gender budgeting, and other such policies. Finally, countries coming out of years of civil conflict were re-creating their polities through the writing of new constitutions and other such efforts to reorder society. Women inserted themselves into these propitious moments of flux to demand greater rights and representation. They took advantage of these openings to press their agendas. Although no one would advocate societal upheaval to advance a women's agenda, we have observed the political opportunities that presented themselves to women's movements in these otherwise most tragic of situations.

PARADOXES OF CHANGE

There are several paradoxes or puzzles that emerge from our study. First, what made it possible for some countries to expand rights without tremendous pressure from women's movements while other countries, such as Cameroon, Kenya, and Mali have had active women's movements with slower legislative and other outcomes? Mozambique, for example, has a women's movement but not a large and influential one compared with some other African countries. Yet the government has moved ahead with key reforms in family and land law affecting women and the ruling party has promoted women representatives in parliament in ways not often found elsewhere in Africa. The government has adopted a gender budgeting initiative and has readily ratified all international and AU treaties and protocols pertaining to women. We believe other factors such as international pressures from the AU, SADC, and UN converged powerfully with the activities of Mozambican women's organizations, while Mozambique's postconflict status created other incentives for change along with an influx of donor funds directed at efforts such as the gender budgeting initiative and various legal reforms. In Mozambique, it was clearly not the size of the women's movement that mattered, but rather the ways in which women's organizations interacted with the parties, national machinery, ministries, and donors, and the independence that they wielded in forming their agenda.

In Mozambique's case one can also attribute many of its gender-related reforms to the orientation of the ruling party, Frente de Libertação de Moçambique (FRELIMO), which as a left leaning party has always seen itself as interested in advancing gender equality. Like many parties, FRELIMO has realized that being seen as enhancing women's status has garnered enormous payoffs at the polls, especially since women vote in proportionately larger numbers than men in Mozambique (Jacobson 1995). Although FRELIMO was favorably disposed toward women's concerns, women's organizations still found themselves at odds over many of the ways in which women's rights policies were framed by the party.

This brings us to a second paradox: Why were some countries slower to embrace women's rights even with the presence of large and active women's movements? We explored the case of Cameroon to better understand some of the obstacles in the way of reform. Cameroon, like many other African countries, faced many of the same pressures from the international community. Yet, unlike many African countries, Cameroon has not seen the emergence of a large number of political advocacy groups, and most women's organizations remain "developmental" in their approach.

Cameroon did not face the same urgent pressures for reform as did postconflict countries and did not undergo constitutional changes of the kind seen in Mozambique and Uganda. Thus, Cameroon shares with Kenya and Mali a conundrum: In spite of having an active women's movement that has generated and tabled necessary drafts for legislation seeking to address key constraints faced by women, they have experienced challenges within the legislative process in moving ahead with adopting changes, suggesting that the presence of a women's movement may be necessary but not sufficient for change to occur.

A third puzzle that we have explored questions why some legislative reforms have been easier to pass than others. Here we need to distinguish between laws that reach into the public and the private spheres, as defined in African contexts. There appears to have been greater resistance in legal change affecting familial, clan, and kin institutions, with lesser opposition to changes relating most directly to state and market-related institutions. Chapter 5 explored some of these obstacles and the role that they played in preventing the passage of legislation pertaining to family and land laws. Generally, this resistance reflected the general status quo and has come from clan-based or religious institutions as well as from indigenous institutions. If politically mobilized and influential, these challenges can prevent the passage of key legislation and policy reforms. In the case of Uganda, key provisions in land legislation regarding common property provisions were not included as a result of pressures from clan elders. Objections from Muslim leaders have been one of the main factors preventing a Domestic Relations Bill from passing because it deals with controversial matters pertaining marriage, divorce, maintenance, and child custody.

Thus, the policies that have been the hardest to change have involved challenges to traditional authority, to the clan, to chiefs, and to older power arrangements, especially those tied to resources. Hence, land, inheritance, and marriage laws generally have been the most challenging to reform. Those that have been the easiest to change – such as those introducing electoral quotas, gender budgeting, and educational policies – have affected institutions that are more removed from people's daily lives and from local power structures and property arrangements.

As much as these older arrangements protected women in the past, the introduction of capitalism and individualized property rights has transformed communities and economies in ways that make it difficult for women to attain a secure livelihood within the framework of the older arrangements. They no longer provide women the safety net that they once might have, and for this reason, women are demanding changes in laws, not just for symbolic purposes as an assertion of modernity or because they have succumbed to Western feminism, but as a way of protecting their livelihood in a very real sense.

A fourth puzzle has to do with why democratization has not featured more as a factor driving policy regarding women's rights, especially because women were active in democratizing movements and political liberalization opened space for women's movements. Countries have often exhibited the same readiness to pass woman-friendly legislation regardless of their level of democratization. Whether they are as likely to actually enforce the legislation is another matter that needs empirical study and goes beyond the scope of this book. Nevertheless, they have passed woman-friendly legislation for a variety of reasons: in response to changing global norms, international and regional pressures, and donor incentives. Rwanda, which is an authoritarian state, has basked in the warm glow of international limelight for increasing the number of women representatives in parliament to 49 percent. Some authoritarian states also seek to curry women's votes and support; others wish to appear to be seen as modernizers, and in some countries they seek to drive a wedge between themselves and religious leaders.

Even in countries that have democratized more than others, there are new challenges. This is because the same democratic openings that allowed for women's rights groups to emerge also allowed for the increased mobilization of other societal groups that may be opposed to the women's rights agenda.

## AFRICAN INFLUENCES ON WOMEN'S RIGHTS GLOBALLY

Although much of this book has focused on the impact of women's movements in Africa in terms of policy change, it also provides us with an opportunity to recognize the global and political impact of these changes. Africa not only has absorbed international norms and been the recipient of new ideas and ways of thinking about gender relations. It has been integral to these changes. Ideas and practices have emerged from Africa and spread elsewhere. It is important to acknowledge the ways in which African women's movements have and are influencing these global trends.

The marginalized position of Africa in the global context has often blurred the contribution of African women to many discourses of the global women's movement. The decline in economic and social development of the 1980s and 1990s, famine, floods, the HIV/AIDS pandemic, and interstate and intrastate conflicts coupled by inequitable world trade terms have shifted the focus of discussion to these pressing and urgent concerns. Also, the international media have had little interest in African women, except to portray them as hopelessly mired in traditional "inhuman" practices such as genital mutilation or as helpless victims of war and famine.

The extensive documentation of the women's movement in Europe and the United States has often overshadowed the contributions of the women's movements outside these regions, creating the misinformed perception that women's activism globally was a byproduct of Western feminist movements. Women from developing countries, especially in the 1980s, started protesting such characterizations and increased efforts in documenting their own movements.

Among the first regionally based organizations, the Association of African Women for Research and Development (AAWORD) was formed in 1976 in response to experiences at the first UN conference on women held in Mexico in 1975 and the 1976 Wellesley College conference. AAWORD sought to promote scholarship among African women scholars, in part as a response to the domination of research on women in Africa by Western scholars and the lack of availability of their work in Africa. African scholars were critical of the many condescending and patronizing assumptions of Western scholars that did not regard African women as capable of looking after their own interests (AAWORD 1982: 107). African women participants presented a written criticism that was both procedural and substantial.

The concerns that AAWORD raised at the time are still relevant today. In colonial times, anthropologists, missionaries, and travelers took it upon themselves to raise issues concerning women. In more recent times, development practitioners, human rights activists, and Western scholars and donors have been increasingly documenting African women's experiences. Much of this scholarship, although not all, has been critiqued for adopting a "safari" stance. In other words, the research is not always grounded in the fabric of African societies and therefore is likely to draw erroneous conclusions. False parallels are drawn between patriarchy in Western and African societies, and overgeneralization, oversimplification, or misinterpretation of African realities has led some African scholars to raise questions about who should reflect on the experiences of African women and to promote research that is produced by those who themselves are part of a particular society and understand its dynamics and complexities (Basu 1995; Ogundipe-Leslie 1994; Oyewumi 2003).

The trajectory of post-1990s women's mobilization in Africa, as explored in Chapters 2 and 3, while influenced by global trends and norms and women's activism, has had its own sources arising out of Africa's democratizing trends, the economic crisis in the 1980s and 1990s, the influence of African regional institutions, and the expansion of new communications mechanisms. The contemporary movements in Africa have also drawn on their roots in indigenous women's strategies that predated Islamicization, Christianization, and colonization. They have drawn on women's experiences in anticolonial resistance and national liberation movements, as well as women's experiences in party/state-directed women's organizations in the era of single parties and military rule.

In spite of important global influences, women's movements in Africa have defined themselves and their vision of change with respect to local conditions. Non-Western countries continue to define their own agendas actively and today have, in fact, claimed much of the momentum of feminist and women's rights advocacy globally. They have helped influence the combination of the rights-based and development-based approaches to women's advancement, which has energized activists in the global South. Global feminism is a more South-centered movement than ever before and African women leaders have helped significantly in bringing about this transformation. In the past decade, many of the specific initiatives pertaining to women's rights have come from the global South.

African contributions to transnational women's rights activism have been especially important in the areas of violence against women, women and conflict, the girl child, financing women's entrepreneurship, resisting female genital cutting, the role of government versus nongovernmental organizations (NGOs) in service provision, and increasingly in discussions about women and political decision making (Madunagu 2001; Snyder 2003; Tripp 2006).

## AFRICAN WOMEN AND UN WOMEN'S INITIATIVES

Margaret Snyder has characterized the United Nations as the "unlikely god-mother" of the global feminist movement. Women the world over have relied on the UN to help define and coalesce women's concerns, put forward programs for legislative change, provide fora for meeting across borders, and participate in discussions on issues of concern to women's lives (Snyder 2006). By sheer numbers, African women have been visible in the various international conferences, starting with the First World Conference on Women in Mexico (1975) and Copenhagen (1980), but especially after Nairobi (1985) and Beijing (1995), as well as the follow-up Beijing + 5 conference in New York (2000). They have also effectively participated in the other related international conferences: the UN Conference on Environment and Development (UNCED) in Rio de Janeiro (1992), the Human Rights Conference in Vienna (1993), the International Conference on Population and Development in Cairo (1994), and the Copenhagen World Summit for Social Development (1995).

African women attended the conferences in various capacities as NGO representatives, on official national delegations, as members of UN agencies, as professionals, and as organizers.[1] They were visible in planning and running these conferences. Gertrude Mongella was general secretary of the UN Beijing conference, whereas Filomena Steady was one of the key convenors of the Earth Summit (1992). The Kenya Women's Group helped in the planning and running of the Nairobi conference (1985).

These international fora provided a range of opportunities for African women to bring their unique experiences to the rest of the UN community.

---

[1] As with the other four world regions, Africa had two representatives on the NGO Forum Facilitating Committee: Soukeyna Ndiaye Ba of Senegal and Njoki Wainaina of Kenya, both officials of the African Women's Communications and Development Network (FEMNET). Of the twenty-seven Editing Committee members for the NGO Forum report, the Africa region had seven members: Hoda Badran of Egypt, Winnie Byanyima of Uganda, Sara Hlu-pekile Longwe of Zambia, Veronica Mullei of Senegal, Bernadette Palle of Burkina Faso, Primila Patten of Mauritius, and Linda Vilarazi-Tselane of South Africa. Plenary speakers at the NGO Forum included Bisi Adeleye-Fayemi, Akina Mama wa Afrika (UK); Reine-Brigitte Agbassy-Boni, the African Women Leaders in Agriculture and the Environment (AWLAE), Winrock International Institute, Cote d'Ivoire; Florence Butegwa, Women in Law and Development in Africa (based in Zimbabwe), Uganda; Winnie Byanyima, Women's Caucus, Constituent Assembly, Uganda; Cheryl Carolus, African National Congress (ANC), South Africa; Misrak Elias, Effective Gender Equality Strategies – the United Nations Children's Fund (UNICEF), Ethiopia; Francoise Kaudjhis-Offoumou, International Association for Democracy in Africa, Côte d'Ivoire; Miria R. K. Matembe, Constituent Assembly, Uganda; and Esther Ocloo, Sustainable End of Hunger Foundation, Ghana.

These conferences served as a stimulus for many programs for women's advancement on the continent, but they also provided fora for African women to share their experiences and influence the global women's movement.

For example, one of the six organizations involved in drafting the 1979 Convention on the Elimination of Discrimination against Women (CEDAW) together with representatives of member states was the All African Women's Conference, which was the only regional organization involved (Zwingel 2005: 12). African women have continued to be part of the Monitoring International Group for CEDAW.

In the preparations for the 1995 Beijing conference, many African-based and/or -oriented organizations formed part of the NGO Forum Planning Committee, including the African Women's Communication and Development Network (FEMNET), which was also charged with the overall coordination of the African regional input.[2] In addition, African women were members of international bodies on this planning committee, such as the Federation of University Women, the Girl Guides Association, Women's World Banking, the Young Women's Christian Association (YWCA), and many others.

African women's organizations pressed the UN Economic Commission for Africa to establish a training center for women already in the 1970s. The African Training and Research Centre for Women (ATRCW), which was formed in Addis Ababa, became the first regional center in the world and soon became a model for the UN system as other such centers were established. It provided a national machinery for the advancement of women within the UN structure. This center has played a major role in articulating the role of women and ensuring the formulation of relevant policies and conventions and charters from the women's perspective. The center was deeply involved in planning and facilitating women's participation at the various conferences, including the Beijing+ conference and related activities.

When they came to the 1980 world conference on women in Copenhagen, African women representatives were prepared with draft policy proposals regarding women and development, having worked on them in advance at a Lusaka regional conference that drew on research carried out by ATRCW. The proposals became the Women and Development section of the OAU's

---

[2] Other participating organizations included AAWORD, Akina Mama Wa Afrika London Women's Centre, the Association of Uganda Women Medical Doctors/Advocacy for Women's Health, and Comité d'Action pour les Droits de l'Enfant et de la Femme (CADEF) in Mali, Country Women of Nigeria, Women in Africa/The African Diaspora.

1982 Lagos Plan of Action and served as a blueprint for women's economic empowerment, detailing education strategies, plans to claim administrative and political power, the need for research and the exchange of information regarding economic changes as they affected women, and ways to build strategic collaborations between governments, international agencies, and women's NGOs. As Devaki Jain put it, "African women were several steps ahead of the rest of the world's women during the 1960s and 1970s" as they were already conducting research and translating it into policy recommendations for government officials and regional bodies (Jain 2005: 100–1). The notion of gender mainstreaming was articulated by women like Jacqueline Ki-zerbo already in 1960 when at a meeting of the United Nations Economic Commission for Africa she argued for the need to "keep a double stream, to have specific support for women while at the same time trying to involve them in the mainstream of decisions and actions" (Snyder and Tadesse 1995: 38).

Similarly, Women's World Banking was inspired by women's economic activity in Africa. A pre-conference seminar before the 1975 Mexico City UN Conference on Women discussed how women might be able to access capital to improve their economic situation. There the successful Ghanaian entrepreneur, industrialist, and philanthropist Esther Ocloo pioneered the idea of formalizing local women's credit associations. Ocloo worked with Ela Bhatt, founder of the Self Employed Women's Association in India and Michaela Walsh, a New York investment banker, and together they founded Women's World Banking in 1979. Ocloo became the first chairperson of its board, serving in that capacity from 1980 to 1985. As of 2005, Women's World Banking operates in forty-five countries around the world.

Following Ocloo's lead, other African women funders have emerged on the continent to provide resources also for women's rights advocacy. Bisi Adeleye-Fayemi (Nigeria and the United Kingdom), Joana Foster (Ghana), and Hilda Tadria (Uganda) formed the African Women's Development Fund (AWDF), based in Accra, Ghana, which supports local, national, and regional organizations in Africa working on women's empowerment. Since its creation in 2001, it has funded 575 women's organizations in forty-one African countries.

At the 1985 Nairobi conference, African women were able to influence official discussions of the UN conference to focus on issues of national liberation and apartheid that were not receiving the deserved attention. A decade later at the UN Conference on Women held in Beijing in 1995, African women once again played a key role in promoting among other things, their concerns regarding the girl child, which became one of the twelve areas of critical concern in the core of the Beijing Platform for Action. This had been part of a proposal coming out of the NGO Forum for the region (Fifth Conference on African Women, Dakar, Senegal, 1994) and was accepted by the official African Conference. As the final report for the NGO Forum explained:

Perhaps the most significant achievements were the successful participation of rural African women in the Conference and the historic collaboration between African NGOs and their official counterparts. Rural African women's participation held center-stage in the African women's agenda. Their presence and vision were evident throughout the region's activities and culminated in the launching of an African rural women's bank. The cross-sector collaboration of the region's representatives made the issue of the girl-child a priority for the Conference and helped ensure the recognition of women's rights as human rights. ("Final Report..." 1995: 46)

LEADERS IN POLICY

Ever since Rwanda's women parliamentarians claimed 49 percent of the legislative seats, the highest in the world, advocates for greater female political representation around the globe have been looking to Africa to understand better how to improve women's political standing. This was further underscored by the election of Ellen Johnson-Sirleaf as president of Liberia. It gave women in Africa new visibility in politics on a global scale and has resulted in a new discussion about the strategies to enhance women's political representation. As we saw in Chapter 6, a key demand of many women's movements in Africa is equal representation of women in legislative bodies, local government, and other decision-making bodies. In various African countries such as Kenya, Namibia, Sierra Leone, South Africa, and Uganda, there are 50/50 movements advocating that women claim half of all parliamentary seats. Regional bodies such as the African Union, ECOWAS, and SADC have been debating the use of quotas to promote women's parliamentary representation in these bodies. Drude Dahlerup and Lenita Freidenvall (2005) have argued that the incremental model of increasing women's representation in parliament that led to high rates of female representation in the Nordic countries in the 1970s has been replaced by the fast track model one finds in developing countries where dramatic jumps in parliamentary representation are brought about by the introduction of electoral quotas. African women have played an important role in advancing the debate regarding both the advantages and disadvantages of the use of quotas.

Another area that has generated considerable momentum in Africa has been the adoption of "gender budgets," or attempts to make the gender implications of national spending priorities more explicit and ultimately fairer. As described in Chapter 7, after the 1995 Beijing UN Women's Conference, many countries in Africa adopted women's budgets patterned along the lines of South Africa's 1994 budget exercise, which itself was inspired by the budgets of federal and state governments in Australia in 1984. Approximately thirty gender-sensitive budget initiatives were under way globally by 2006, the largest number of which were in Africa, including Botswana, Malawi, Mozambique, Namibia, Tanzania, Uganda, and Zimbabwe. Gender budgeting as an approach has subsequently spread more widely in the West; the European Union has endorsed this as an approach as have the parliaments of some of its member states such as Germany. African experiences with this form of mainstreaming have been an important factor in increasing their popularity.

African women's contributions to policy were also to be seen in global fora. Coming from a continent that has experienced a great many of the world's civil conflicts, African women also were very proactive in promoting issues of peace and peacemaking in international fora and in confronting various heads of states. Because of women's marginalization from politics, they brought a different set of interests to bear on peace processes and talks. African women, in particular, made peace a central issue at the UN Beijing Conference on Women in 1995. Their efforts contributed greatly to the passing of the UN Security Council Resolution 1325 on 31 October 2000 to include women in peace negotiations and give them roles in peace-keeping missions around the world. The resolution requires protection of women and girls against sexual assault in civil conflicts and heightened efforts to place women in decision-making positions in international institutions.

These are just a few areas where women in Africa have contributed to policy debates globally. There are many others, ranging from women and peacemaking, to women's role in informal economies, to understanding the relationship between HIV/AIDS and violence against women.

## CULTURAL RIGHTS AND WOMEN'S RIGHTS

African women were also among the first to discuss openly the tensions between women's rights and cultural rights that are so contentious today. Professor Seble Dawit (Ethiopia), Mme. Diakité (Mali), Asha Elmi Hagi (Somalia), Dr. Amna Hassan (Sudan), Jane Frances Kuka (Uganda), Salem Mekuria (Ethiopia), Dr. Nawal es-Sadaawi (Egypt), and Dr. Nahid Toubia (Sudan) are a few of the many leaders in the struggle to eradicate female genital cutting in Africa.

The Inter-African Committee on Traditional Practices Affecting the Health of Women and Children was formed in 1984 and works with governments, international organizations, and donors to develop and evaluate policies, laws, and programs to protect and promote the bodily integrity of women and young girls. Groups such as Somalia National Committee on Female Genital Mutilation and Harmful Traditional Practices, Tostan in Senegal, and Women Wake Up (WOWAP) in Tanzania have led the way in their respective countries advocating for change in the area of female genital mutilation (FGM).

As Seble Dawitt explains:

Current practice has it that when the treatment of women in the "private" context is questioned, we are suddenly not members of families and communities but family and community itself. Our lives become secondary to the preservation of communal identity. The challenge we pose is to the structure itself, and not merely to its outward manifestations – in the final analysis, if what goes on in families and communities is not open to scrutiny and adjudication, then no human right can be protected. This is where we are today. (Dawit 1994: 39)

Today there are women's movements in Africa challenging constructions of culture – and of the family, clan, tribe, and community – that deny women their human rights in the name of preserving culture. Beyond the debates regarding FGM, there are numerous conflicts between those claiming the right to religious and cultural freedom and women's rights advocates in other countries over issues like polygamy, child marriage, and inheritance rights.

Thus, as women's movements have responded to the challenges of poverty, conflict, domestic violence, and political marginalization in their own societies, they have engaged regional and global actors in order to advance their own goals at home. They have been linked with international women's movements to lobby the UN and other multilateral agencies as well as foreign donors. They have relied on international treaties and conventions to press their own agenda at home. And they have engaged regional organizations such as SADC as well as ECOWAS and ECCAS to do the same.

Finally, as African women's movements have taken advantage of changing international gender norms and transnational feminist movements to advance their own agendas domestically, they themselves have in turn influenced international women's movements in areas such as the political representation of women, gender budgeting, micro-credit, peace and conflict, and dealing with cultural constraints on gender-based change. Although our focus has been on women's agency, we have shown how it interacts with structural factors to bring about change. The change in international norms and the popularity of rights-based approaches as advocated by women's movements provided an important rationale for the UN, African regional associations, and other multilateral and bilateral donors to press governments to adopt more woman-friendly legislation. These pressures were, as we have seen, felt most sharply in postconflict contexts given the disruptions in gender and other societal relations.

# Bibliography

AAWORD. 1982. "The Experience of the Association of African Women for Research and Development." *Development Dialogue* 1–2.

Abdul-Raheem, Tajudeen. 2000. Paper presented at the conference "The Challenges to the Social Sciences in Africa in the Twenty-First Century." October, at Makerere University, Kampala, Uganda.

Abdullah, Hussaina. 1993. "'Transition Politics' and the Challenge of Gender in Nigeria." *Review of African Political Economy* 56: 27–41.

———. 1995. "Wifeism and Activism: The Nigerian Women's Movement." In *Challenge of Local Feminisms*, ed. A. Basu. Boulder: Westview Press.

Accampo, Elinor Ann, and Rachel Ginnis Fuchs. 1995. *Gender and the Politics of Social Reform in France, 1870–1914.* Baltimore: Johns Hopkins University Press.

ACFODE. 2005. *Gender Responsive Budgeting (GRB): ACFODE's Experiences at the Local Level 2004.* Kampala: Action for Development.

Adams, Melinda. 2003. "Cameroon." In *Sub-Saharan Africa: The Greenwood Encyclopedia of Women's Issues Worldwide*, ed. Aili Mari Tripp. Westport: Greenwood Press.

———. 2004a. "Appropriating Global Discourses for Domestic Aims: National Machinery for the Advancement of Women." In *Annual Meeting of the American Political Science Association*. Chicago.

———. 2004b. "Women's Organizations, and the State in Cameroon." Ph.D., Political Science, University of Wisconsin–Madison, Madison.

Adams, Melinda, and Alice Kang. 2007. Regional Advocacy Networks and the Protocol on the Rights of Women in Africa. *Politics & Gender* 3 (4): 451–74.

Ahooja-Patel, Krishna. 1982. "Another Development with Women." *Development Dialogue* 1 (2): 17–28.

Albertyn, Cathi. 2005. "Defending and Securing Rights through Law: Feminism, Law and the Courts in South Africa." *Politikon* 32 (2): 217–37.

All-Party Burundi Women's Peace Conference. "Final Declaration." 2000. 17–20 July, at Arusha.

Alvarez, Sonia. 1998. "Latin American Feminisms 'Go Global.'" In *Cultures of Politics/Politics of Cultures: Revisioning Latin American Social Movements*, ed. S. E. Alvarez, E. Dagnino, and A. Escobar. Boulder: Westview Press.

Amadiume, Ifi. 2000. *Daughters of the Goddess, Daughters of Imperialism: African Women Struggle for Culture, Power and Democracy*. London: Zed.

Anderlini, Sanam N. 2000. "Women at the Peace Table: Making a Difference." New York: UNIFEM.

Andersen, Margrethe Holm. 1992. "Women in Politics: A Case Study of Gender Relations and Women's Political Participation in Sukumaland, Tanzania." Ph.D., Aalborg University, Denmark.

Ankrah, Maxine E. 1996. "ACFODE: A Decade and Beyond." *Arise* 17 (January–June): 21–2.

Antrobus, Peggy. 2004. *The Global Women's Movement: Origins, Issues and Strategies*. London: Zed.

Arnfred, Signe. 1988. "Women in Mozambique: Gender Struggle and Gender Politics." *Review of African Political Economy* 41: 5–16.

———. 2001 "Questions of Power: Women's Movements, Feminist Theory and Development Aid." *Sidastudies* No. 3, *Discussing Women's Empowerment – Theory and Practice*. Stockholm: SIDA.

Arthur, Maria Jose, Amida Maman, and Helena Pedro 2000. "Politicas da Desigualdade? Primeiros Elementos para uma Avaliacao das Politicas e Programas de Genero do Governo e ONGs apos Beijing, 1995–1999." [Politics of Inequality? Basic Elements for an Evaluation of the Politics and Programs of the Government and NGOs after Beijing, 1995–1999.] Maputo: Fórum Mulher.

Awasom, Sussana Yene. 2002. "A Critical Survey of the Resuscitation, Activation, and Adaptation of Traditional African Female Political Institutions to the Exigencies of Modern Politics in the 1990s: The Case of the Takumbeng Female Society in Cameroon." Paper for the CODESRIA Tenth General Assembly, 8–12 December 2002 at Kampala. Available online at http://www.codesria.org/Archives/ga10/Abstracts%20GA%201-5/gender_Awasom.htm, accessed 21 May 2008.

Babalola, Stella. 2004. "Invisibility and Women in the Constitution." *This Day*, September 1.

Bacchi, Carol Lee. 1999. *Women, Policy and Politics: The Construction of Policy Problems*. London: Sage.

Baden, Sally, and Anne Marie Goetz. 1997. "Who Needs [Sex] When You Can Have [Gender]? Conflicting Discourses on Gender at Beijing." *Feminist Review* 56: 3–25.

Bainomugisha, A. 1999. "The Empowerment of Women." In *Uganda's Age of Reforms: A Critical Overview*, ed. J. Mugaju. Kampala: Fountain.

Banda, Fareda. 2005. *Women, Law and Human Rights: An African Perspective*. Oxford and Portland: Hart.

Bangura, Yusuf. 1996. "The Concept of Policy Dialogue and Gendered Development: Understanding Its Institutional and Ideological Constraints." Paper presented at UNRISD/CPD workshop "Working towards a More Gender Equitable Macro-Economic Agenda, 26–28," November, at Rajendrapur, Bangladesh.

Barrig, Maruja. 1999. "The Persistence of Memory: Feminism and the State in Peru in the 1990s, Civil Society and Democratic Governance in the Andes and the Southern Cone." Comparative Regional Project, Ford Foundation–Department of Social Sciences. La Pontificia Universidad Católica del Perú (PUCP), Lima. Peru.

Basu, Amrita, ed. 1995. *Challenge of Local Feminisms*. Boulder: Westview Press.

"Batswana Stage Street Protests against Rape" 2002. Panafrican News Agency, 1 March.

Bauer, Gretchen, and Hannah Evelyn Britton. 2006. *Women in African Parliaments*. Boulder: Lynne Rienner.

Biyong, Pauline. 1998. "Stronger NGOs Needed for Grassroots Work." *Africa Recovery* (August): 32.

Blofield, Merike H., and Liesl Haas. 2005. "Defining a Democracy: Reforming the Laws on Women's Rights in Chile, 1990–2002." *Latin American Politics and Society* 47 (3): 35–68.

Brand, Laurie A. 1998. *Women, the State, and Political Liberalization: Middle Eastern and North African Experience*. New York: Columbia University Press.

Bratton, Michael. 1989. "The Politics of Government-NGO Relations in Africa." *World Development* 17 (4): 569–87.

Britton, Hannah. 2002. "Coalition Building, Election Rules, and Party Politics: South African Women's Path to Parliament." *Africa Today* 49 (4): 33–67.

———. 2005. *Women in the South African Parliament: From Resistance to Governance*. Urbana: University of Illinois Press.

Buckley, Mary. 1997. *Post-Soviet Women: From the Baltic to Central Asia*. Cambridge and New York: Cambridge University Press.

Budlender, Debbie. 2000. "The Political Economy of Women's Budgets in the South." *World Development* 28 (7): 1365–78.

Burke, Enid, Jennifer Klot, and Bunting Ikaweba, eds. 2001. *Engendering Peace: Reflections on the Burundi Peace Process*. UNIFEM, African Women for Peace Series.

Cahen, Michel. 1984. "I. Corporatisme et Colonialisme. Approche du Cas Mozambicain, 1933–1979. II. Crise et Survivance du Corporativisme Colonial, 1960–1979." [I. Corporatism and Colonialism. The Case of Mozambique, 1933-1979. II. Crisis and Survival of Colonial Corporatism 1960–1979]. *Cahiers d'Études Africains* 98 (24): 5–24.

Callan, Hilary, and Shirley Ardener, eds. 1984. *The Incorporated Wife*. London: Croom Helm.

"Cape Town Men to March against Women and Child Abuse." 2002. *BuaNews*, 25 November.

Casimiro, Isabel. 1986. "Transformação nas Relações Homem/Mulher em Moçambique, 1964–74" [Changing Gender Relations in Mozambique, 1964–74]. Licenciatura, Universidade Eduardo Mondlane, Maputo.

———. 1999. "Peace in the Country, War at Home'. Feminism and Women Organisations in Mozambique, 1987–97." M.A., Sociology, Universidade de Coimbra, Coimbra, Portugal.

———. 2004. *"Paz na Terra, Guerra em Casa". Feminismo e Organizações de Mulheres em Moçambique, Maputo*. ["Peace on Earth, War at Home." Feminism and Women Organizations in Mozambique.] Maputo: PROMÉDIA, Colecção Identidades.

"Chadian Police Forces Shot Grenades at a Peaceful Assembly of Women," *Africa News*, 14 June 2001.

Chanock, Martin. 1980. "Neo-Traditionalism and the Customary Law in Malawi." In *African Women and the Law*, ed. M. Hay and M. Wright. Boston: Boston University Press.

Chappell, Louise A. 2002. *Gendering Government: Feminist Engagement with the State in Australia and Canada*. Vancouver: UBC Press.

Chilaizya, Joe. 1995. "Zambia-Gender: Women Split on Constitutional Rights Issue." *Inter Press Service*, November 9.

Clark, Cal, and Rose J. Lee. 2000. "Democracy and 'Softening' Society." In *Democracy and the Status of Women in East Asia*, ed. R. J. Lee and C. Clark. Boulder: Lynne Rienner.

Clark, Cindy, Ellen Sprenger, and Lisa VeneKlasen. 2005. "Where is the Money for Women's Rights: Assessing Resources and the Role of Donors in the Promotion of Women's Rights and the Support of Women's Organizations." Association for Women's Rights in Development. Available at http://www.awid.org/publications/money_report_2005_en.pdf, accessed 21 May 2008.

Connell, Dan. 1998. "Strategies for Change: Women and Politics in Eritrea and South Africa." *Review of African Political Economy* 25 (76): 189–206.

Cooper, Barbara. 1995. "The Politics of Difference and Women's Associations in Niger: Of 'Prostitutes,' the Public and Politics." *Signs* 20 (4): 851–82.

Council of Europe. 1998. Committee of Ministers Recommendation No. R (98) 14 of the Committee of Ministers to Member States on Gender Mainstreaming. Adopted by the Committee of Ministers on 7 October 1998 at the 643rd Meeting of the Ministers' Deputies.

Dahlerup, Drude, and Lenita Freidenvall. 2005. "Quotas as a 'Fast Track' to Equal Representation for Women," *International Feminist Journal of Politics*, 7 (1): 26–48.

Dakar Declaration. 1982. *Development Dialogue* 1–2: 11–6.

Dawit, Seble. 1994. "Culture as a Human Rights Concern: Highlights for Action with the African Charter on Human and Peoples' Rights." In *Gender Violence and Women's Human Rights in Africa*, Center for Women's Global Leadership, Douglass College, Rutgers, New Brunswick.

Dei, George J. Sefa. 1994. "The Women of a Ghanaian Village: A Study of Social Change." *African Studies Review* 37 (2): 121–45.

DENIVA 2006. *Civicus Civil Society Index Project: Civil Society in Uganda: At the Crossroads?* Kampala: DENIVA.

Denzer, LaRay. 1987. "Women in Freetown Politics, 1914–61: A Preliminary Study." *Africa: Journal of the International African Institute* 57 (4): 439–56.

———. 1992. "Domestic Science Training in Colonial Yorubaland, Nigeria." In *African Encounters with Domesticity*, ed. K. Hansen. New Brunswick: Rutgers University Press.

———. ed. 1995. *Constance Agatha Cummings-John: Memoirs of a Krio Leader*. Ibadan: Humanities Research Center.

Diduk, Susan. 1989. "Women's Agricultural Production and Political Action in the Cameroon Grassfields." *Africa* 59 (3): 338–55.

Disney, Jennifer. 2005. "Mozambique: Empowering Women through Family Law." In *Women in African Parliaments*, ed. G. Bauer and H. Britton. Boulder: Lynne Rienner.

DRCongo Radio. 2004. "Women Demonstrate in East, Call for Sanctions against Rwanda." 7 December.

Dunbar, Roberta Ann, and Hadiza Djibo. 1992. "Islam, Public Policy and the Legal Status of Women in Niger." Genesys report prepared for Office of Women in Development, Bureau for Research and Development, Agency for International Development.

Edwards, Michael, and Davide Hulme. 1996. "Too Close for Comfort? The Impact of Official Aid on Nongovernmental Organizations." *World Development* 24 (6): 961–73

Einhorn, Barbara. 1993. *Cinderella Goes to Market: Citizenship, Gender, and Women's Movements in East Central Europe.* London and New York: Verso.

Elliott, C. 1987. "Some Aspects of Relations between the North and South in the NGO Sector." *World Development* 15: 57–68.

Endeley B. Joyce. 2004. "Establishment of the Department of Women and Gender Studies of the University of Buea, Cameroon." *AGI Newsletter* 13 (October). Available online at http://web.uct.ac.za/org/agi/pubs/newsletters/vol13/buea.htm, accessed 1 December 2007.

Essof, Shereen. 2005. "She-murenga: Challenges, Opportunities and Setbacks of the Women's Movement in Zimbabwe." *Feminist Africa* (4): 29–45.

Facio, Alda. 1997. "Campaña Mundial 1998: Un Año para Celebrar y Exigir [1998 Worldwide Campaign: A Year of Celebration and Activism]." In *Boletín Red Contra la Violencia*, N°17 Septiembre. ISIS International. 5–7.

Fallon, Kathleen. 2003. "The Status of Women in Ghana." In *Sub-Saharan Africa: The Greenwood Encyclopedia of Women's Issues Worldwide*, ed. A. M. Tripp. Westport:. Greenwood Press.

———. Forthcoming. *Big Men, Small Girls, and the Transition to Democracy: Ghanaian Women Mobilizing within Gendered and Political Terrains.* Baltimore: Johns Hopkins University Press.

Feldman, Rayah. 1983. "Women's Groups and Women's Subordination: An Analysis of Politics towards Rural Women in Kenya." *Review of African Political Economy* 27/28: 67–85.

Feminia. 2002. "Empowerment Mechanisms, How Women Wield Power in a Traditional Milieu." Available online at http://www.mediacommunity.org/feminia/index.php?nav=iap.php&screen=1&crit=&p=10&id=122, accessed 1 December 2007.

Ferguson, Anne E. with Beatrice Liatto Katundu. 1994. "Women in Politics in Zambia: What Difference has Democracy Made?" *African Rural and Urban Studies* 1 (2): 11–30.

Ferguson, Anne, Kimberly Ludwig, Beatrice Liatto Katundu, and Irene Manda. 1995. "Zambian Women in Politics: An Assessment of Changes Resulting from the 1991 Political Transition." Working paper, Michigan State University.

Ferree, Myra Marx. 2006. "Globalization and Feminism: Opportunities and Obstacles for Activism in the Global Arena." In *Transnational Feminisms: Women's Global Activism and Human Rights*, ed. Myra Marx Ferree and Aili Mari Tripp. New York: New York University Press.

"Final Report of the NGO Forum on Women." 1995. Paper presented at the NGO Forum on Women, at Beijing. 30 August–8 September.

Fleshman, Michael. 2002. "'Gender Budgets' Seek More Equity: Improved Spending Priorities Can Benefit All Africans." *Africa Recovery* 16 (1): 4.

———. 2003. "African Women Struggle for a Seat at the Peace Table." *Africa Recovery* 16 (4): 1.

Fonchingong, Charles. 2004. "The Travails of Democratization in Cameroon in the Context of Political Liberalisation since the 1990s." *African and Asian Studies*, 3 (1): 33–59.

"For Women, Constitution Is a Curate's Egg." 2005. *Inter Press Service*, 22 February 2005.

Franceschet, Susan. 2005. *Women and Politics in Chile*. Boulder: Lynne Rienner.

Gal, Susan, and Gail Kligman. 2000a. *Politics of Gender after Socialism: A Comparative-Historical Essay*. Princeton: Princeton University Press.

———. 2000b. *Reproducing Gender: Politics, Publics, and Everyday Life after Socialism*. Princeton: Princeton University Press.

Gawaya-Tegulle, Tom, and Rose Mary Kemigisha. 2000. "Gender Ministry Remains Skeleton." *Other Voice*, 3 (2): 1–8.

Gayflor, Hon. Vabah. 2005. Comments made at the conference Women and Political Participation in Africa: Lessons from Southern and Eastern Africa. Organized by International IDEA, Abantu for Development, Centre Pour Gouvernance Democratique Burkina Faso, 24–25 November, at Accra, Ghana.

Gberie, Lansana. 2003. "Sankoh, the Warlord Is Dead." *Concord Times* (Sierra Leone). 6 August 2003.

Geiger, Susan. 1982. "Umoja wa Wanawake wa Tanzania and the Needs of the Rural Poor." *African Studies Review*, 25 (2, 3): 45–65.

———. 1987. "Women in Nationalist Struggle: TANU Activists in Dar es Salaam." *International Journal of African Historical Studies*, 20 (1): 1–26.

———. 1990. "Woman and African Nationalism." *Journal of Women's History* 2 (1): 227–44.

Geisler, Gisela. 1987. "Sisters under the Skin: Women and the Women's League in Zambia." *Journal of Modern African Studies* 25 (1): 43–66.

———. 1995. "Troubled Sisterhood: Women and Politics in Southern Africa." *African Affairs* 94: 545–78.

———. 2004. *Women and the Remaking of Politics in Southern Africa: Negotiating Autonomy, Incorporation and Representation*. Uppsala: Nordiska Afrikainstitutet.

Gelb, Joyce, and Marian Lief Palley. 1982. *Women and Public Policies*. Princeton: Princeton University Press.

"Gender Activists Protest MP's Anti-Women Remarks," 2006. UN Integrated Regional Information Networks, 11 October.

Ghai, Yash. 2005. "The Constitution Making Process in Kenya." Paper presented at African Politics Colloquium, 11 October 2005 at University of Wisconsin–Madison.

Gilmartin, Christina K. 1995. *Engendering the Chinese Revolution: Radical Women, Communist Politics, and Mass Movements in the 1920s.* Berkeley: University of California Press.

Goetz, Anne Marie, and Shireen Hassim. 2003. *No Shortcuts to Power: African Women in Politics and Policy Making.* London: Zed.

Gouws, Amanda. 2006. "The State of the National Machinery: Structural Problems and Personalised Politics." In *State of the Nation: South Africa,* ed. Sakhela Buhlungu, John Daniel, Roger Southall, and Jessica Lutchman. Cape Town: HSRC Press (Human Science Research Council Press).

Gray, L., and M. Kevane. 1999. "Diminished Access, Diverted Exclusion: Women and Land Tenure in Sub-Saharan Africa." *African Studies Review* 42 (2): 15–39.

Haffajee, Ferial. 1999. "Women Peace It Together." Addis Ababa: FLAME/FLAMME (daily newsletter of the Sixth African Regional Conference on Women, 25 November 1999 at Addis Ababa).

Hassim, Shireen. 2005. "Terms of Engagement: South African Challenges." *Feminist Africa* (4): 10–28.

———. 2006. *Women's Organizations and Democracy in South Africa Contesting Authority.* Madison: University of Wisconsin Press.

Hauser, Ellen. 1999. "Ugandan Relations with Western Donors and the 1990s: What Impact on Democratisation?" *Journal of Modern African Studies* 37 (4): 622.

Henry, Joanne. 2005. "Mobilising Tanzania's Women: Joanne Henry Speaks with Fatma Alloo." *Feminist Africa* (4): 139–50.

Hipsher, Patty, and R. Darcy. 2000. "Women Policies in Asia." In *Democracy and the Status of Women in East Asia,* ed. R. J. Lee and C. Clark. Boulder: Lynne Rienner.

Hirschmann, David. 1991. "Women and Political Participation in Africa: Broadening the Scope of Research." *World Development* 19 (12): 1679–94.

Hollier-Larousse, Juliette. 2000. "Somali Women Win Political Emancipation with Parliamentary Quota." *Agence France Presse.* 1 August.

Holm, John. 1989. "Rolling Back Autocracy in Africa: The Botswana Case." In *Beyond Autocracy in Africa,* ed. R. Joseph. Atlanta: Carter Center.

Htun, Mala. 2003. *Sex and the State: Abortion, Divorce, and the Family under Latin American Dictatorships and Democracies.* New York: Cambridge University Press.

Hughes, Melanie. 2004. "Another Road to Power? Armed Conflict, International Linkages, and Women's Parliamentary Representation in Developing Nations." Paper presented at the Ninety-Ninth American Sociological Association Annual Meeting, 14–17 August 2004 at San Francisco.

Hunt, Nancy. 1989. "Placing African Women's History and Locating Gender," *Journal of Social History* 14 (3): 359–79.

———. 1990. "Domesticity and Colonialism in Belgian Africa; Usumbura's *Foyer Social,* 1946–1960." *Signs* 15 (31): 447–74.

———. 1999. *A Colonial Lexicon of Birth Ritual, Medicalization, and Mobility in the Congo*. Durham: Duke University Press.

Ibrahim, Jibrin. 2004. "The First Lady Syndrome and the Marginalisation of Women from Power: Opportunities or Compromises for Gender Equality?" Available online at http://www.feministafrica.org/, accessed 22 May 2008.

Ibraimo, Maimuna A. 2003. "The Gender Dimension of Mozambique's Budget: An Assessment Report." Report for UNIFEM–Southern Africa Regional Office.

Ifeka-Moller, Caroline. 1973. "'Sitting on a Man: Colonialism and the Lost Political Institutions of Ibo Women': A Reply to Judith Van Allen." *Canadian Journal of African Studies* 7: 317–18.

Imam, Ayesha. 1996. "The Dynamics of WINning: An Analysis of Women in Nigeria (WIN)." In *Feminist Genealogies, Colonial Legacies, Democratic Futures*, ed. M. J. M. Alexander and Chandra Talpade. New York and London: Routledge.

Inglehart, Ronald, Pippa Norris, and Chris Welzel. 2002. "Gender Equality and Democracy." *Comparative Sociology* 1 (3–4): 321–45.

Jacobson, Ruth. 1995. "Women's Political Participation: Mozambique's Democratic Transition." *Gender and Development* 3 (3): 29–35.

Jain, Devaki. 2005. *Women, Development, and the UN – A Six-Year Quest for Equality and Justice*. Bloomington: Indiana University Press.

Jaquette, Jane S., and Sharon L. Wolchik. 1998. *Women and Democracy: Latin America and Central and Eastern Europe*. Baltimore: Johns Hopkins University Press.

Jenje-Makwenda, Joyce. 1998. "The Republic of Dongo: Parliamentarian Margaret Dongo." *WIN (Women International Net) Magazine*. Available online at http://www.geocities.com/Wellesley/3321/win14b.htm, accessed 22 May 2008.

Jirira, K. Ona. 1995. "Gender, Politics and Democracy: Kuvaka Patsva (Reconstructing) the Discourse." *Safere* 1 (2): 1–29.

Johnson, Cheryl. 1982. "Grass Roots Organizing: Women in Anticolonial Activity in Southwestern Nigeria." *African Studies Review* 25 (2/3): 137–57.

Kabira, Wanjiku Mukabi, and Elizabeth Akinyi Nzioki. 1993. *Celebrating Women's Resistance*. Nairobi: New Earth Publishing.

Kamau, Jean N. 1999. "Assessment Report on Women's Participation in the Peace Process: Mid-Decade Review of the Implementation of the Dakar and Beijing Platforms for Action in the African Region." Paper presented at the Economic Commission for Africa Sixth African Conference on Women, 22–26 November, at Addis Ababa.

Kante, M., H. Hobgood, B. Lewis and C. Coulibaly. 1994. *Governance in Democratic Mali: An Assessment of Transition and Consolidation and Guidelines for Near-Term Action*. Washington: Associates in Rural Development.

Kanyinga, Karuti. 1993. "NGOs in Kenya." In *Social Change and Economic Reform in Africa*, ed. P. Gibbon. Uppsala: Scandinavian Institute of African Studies.

Kapinga, Marithe. 2003. "Africa: Women in Congo Form Common Front for Peace." *Ms. Magazine*, (Spring) 25–6. Available online at http://www.msmagazine.com/maro3/kapinga.asp, accessed 22 May 2008.

Kemp, Amanda, Nozizwe Madlala, Asha Moodley, and Elaine Salo. 1995. "The Dawn of a New Day: Redefining South African Feminism." In *Challenge of Local Feminisms*, ed. Amrita Basu. Boulder: Westview Press.

Khadiagala, Lynn. 2001. "The Failure of Popular Justice in Uganda: Local Councils and Women's Property Rights." *Development and Change* 32 (1): 55–76.

Kibwana, Kivutha. 2001. "Women, Politics and Gender Politicking: Questions from Kenya." In *Constitutionalism in Africa: Creating Opportunities, Facing Challenges*, ed. Joe Oloka-Onyango. Kampala: Fountain.

Kivamwo, Simon. 1997. "Keep Off Politics, Kigoda Advises Women Miners." *Daily News*, 30 December, 2.

Kolawole, Yinka. 2006. "Provide for Women in Purdah, INEC Urged." *This Day* (Nigeria), 12 November.

Konopo, Joel. 2005. "Women Hopeful about Gender Parity." *Mmegi/The Reporter*, 22 September.

KULIMA. 1997. "Directório das Organizações Não Governamentais (ONG's) em Moçambique" [Directory of Non-governmental Organizations (NGOs) in Mozambique]. Maputo: Ministério da Cooperação, Departamentos de Documentação e Informação e de ONG's.

Kwesiga, J. C. 2003."The National Machinery for Gender Equality in Uganda: Institutionalised Gesture Politics?" In *Mainstreaming Gender, Democratizing the State?: Institutional Mechanisms for the Advancement of Women*, ed. S. Rai. Manchester: Manchester University Press.

Kwesiga, Joy C., Aramanzan Madanda, Nite Baza Tanzarn, and Eilís Ward. 2003. "Women's Political Space: the Experience of Affirmative Action in Eritrea, Tanzania and Uganda." London: British Council and Department for International Development (DFID).

Kwesiga, Joy C. and Elizabeth N. Ssendiwala. Forthcoming. "Gender Mainstreaming in the University Context: Prospects and Challenges at Makerere University, Uganda." *Women's Studies International Forum* 29 (6): 592–605.

Lacina, Bethany, and Nils P. Gleditsch. 2005. "Monitoring Trends in Global Combat: A New Dataset of Battle Deaths." *European Journal of Population* 21 (2–3): 145–66.

"Lack of Legal Status Hinders the Progress of Women." 2005. UN Integrated Regional Information Networks. 18 August. Available online at http://www.irinnews.org/PrintReport.aspx?ReportId=55910, accessed 22 May 2008.

"Learning to Live without Husbands: Upper East Single Mothers Show the Way." 2005. *Public Agenda*, 8 August.

Lee, Rose J. 2000a. "Democratic Consolidation and Gender Politics in South Korea." In *Democracy and the Status of Women in East Asia*, ed. R. J. Lee and C. Clark. Boulder: Lynne Rienner.

———. 2000b. "Electoral Reform and Women's Empowerment: Taiwan and South Korea." In *Democracy and the Status of Women in East Asia*, ed. R. J. Lee and C. Clark. Boulder: Lynne Rienner.

Leith-Ross, Sylvia. 1965. *African Women*. London: Routledge and Paul Kegan.

Lemarchand, Réné. 1994. *Burundi: Ethnocide as Discourse and Practice*. Washington: Woodrow Wilson Center Press and Cambridge University Press.

"Liberia Politics: Peace Isn't Enough." 2006. *EIU ViewsWire*. 15 December.

Lindberg, Staffan I. 2004. "Women's Empowerment and Democratization: The Effects of Electoral Systems, Participation and Experience in Africa." *Studies in Comparative International Development* 39 (1): 28–53.

Lister, Sarah. 2000. "Power in Partnership? An Analysis of an NGO's Relationships with Its Partners." *Journal of International Development* 12: 227–39.

Longwe, Sara, and Clarke, Roy. 1991. "A Gender Perspective on the Zambian General Election of October 1991." Working paper, Zambia Association for Research and Development, Lusaka, Zambia.

Lueker, Lorna L. 1998. "Fighting for Human Rights: Women, War, and Social Change in Zimbabwe." *Instraw News* 28: 34–44.

Maathai, Wangari. 2006. *Unbowed: A Memoir*. New York: Alfred Knopf.

Madunagu, Bene E. 2001. "Reflections on New Directions for African Women." Paper presented at the Joint Meeting of the Society for Development (SID) and Development Alternatives with Women for a New Era (DAWN), African Chapter, 13–16 December, at Dar es Salaam, Tanzania.

Makanya, Stella. 1999. "Situation Analysis of Women in Politics in Selected SADC Countries." Paper presented at Women in Politics and Decision Making in SADC: Beyond 30% in 2005, 28 March–1 April, at Gaborone, Botswana.

Mama, Amina. 1995. "Feminism or Femocracy? State Feminism and Democratisation in Nigeria." *Africa Development* 20 (1): 37–58.

———. 1996. "Women's Studies and Studies of Women in Africa during the 1990s." In *CODESRIA Working Paper Series* 5/96. Dakar: CODESRIA.

———. 2004. "Critical Capacities: Facing the Challenges of Intellectual Development in Africa." Inaugural Address as Professor to the Prince Claus Chair in Development and Equity, 28 April 2004. The Hague: Institute of Social Studies.

———. 2005. "The Ghanaian Women's Manifesto Movement: Amina Mama Speaks with Dzodzi Tsikata, Rose Mensah-Kutin and Hamida Harrison." *Feminist Africa* (4): 124–38.

Manuh, Takyiwaa. 1998. "Women in Africa's Development: Overcoming Obstacles, Pushing for Progress." In *Africa Recovery Briefing Paper* 11 (April).

Masemann, Vandra Lea. 1974. "The Hidden Curriculum of a West African Girls' Boarding School." *Canadian Journal of African Studies* 8 (February): 479–94.

Matembe, Miria. 2002. *Gender, Politics, and Constitution Making in Uganda*. Kampala: Fountain.

Mbaku, John 2002 "Cameroon's Stalled Transition to Democratic Governance: Lessons for Africa's New Democrats." *African and Asian Studies* 1 (2): 125–63.

"Mbarara Stages Demo against Defilement." 2002. *New Vision* (Kampala), 13 March.

Mbikusita-Lewanika, Inonge. 1995. Paper presented at USAID Gender and Democracy in Africa Workshop, 28 July 1995 at Washington.

Mbire-Barungi, Barbara. 1999. "Ugandan Feminism: Political Rhetoric or Reality." *Women's Studies Forum International* 22 (4): 435–9.

Mbunwe, Chris. 2007. "We're Bored with Singsongs by CPDM Resource Persons – Bali Fon." *Post*. Available online at http://www.Postnewsline.com, accessed 16 November 2007.

McEwan, Cheryl. 2000. "Engendering Citizenship: Gendered Spaces of Democracy in South Africa." *Political Geography* 19 (5): 627–51.

McFadden, Patricia. 1997. "Challenges and Prospects for the African Women's Movement into the 21st Century." *Women in Action*, 1.

McKinley, James C. 1996. "In Peace, Warrior Women Rank Low." *New York Times*, 4 May, 4.

Media Monitoring Project. 1999. "Biased? Gender, Politics and the Media." In *Redefining Politics: South African Women and Democracy*, ed. S. Boezak. Johannesburg: Commission on Gender Equality, Parliamentary Women's Group, Gender Equity Unit (University of the Western Cape), Gender Advocacy Programme, School of Public and Development Management (University of Witwatersrand), and Women'sNet.

Meena, Ruth, ed. 1992. *Gender in Southern Africa – Conceptual and Theoretical Issue*. Harare: Sapes.

Mianda, Gertrude. 2002. "Colonialism, Education, and Gender Relations in the Belgian Congo: The Évolué Case." In *Women in African Colonial Histories*, ed. Jean Allman, Susan Geiger, and Nakanyike Musisi. Bloomington and Indianapolis: Indiana University Press.

Mikell, Gwendolyn. 1984. "Filiation, Economic Crisis and the Status of Women in Rural Ghana." *Canadian Journal of African Studies* 18 (1): 195–218.

Molyneux, Maxine. 1985. "Mobilisation without Emancipation? Women's Interests, the State, and Revolution in Nicaragua." *Feminist Studies* 2 (2): 227–54.

———. 1998. "Analysing Women's Movements." *Development and Change* 29 (1): 219–45.

Moran, Mary H., and M. Anne Pitcher. 2004. "The 'Basket Case' and the 'Poster Child': Explaining the End of Civil Conflicts in Liberia and Mozambique." *Third World Quarterly*, 25 (3): 501–19.

Morna, Colleen Lowe. 2003. "Beyond Numbers – Quotas in Practise." In *Parliamentary Forum Conference*. Pretoria: International Institute for Democracy and Electoral Assistance (IDEA)/Electoral Institute of Southern Africa (EISA)/Southern African Development Community (SADC).

———. 2004. *Ringing Up the Changes: Gender in Southern African Politics*. Johannesburg: Gender Links.

Mtintso, Thenjiwe. 1999. "The Contribution of Women Parliamentarians to Gender Equality." Unpublished thesis of an M.D. in public and development management, University of Witwatersrand, Johannesburg.

Mucunguzi, Julius, "NGOs ask Govt to Ammend [sic] Land Law." *Monitor*, 19 December.

Mugabe, Robert. 1984. "An Opening Address by the President of ZANU(PF)." Presented at Women's League Conference, 15–17 March, at Harare, Zimbabwe.

Mumba, Tafadzwa. 1997. "Shattering the Glass Ceiling in Politics." *Woman Plus*. May–August, 3–6.

Munachonga, Monica. 1989. "Women and the State: Zambia's Development Policies and Their Impact on Women." In *Women and the State in Africa*, ed. Jane L. Parpart and Kathleen A. Staudt. Boulder: Lynne Rienner.

Murphy, Emma C. 2003. "Women in Tunisia: Between State Feminism and Economic Reform." In *Women and Globalization in the Arab Middle East: Gender, Economy, and Society*, ed. Eleanor A. Doumato and Marsha P. Posusney. Boulder: Lynne Rienner.

Mwaniki, Nyaga. 1986. "Against Many Odds: The Dilemmas of Women's Self-Help Groups in Mbeere, Kenya." *Africa* 56 (2): 210–28.

Mwavita, Yvette B., 2002. "Violence against Women during the War: The Case of the Southern Kivu Province in Democratic Republic of Congo." *Women's Global Network for Reproductive Rights: Newsletter* 77 (October).

Negrão, José. 1998. "Terra e Desenvolvimento Rural em Moçambique" [Land and Rural Development in Mozambique]. Paper presented at Memórias do V Congresso Luso-Afro-Brasileiro de Ciências Sociais, at Maputo.

Ngugi, Mumbi. c. 2001. "The Women's Rights Movement and Democratization in Kenya." Unpublished paper.

Nkwi, Paul, and Antoine Socpa. 1997. "Ethnicity and Party Politics in Cameroon: The Politics of Divide and Rule," in *Regional Balance and National Integration in Cameroon: Lessons Learned and the Uncertain Future*, P. Nkwi and F. Nyamnjoh, eds. Leiden: African Studies Center, 139–49.

Nordstrom, Carolyn. 1997. *A Different Kind of War Story (Ethnography of Political Violence)*. Philadelphia: University of Pennsylvania Press.

Nyangoro, Julius, ed. 1999. *Civil Society and Democratic Development in Africa: Perspectives from Eastern and Southern Africa*. Harare: Mwengo.

Nzegwu, Nkiru. 1995. "Recovering Igbo Traditions: A Case for Indigenous Women's Organizations in Development." In *Women, Culture and Development: A Study of Human Capabilities*, ed. M. Nussbaum and J. Glover. Oxford: Clarendon Press.

Nzomo, Maria. 1994. "Empowering Women for Democratic Change in Kenya: Which Way Forward?" In *Empowerment of Women in the Process of Democratisation – Experiences of Kenya, Uganda and Tanzania*, ed. D. L. Klemp: Friedrich Ebert Stiftung.

———. 1995. Presentation to USAID Gender and Democracy in Africa Workshop, 28 July, at Washington.

O'Barr, Jean. 1976. "Pare Women: A Case of Political Involvement." *Rural Africana* 29: 121–34.

Obiorah, Ndubisi. 2001. "To the Barricades or the Soapbox: Civil Society and Democratization in Nigeria." Paper presented at Berkeley-Stanford Joint Center for African Studies Conference, 28 April, at Stanford University, Palo Alto.

O'Connor, Julia S., Ann Shola Orloff, and Sheila Shaver. 1999. *States, Markets, Families: Gender, Liberalism and Social Policy in Australia, Canada, Great Britain and the United States*. Cambridge: Cambridge University Press.

Ogundipe-Leslie, Molara. 1994. *Re-creating Ourselves: African Women & Critical Transformations*. Trenton: Africa World Press.

Ojiambo Ochieng, Ruth. 1998. "Information Services: Tools for Politicians and Policy Makers." *Impact Magazine* (Uganda) 1 (1): 33–6.

Okeke-Ihejirika, Philomina E., and Susan Franceschet. 2002. "Democratization and State Feminism: Gender Politics in Africa and Latin America." *Development and Change* 33: 439–66.

Okonjo, Kamene. 1994. "Reversing the Marginalization of the Invisible and Silent Majority: Women in Politics in Nigeria." In *Women and Politics Worldwide*, ed. B. J. Nelson and N. Chowdhury. New Haven and London: Yale University Press.

Okurut, Mary Karooro. 2006. "Thank You Women for the Peace Torch," *New Vision*, 11 November.

Olojede, Iyabo. 1999. *Women Interest Organizations: Encounters with the State on Issues of Good Governance*. Kano: Centre for Research and Documentation.

"OMM Returns to FRELIMO." 1996. *Mozambiquefile* 1 (August 24): 4–5.

Osei-Hwedie, Bertha Z. 1998. "Women's Role in Post-Independence Zambian Politics." *Atlantis* 22.2 (Spring/Summer): 85–96.

Ottaway, Marina, and Thomas Carothers. 2000. "Toward Civil Society Realism." In *Funding Virtue: Civil Society Aid and Democracy Promotion*, ed. M. Ottaway and T. Carothers. Washington: Carnegie Endowment for International Peace.

Otu, Martin Luther. 2004. "Govt Urged to Strengthen Institutions That Promote Women's Rights." *Public Agenda* (Accra), 5 July.

Owiti, Jeremiah. 2000. *Political Aid and the Making and Re-Making of Civil Society.* Brighton: Civil Society and Governance Programme, Institute of Development Studies, University of Sussex, Brighton.

Oyewumi, Oyeronke, ed. 2003. *African Women and Feminism: Reflecting on the Politics of Sisterhood.* Lawrenceville, NJ: Africa World Press.

Packard, Gabriel. 2003. "Somalian Seeks to Become Africa's First Female President," *Inter Press Service*, 15 July.

Palmer, Robin. 1998. "Oxfam GB's Land Advocacy Work in Tanzania and Uganda: The End of an Era?" Oxford: Oxfam.

"Paper Hails Liberian Women for Holding Peace Talks Delegates 'Hostage.'" 2003. *Accra Mail*, 24 July.

Parpart, Jane. 1988. "Women and the State in Africa." In *The Precarious Balance: State and Society in Africa*, ed. D. Rothchild and N. Chazan. Boulder: Westview Press.

Parpart, Jane L., and Kathleen A. Staudt. 1989. "Women and the State in Africa." In *Women and the State in Africa*, ed. J. L. Parpart and K. A. Staudt. Boulder: Lynne Rienner.

Pennell, C. Richard. 1987. "Women and Resistance to Colonialism in Morocco: The Rif 1916–1926." *Journal of African History* 28 (1): 107–18.

Peter, Chris Maina. 1999. "The State and Independent Civil Organisations: The Case of Tanzania Women Council (BAWATA)." Unpublished case study provided for the Civil Society and Governance in East Africa Project (Tanzania Side).

Phiri, Brighton. 2006. "Ministry of Women's Affairs Was Created for a Party Cadre – Sikazwe." *The Post*, 2 April.

Pineau, Carol. 2005. "The Africa You Never See." *Washington Post*, 17 April, B02.

Pitamber, Sunita, and Esther Hanoomanjee. 2004. "Mozambique. Multi-Sector Country Gender Profile. Agriculture and Rural Development North and East and South Region (ONAR)." African Development Bank report.

Polgreen, Lydia. 2008. "Congo's Death Rate Unchanged since War Ended," *New York Times*, 23 January. Available online at http://www.nytimes.com/2008/01/23/world/africa/23congo.html, accessed 31 January 2008.

"Polygamy Somewhat Out of Bounds – If Not Out of Fashion." 2004. *Inter Press Service*, 21 June.

Pool, David. 2001. *From Guerrillas to Government: The Eritrean People's Liberation Front.* Oxford: James Currey.

Predelli, Line Nyhagen. 2000. "Sexual Control and the Remaking of Gender: The Attempt of Nineteenth-Century Protestant Norwegian Women to Export Western Domesticity to Madagascar." *Journal of Women's History* 12 (2): 81–103.

Primo, Natasha. 2003. "Gender Issues in the Information Society." UNESCO Publications for the World Summit on the Information Society, 10–12 December,
Geneva.

*Proceedings of the Constituent Assembly (Uganda)*. 1994. "Official Report."
(3 August): 1490.

Radloff, Jennifer. 2005. "Claiming Cyberspace: Communication and Networking for Social Change and Women's Empowerment." *Feminist Africa* (4): 85–
98.

Rai, Shirin. 2003. "Institutional Mechanisms for the Advancement of Women: Mainstreaming Gender, Democratizing the State?" In *Mainstreaming Gender, Democratizing the State?: Institutional Mechanisms for the Advancement of Women*, ed.
S. Rai. Manchester: Manchester University Press.

Ranchod-Nilsson, Sita. 2006. "Gender Politics and the Pendulum of Political and
Social Transformation in Zimbabwe." *Journal of Southern African Studies* 32 (1):
49–67.

Razavi, Shahra, and Carol Miller. 1995. *Gender Mainstreaming: A Study of Efforts
by the UNDP, the World Bank, and the ILO to Institutionalise Gender Issues*.
Geneva: UNRISD.

Rees, Teresa. 2000. "Mainstreaming Gender Equality in Science in the European Union: The 'ETAN Report.'" Paper prepared for the Mainstreaming Gender in European Public Policy Workshop, 14–15 October, at the University of
Wisconsin–Madison.

Robertson, Claire. 1986. "Women's Education and Class Formation in Africa, 1950–
1980." In *Women and Class in Africa*, ed. C. Robertson and I. Berger. New York:
Africana.

Rogers, Susan G. 1980. "Anti-Colonial Protest in Africa: A Female Strategy Reconsidered." *Heresies* 3: 22–5.

———. 1983. "Efforts toward Women's Development in Tanzania: Gender Rhetoric
vs. Gender Realities." In *Women in Developing Countries: A Policy Focus*, ed. K.
Staudt and J. Jaquette. New York: Haworth Press.

Rweyemamu, Robert. 1997. "The Women Who Scared the Men of Power." *East
African* (Nairobi), 11 June.

Sahle, Eunice Njeri. 1998. "Women and Political Participation in Kenya: Evaluating
the Interplay of Gender, Ethnicity, Class and State." In *Multiparty Democracy
and Political Change: Constraints to Democratization in Africa*, ed. J. M. Mbaku
and J. O. Ihonvebere. Brookfield, Singapore, and Sydney: Ashgate.

Sall, Ebrima, ed. 2000. *Women in Academia: Gender and Academic Freedom in
Africa*. Dakar: CODESRIA.

Santos, Boaventura de Sousa, and João Carlos Trindade, eds. 2003. *Conflito e
Transformação Social: Uma Paisagem das Justiças em Moçambique* [Conflict and
Social Transformation: An Overview of Justice in Mozambique] (2 volumes).
Porto: Edições Afrontamento.

SARDC. 2004. *The African Gender and Development Index, Mozambique*. Maputo:
Economic Commission for Africa and African Centre for Gender and Development.

Schild, Veronica. 1998. "New Subjects of Rights? Women's Movements and the
Construction of Citizenship in the 'New Democracies.'" In *Cultures of Politics,*

*Politics of Cultures: Revisioning Latin American Social Movements*, ed. Sonia Alvarez, Evelina Dagnino, and Arturo Escobar. Boulder: Westview Press.

Schmidt, Elizabeth. 2002. "'Emancipate Your Husbands!' Women and Nationalism in Guinea, 1953–1958." In *Women in African Colonial Histories*, ed. Jean Allman, Susan Geiger, and Nakanyike Musisi. Bloomington and Indianapolis: Indiana University Press.

———. 2005a. "Top Down or Bottom Up? Nationalist Mobilization Reconsidered, with Special Reference to Guinea (French West Africa)." *American Historical Review* 110 (4): 975–1014.

———. 2005b. *Mobilizing the Masses: Gender, Ethnicity, and Class in the Nationalist Movement in Guinea, 1939–1958.* Portsmouth: Heinemann.

Schuster, Ilsa. 1983. "Constraints and Opportunities in Political Participation: The Case of Zambian Women." *Genévè-Afrique* 21 (2): 13–9.

Selolwane, Onalenna Doo. 2004. "The Emang Basadi Women's Association." Available online at http://www.feministafrica.org/, accessed 22 May 2008.

Semu, L. 2002. "Kamuzu's Mbumba: Malawi Women's Embeddedness to Culture in the Face of International Political Pressure and Internal Legal Change." *Africa Today* 49 (2): 77–99.

SIDA. 2007. *A Profile on Gender Relations Update 2006. Towards Gender Equality in Mozambique.* Paper prepared for SIDA by Edda Collier. Available online at http://www.sida.se/publications, accessed 22 May 2008.

Silva, Benedita da, Benilde Nhalivilo, Celeste Nobela, Conceição Osório, Fernanda Machungo, Lara da Silva Carrilho, Lucia Maximiano do Amaral, Margarita Mejia, Maria José Arthur, and Terezinha da Silva. 2005. *Beyond Inequalities: Women in Mozambique.* Maputo: Fórum Mulher and Women in Development Southern Africa Awareness (WIDSAA) Programme of the Southern African Research and Documentation Centre (SARDC).

Slackman, Michael. 2007. "A Quiet Revolution in Algeria: Gains by Women." *New York Times*, 26 May, 1.

Smyth, Rosaleen. 2004. "The Roots of Community Development in Colonial Office Policy and Practice in Africa." *Social Policy and Administration* 38 (4): 418–36.

Snyder, Margaret C. 2000. *Women in African Economies: From Burning Sun to Boardroom.* Kampala: Fountain.

———. 2003. "African Contributions to the Global Women's Movement." Paper presented at National Feminisms, Transnational Arenas, Universal Human Rights, Havens Center Colloquium Series, 14 April, at Madison, Wisconsin.

———. 2004. "Women Determine Development: The Unfinished Revolution." *Signs: Journal of Women in Culture and Society* 29 (2): 619–32.

———. 2006. "Unlikely Godmother: The UN and the Global Women's Movement." In *Global Feminism: Transnational Women's Activism, Organizing, and Human Rights*, ed. Myra Marx Ferree and Aili Mari Tripp. New York: New York University Press.

Snyder, Margaret, and Mary Tadesse. 1995. *African Women and Development.* Atlantic Highlands: Zed.

Soiri, Ilina. 1996. *The Radical Motherhood: Namibian Women's Independence Struggle.* Research Report No. 99. Uppsala: Nordiska Afrikainstitutet.

Staudt, Kathleen. 1985. "Women's Political Consciousness in Africa: A Framework for Analysis." In *Women as Food Producers in Developing Countries*, ed. Jamie Monson and Marion Kalb. Los Angeles: UCLA African Studies Centre.

Staunton, Irene. 1990. *Mothers of the Revolution: The War Experiences of Thirty Zimbabwean Women*. London: James Currey.

Steady, Filomina. 1975. *Female Power in African Politics: The National Congress of Sierre Leone Women*. Pasadena: Munger Africana Library, California Institute of Technology.

———. 2006. *Women and Collective Action in Africa*. New York: Palgrave.

Strobel, Margaret. 1979. *Muslim Women in Mombasa, 1890–1975*. New Haven: Yale University Press.

———. 1991. *European Women and the Second British Empire*. Bloomington and Indianapolis: Indiana University Press.

Summers, Carol. 1991. "Intimate Colonialism: The Imperial Production of Reproduction in Uganda, 1907–1925." *Signs* 16 (4): 787–807

Sylvester, Christine. 1989. "Patriarchy, Peace, and Women Warriors." In *Peace: Meanings, Politics, Strategies*, ed. L. R. Forcey. New York: Praeger.

Tamale, Sylvia. 1999. *When Hens Begin to Crow: Gender and Parliamentary Politics in Uganda*. Boulder: Westview Press.

Tandon, Yash. 1991. "Foreign NGOs, Uses and Abuses: An African Perspective." *Associations Transnationales* 3: 141–5.

Terretta, Meredith. Forthcoming. "A Miscarriage of Nation: Cameroonian Women and Revolution, 1949–1971." *Stichproben: Vienna Journal of African Studies*, special issue on Fracturing Binarisms: Gender and Colonialisms in Africa.

Tibbetts, Alexandra. 1994. "Mamas Fighting for Freedom in Kenya." *Africa Today* 41 (4): 27–48.

Tobar, Marcela Ríos. 2003. "Paradoxes of an Unfinished Revolution." *International Feminist Journal of Politics* 5 (2): 256–80.

Toyo, Nkoyo. 2006. "Revising Equality as a Right: The Minimum Age of Marriage Clause in the Nigerian Child Rights Act, 2003." *Third World Quarterly* 27 (7): 1299–1312.

Tripp, Aili Mari. 2000. *Women and Politics in Uganda*: Madison: University of Wisconsin Press, James Currey, and Fountain Press.

———. 2001a. "Women and Democracy: The New Political Activism in Africa." *Journal of Democracy* 12 (3): 141–55.

———. 2001b. "Women's Movements and Challenges to Neopatrimonial Rule: Preliminary Observations from Africa." *Development and Change*. 32 (1): 33–54.

———. 2002. "Women's Mobilization in Uganda (1945–1962): Non-Racial Ideologies within Colonial-African-Asian Encounters." *International Journal of African Historical Studies* 35 (1): 1–22.

———. 2004. "A New Look at Colonial Women: British Teachers and Activists in Uganda (1898–1962)," *Canadian Journal of African Studies*. 38 (1): 123–56.

———. 2006. "The Evolution of Transnational Feminisms: Consensus, Conflict and New Dynamics." In *Global Feminism: Transnational Women's Activism, Organizing, and Human Rights*, ed. Myra Marx Ferree and Aili Mari Tripp. New York: New York University Press.

————. 2007. "Women's Rights and Legislative and Constitutional Reform in Post-Conflict Africa." Paper presented at UNESCO conference on "Women's rights, peace and security in post-conflict democracies in Africa," 29–30 August, at Pretoria.

————. 2008. "Gender, Power and Peacemaking in Africa." Presentation to Woodrow Wilson International Center for Scholars, 15 January.

Tripp, Aili Mari, and Alice Kang. 2008. "The Global Impact of Quotas: On the Fast Track to Increased Female Legislative Representation." *Comparative Political Studies* 41 (3): 338–61.

Tripp, Aili Mari, and Joy Kwesiga, eds. 2002. *The Women's Movement in Uganda: History, Challenges and Prospects*. Kampala: Fountain.

True, Jacqui. 2003. *Gender, Globalization, and Postsocialism: The Czech Republic after Communism*. New York: Columbia University Press.

True, Jacqui and Michael Mintrom. 2001. "Transnational Networks and Policy Diffusion: The Case of Gender Mainstreaming." *International Studies Quarterly* 45 (1): 27–57.

Tsikata, Dzodzi. 2001. "National Machineries for the Advancement of Women in Africa: Are They Transforming Gender Relations?" Available online at http://www.socialwatch.org/en/informesTematicos/29.html, accessed 22 May 2008.

Tsikata, Edzodzinam. 1989. "Women's Political Organisations 1951–1987." In *The State, Development and Politics in Ghana*, ed. Emmanuel Hanson and Kwame Ninsin. Oxford: African Books Collective.

Turrittin, Jane. 1993. "Aoua Kéita and the Nascent Women's Movement in the French Soudan." *African Studies Review* 36 (1): 59–89.

Turshen, Meredeth. 2002. "Algerian Women in the Liberation Struggle and the Civil War: From Active Participants to Passive Victims?" *Social Research* (Fall). Available online at http://findarticles.com/p/articles/mi_m2267/is_3_69/ai_94227145, accessed 22 May 2008.

Uganda, Government of. 2003. "Progress on Implementation of the Beijing Platform for Action (1995) and the Commonwealth Plan of Action on Gender and Development (1995) and its Update (2000–2005) Submitted to the Commonwealth Secretariat. Available at http://www.thecommonwealth.org/, accessed 22 May 2008.

UNDP. 2005. "International Cooperation at a Crossroads: Aid, Trade, and Security in an Unequal World." In *Human Development Report 2005*. New York: United Nations Development Programme.

Urdang, Stephanie. 1978. "'Precondition for Victory': Women's Liberation in Mozambique and Guinea-Bissau." *Issue: A Journal of Opinion* 8 (1): 25–31.

Van Allen, Judith. 1972. "'Sitting on a Man': Colonialism and the Lost Political Institutions of Igbo Women." *Canadian Journal of African Studies* 6 (2): 165–82.

————. 1976. "'Aba Riots' or Igbo Women's War? Ideology, Stratification and the Invisibility of Women." In *Women in Africa: Studies in Social and Economic Change*, ed. N. H. Hafkin and E. Bay. Stanford: Stanford University Press.

————. 2000. "Must A Woman (Politician) Be More Like A Man? Constructing Female Political Power and Agency in Botswana." Paper presented at the Forty-Third Annual Meeting of the African Studies Association, 16–19 November, at Nashville, Tennessee.

Verloo, Mieke. 2005. "Displacement and Empowerment: Reflections on the Concept and Practice of the Council of Europe Approach to Gender Mainstreaming and Gender Equality." *Social Politics: International Studies in Gender, State and Society* 12 (3): 344–65.

Wallerstein, Immanuel. 1964. "Voluntary Associations." In *Political Parties and National Integration in Tropical Africa*, ed. J. Coleman and C. Rosberg. Berkeley: University of California Press.

Wanyeki, L. Muthoni. 2005. "The African Women's Development and Communication Network (FEMNET): Experiences of Feminist Organising." *Feminist Africa* (4): 105–15.

Warioba, Christine. 2004. "The Role of National Mechanisms in Promoting Gender Equality and the Empowerment of Women: SADC Experience." In *The Role of National Mechanisms in Promoting Gender Equality and the Empowerment of Women: Achievements, Gaps and Challenges*. Rome, Italy: United Nations Division for the Advancement of Women (DAW).

Watson, Catherine. 1988. "Uganda's Women: A Ray of Hope." *Africa Report* (July–August): 26–33.

Waylen, Georgina. 1994. "Women and Democratisation: Conceptualising Gender Relations in Transition Politics." *World Politics* 46 (3): 327–54.

———. 2007a. *Engendering Transitions: Women's Mobilization, Institutions, and Gender Outcomes*. Oxford and New York: Oxford University Press.

———. 2007b. "Women's Mobilization and Gender Outcomes in Transitions to Democracy – The Case of South Africa." *Comparative Political Studies* 40 (5): 521–46.

"We're Capable of Fighting MMD Women – Chipeta." 2002. *Post.* 11 January.

White, Carolyn Day. 1973. "The Role of Women as an Interest Group in the Ugandan Political System." M.A., Makerere University.

Wicken, Joan E. 1958. "African Contrasts." Unpublished report of Alice Horsman Travelling Fellow, 1956–7. Bodleian Library of Commonwealth and African Studies at Rhodes House, Oxford University, Mss.Afr.s172b.

Wilson, Amrit. 1993. "Eritrean Women: The Beginning of a New Struggle." *Africa World Review* (May-October): 12–3.

Wilson, Gretchen. 2007. "African Female Scholars Share Virtual Lifeline." *Women's eNews 2007* (cited 23 January 2007). Available online at http://www.womensnews.org/article.cfm?aid=2998, accessed 22 May 2008.

Wing, Susanna D. 2002. "Women Activists in Mali: The Global Discourse on Human Rights." In *Women's Activism and Globalization: Linking Local Struggles and Transnational Politics*, ed. N. A. Naples and M. Desai. New York: Routledge.

Wipper, Audrey. 1975. "The Maendeleo ya Wanawake Movement: Some Paradoxes and Contradictions." *African Studies Review* 18 (3): 99–120.

"Women Legislators Fall below Target Figure." 2007. *Inter Press Service* 26 March.

"Women's Unequal Rights." 2006. *Standard Times* (Sierra Leone). 2 June.

Wunsch, James S. 1991. "Centralization and Development in Post-Independence Africa." In *The Failure of the Centralized State: Institutions and Self-Governance in Africa*, ed. J. S. Wunsch and D. Olowu. Boulder: Westview Press.

Yates, Barbara A. 1982. "Colonialism, Education, and Work: Sex Differentiation in Colonial Zaire." In *Women and Work in Africa*, ed. E. G. Bay. Boulder: Westview Press.

Yoon, Mi Yung. 2004. "Explaining Women's Legislative Representation in Sub-Saharan Africa." *Legislative Studies Quarterly* 29 (3): 447–68.

Zaffiro, James J. 2000. "Women's Political Empowerment in Botswana." Unpublished paper.

"Zim's Marriage Laws Not Harmonised – Official." 2006. *Herald*. 19 May.

Zwingel, Susanne. 2005. "From Intergovernmental Negotiations to (Sub)national Change." *International Feminist Journal of Politics* 7 (3): 400–24.

Zziwa, Hassan Badru. 1996. "Women Soccer Should Be Supported." *Monitor*, 29 April–1 May, 15.

# Index